365 DAILY DEVOTIONALS - FROM THE - Old Testament

Women Read Scripture

365 DAILY DEVOTIONALS - FROM THE - Old Testament

MARIANNA RICHARDSON, MBA, EdD, JD
CHRISTINE THACKERAY,
MICHELLE WILSON & KRISTA M. ISAACSON

CFI
An imprint of Cedar Fort, Inc.
Springville, Utah

Paperback ISBN 13: 978-1-4621-5060-1
eBook ISBN 13: 978-1-4621-5061-8

Published by CFI, an imprint of Cedar Fort, Inc.
2373 W. 700 S., Suite 100 Springville, UT 84663
Distributed by Cedar Fort, Inc., www.cedarfort.com

LIBRARY OF CONGRESS REGISTRATION NUMBER: 2025944888

Cover design by Shawnda Craig

Printed in the United States of America

10 9 8 7 6 5 4 3 2 1

Printed on acid-free paper

We dedicate this book to those who loved the Word of the Lord and who were faithful stewards across the centuries, devoting their hearts, minds, and lives to preserve and translate the prophetic books and sacred writings that form the Old Testament.

We also dedicate this book to the Saints of today who gain renewed strength by turning to the scriptures. We hope the words of Jehovah and His holy prophets will light your way as you prepare for Christ's Second Coming.

Introduction

The Old Testament is foundational to our understanding of the gospel of Jesus Christ and to our preparations for His Second Coming. Through the law of Moses, the ancient Saints were symbolically taught about Christ's eternal mission—just as our ordinances do for us today. Studying their faith in His First Coming can strengthen our own faith as we prepare for Him to come again as King of Kings and Lord of Lords.

As women of faith, the authors of this book testify of the truthfulness of this sacred scripture and have found a witness of Jesus Christ in its pages.

Marianna loves to read the words of Isaiah and other Old Testament prophets who use symbolic poetry to describe the majesty of Christ's eternal purpose and His earthly mission.

Christine gained her testimony of prophets from the face-to-face interactions with Deity of Abraham, Jacob, Ezekiel, and Isaiah, which made her know Joseph Smith had the same.

Michelle loves to see the Old Testament not just as old scripture stories but as *her* story. From before Eve's first bite, she can see the beauty of the Lord's redemptive plan—a divine effort to save her and her family, offering chance after chance to experience the greatest joy here and in the life to come.

Krista loves the challenge of working with the Spirit to discover how the teachings and prophecies written anciently resonate with Christ's familiar love and ongoing guidance for the challenges she faces in her modern life.

That is our purpose: to share our different perspectives as we journey with you on the road of light and understanding. Thank you for joining us!

Translators of the Bible

But among all our joys, there was no one that more filled our hearts, than the blessed continuance of the preaching of God's sacred Word among us; which is that inestimable treasure, which excelleth all the riches of the earth.

The Joy of Reading the Word

At the beginning of the King James Version of the Bible, there is a dedicatory page written by the men who translated the Hebrew and Greek books of the Bible into English. In 1604, King James I gathered forty-seven scholars to create an English translation of the Bible that would be accepted by the king, the Church of England, and the English people. Previous English translations—such as the Great Bible (1538) authorized by King Henry VIII, and the Bishop's Bible (1568)—contained major inconsistencies and were not accepted by all classes of people. The scholars used the original Hebrew and Greek texts, incorporated the earlier partial English translation by William Tyndale (1490–1536), and consulted Jewish commentaries to guide their work. The completed Bible was published by King James I in 1611, a process that took seven years to complete.

The Bible is a collection of books that have been selected and canonized as sacred over the centuries. I am grateful for the work of these righteous men who translated and compiled this version of the Bible. I add my testimony to theirs that these sacred words are priceless and applicable to our lives today.

—Marianna

"It is a miracle that the Bible literally contains within its pages the converting, healing Spirit of Christ, which has turned men's hearts for centuries."

M. Russell Ballard

"The Miracle of the Holy Bible," Apr. 2007

Genesis 1:3–4

And God said, Let there be light: and there was light. And God saw the light, that it was good: and God divided the light from the darkness.

Let There Be Light

If you have teenagers who love electronics like mine did, then you know the effort they make to block out certain types of light. When watching a movie or playing a game in the living room, my boys would often tape paper over the windows or use multiple blankets in addition to our curtains so that their only light source came from the show they wanted to focus on.

A dear childhood friend recently shared a social media post in which she talked about loving others as her reason for not staying close to her covenants. I thought of my boys and wondered if, in our confusing times, it is more important than ever that we focus on the Light of Jesus Christ first and not be distracted by other good things. That may mean we spend time blocking out other good voices or activities for a time so that we can truly gather His light within us. Then, when we are filled, we can open the windows and share that light with others in need.

—Christine

> "We need to simplify, focus our efforts, and be gatherers of the Light of Jesus Christ. We need more holy and revelatory experiences."
>
> Amy A. Wright
>
> "Abide the Day in Christ," Oct. 2023

Genesis 2:18

And the Lord God said, It is not good that the man should be alone; I will make him an help meet for him.

A Help Meet

During a business trip, my husband called me after checking into his hotel room. He had been given an executive suite decorated all in white, with a lovely large sitting room and spacious bathroom. It sounded like paradise to me. But Steve didn't see it that way. Instead, he said that he was lonely and missed me and the family. He said, "Paradise does not exist for me without my family." (Good answer!)

Adam was alone in the Garden of Eden. Even though it was a paradise, Heavenly Father knew that Adam would eventually become lonely without a companion. Then, it would no longer feel like paradise. So, He created Eve, who would be "a helper suited to, worthy of, or corresponding to him" (footnote 18b).

Adam was told to cleave unto his wife. The word *cleave* has two meanings that may seem contradictory. One definition means "to adhere firmly, closely, or unwaveringly." The other means to "divide by a cutting blow" (Merriam-Webster's Dictionary). In our marriage relationship, we need to adhere firmly and loyally to each other. Then, as a couple, we make a "cutting blow" between our relationship and the world. As we do so, we will find paradise in simply being together.

—Marianna

"In the Lord's plan, a 'help meet' was a companion who would walk shoulder to shoulder with Adam in full partnership. In fact, Eve was a heavenly blessing in Adam's life."

Ulisses S. Soares

"In Partnership with the Lord," Oct. 2022

Genesis 3:16

Unto the woman he said, I will greatly multiply thy sorrow and thy conception; in sorrow thou shalt bring forth children.

Worth It

Our Mother Eve was such a brave woman. She lived in paradise without worry, and yet, I believe she understood why she'd been sent to the earth. Eve was the first, and if she didn't make the hard decision to partake of the fruit and the Fall, there would be no progression and no children. She chose sorrow, hardship, and struggle because that was the way forward for her, and for us all. Was it worth it? We can look to Eve's own words for the answer: "Were it not for our transgression we never should have had seed, and never should have known good and evil, and the joy of our redemption, and the eternal life which God giveth unto all the obedient" (Moses 5:11).

Eve has always been an example of courage. Like her, we chose to follow Christ in premortality, and leave the peace and safety of heaven to journey on this earth. Is it worth it? I add my testimony to Eve's: Though this life has presented many struggles, some of those hardships have resulted in my greatest blessings. As I've reached out to Christ for relief, I've come to know and love Him. He has kept His promise to be with me always. And when I return to my heavenly home, all that I've gained by living will be precious to me. Worth it.

—Krista

> "Leaving the comfort and security of His immediate presence . . . would mean coming to earth for a journey filled with unknown danger and trial. . . . But we also knew that we would gain precious treasures."
>
> Dieter F. Uchtdorf
>
> "Your Great Adventure," Oct. 2019

Genesis 4:9

Am I my brother's keeper?

My Brother's (and Sister's) Keeper

Years ago, after struggling with medical issues, I underwent a complete hysterectomy. It was a difficult recovery, physically and emotionally. I felt I'd failed my husband and perhaps even the children who had been waiting to be born into my family. Perhaps the deepest ache was that I didn't feel like me. I didn't feel whole.

At this same time, a sweet sister in my ward had the random thought to buy me a gift. She walked around the store, trying to ignore the repeated prompting. She was shy and didn't know me very well. Finally, she grabbed some things, drove to my house, and sheepishly handed me a candle and some lotion.

A few weeks later, I was draining my first post-op bath when I remembered her gift. As I applied the floral-scented lotion, tears fell down my cheeks. It was the first time I felt like a woman, like me. After that, other tender mercies came. I hadn't failed anyone. I was okay.

We don't need to be "assigned" to minister to one another. As we listen to the Spirit, we can be God's hands in the lives of others. We can help each other heal. We can help each other feel whole.

—Michelle

> "As disciples of the Lord Jesus Christ, we have a responsibility to care for and serve our brothers and sisters."
>
> Dallin H. Oaks
>
> "Unselfish Service," Apr. 2009

Genesis 6:9

Noah was a just man and perfect in his generations, and Noah walked with God.

Perfect in His Generation

John and Janice made intentional decisions to make their home a place different from the world. They encouraged board games over video games. They were a book-loving family and went to the library every week. They read the scriptures as a family and as individuals every day. When Steve and I entered their home, we felt a strong spiritual presence. They had created an ark separated from the violent and divisive world around them.

Noah was perfect for his generation. He walked with God. He protected his family from the evils of the world by building a physical ark. This protection enabled them to live through the devastation and destruction that filled the earth.

We, too, can build an ark for our families to enter—a safe place set apart from the turmoil of the world. Our homes can serve as sanctuaries, allowing us to weather the storms that will certainly come as the world experiences the Lord's judgment, leading to His return to Earth at His Second Coming.

—Marianna

"We need not be dismayed if our earnest efforts toward perfection now seem so arduous and endless. Perfection is pending. It can come in full only after the Resurrection and only through the Lord. It awaits all who love Him and keep His commandments."

Russell M. Nelson

"Perfection Pending," Oct. 1995

Genesis 7:23

And every living substance was destroyed which was upon the face of the ground . . . and Noah only remained alive, and they that were with him in the ark.

Remain Alive in Christ

My youngest son, William, went on a high-adventure whitewater rafting trip with the boys in his quorum. He wore a life vest, held on tightly, and tried to stay in the boat. Unfortunately, he sat at the very back of the raft beside his friend Ethan, who did not follow any of the instructions.

They struck their first big rapids suddenly. Ethan was not prepared and was thrown backward, shoving William out of the raft. Well, almost out. His feet were pinned under his flailing friend. William's life vest provided little help as he continued down the rapids with his knees lifted over the edge of the raft and his head below the turbulent waters. Miraculously, he was able to free one of his knees, kick off, and hold on to the rope. As the water stilled, he got back on the raft—but this time, he sat in the middle and didn't get near the edge.

In our turbulent times, where the only place of safety is within the "ark" or "life raft" of our covenants, simply holding on may not be enough. We also need to stay in the center of the boat, not let others push us out, and keep our focus on our Leader, even Jesus Christ. Then we will remain alive in Him.

—Christine

> "Rule number one: stay in the boat! Rule number two: always wear a life jacket! Rule number three: always hold on with both hands! . . . God our Father and the Lord Jesus Christ are at the helm and will guide us right."
>
> M. Russell Ballard
>
> "Stay in the Boat and Hold On!" Oct. 2014

Genesis 8:16–17

Go forth of the ark, thou, and thy wife, and thy sons, and thy sons' wives with thee. Bring forth with thee every living thing that is with thee of all flesh.

A Fresh Start

Noah and his family had finally made it through their arduous journey in the ark and looked forward to a fresh start. But starting anew would bring its own challenges. Noah and his family were now starting their lives from scratch. They did not have homes to go back to or neighbors to welcome them. Their mission was similar to that of Adam and Eve: they were building a new world. God gave them the tools to succeed, but their effort and strength were needed to make it happen. They were ready to start a new life with God's help and through their own faith and diligence.

The Prophet Joseph Smith taught about the mission of Noah: "The Priesthood was first given to Adam . . . . Then to Noah, who is Gabriel; he stands next in authority to Adam in the Priesthood; he was called of God to this office and was the father of all living in his day" (*History of the Church*, 4:425).

My life was a mess when our family moved from Washington, DC, to Seattle, Washington. I was six months pregnant with child number nine, and I had neither family nor friends nearby. God gave me the tools to succeed, but it was up to me to put forth the effort. With Christ's help, I enjoyed a fresh start.

—Marianna

"You can have a new beginning and a fresh start. In Gethsemane and on Calvary, Jesus 'took upon Himself . . . all of the anguish and suffering ever experienced by you and me.' . . . You can let go of your pain and leave it at His feet."

Patrick Kearon

"He Is Risen with Healing in His Wings," Apr. 2022

Genesis 11:7

Go to, let us go down, and there confound their language.

The Voices He Gives Us

I have always wanted to be a singer. Singing brought me so much joy as a child. It was my destiny—that is, until I realized I wasn't a good singer.

This has been a source of great sadness for me, even as an adult. I've prayed many times about this, asking God why He didn't give me the voice I wanted. Finally, a few years ago, He answered me. *I gave you the voice* I *wanted you to have.*

Since then, I've come to understand that I can't sing, but I can write. Now, my laptop is my stage, and words are my songs. I've also come to understand that if I had the voice I desired, my life would look very different from what it does now. I really love my life. And I believe God knew I would.

Sometimes, God doesn't give us what we want because He knows it won't bring us the joy we are seeking. Rather than looking at what we don't have, we can prayerfully consider what He *has* given us. He knows you. He loves you. And chances are, He's giving you exactly what you need to have joy in your life right now.

—Michelle

"Each member should know how much he or she is needed. Each person has something important to contribute and has unique talents and abilities that help move this important work along."

Bonnie L. Oscarson

"Young Women in the Work," Apr. 2018

Genesis 12:2–3

And I will make of thee a great nation, and I will bless thee, and make thy name great; . . . and in thee shall all the families of the earth be blessed.

How?

Travis and I were newly married. We lived in a microscopic basement apartment just south of BYU's Provo campus. Student loans covered tuition, and Travis and I had part-time jobs where we barely made enough money to cover rent and some scanty groceries. But a new semester was starting, and with it, additional expenses. Travis came home one evening, heavy with concern. Work was slow, and he didn't know how we'd pay rent and still afford textbooks. We prayed and asked Heavenly Father for help. After the prayer, Travis said, "I have a crazy idea. What if we calculate how much money we need to make and prepay our tithing on that amount? Show Heavenly Father that we believe in miracles." I was all in.

It's the only time in our thirty-year marriage that we prepaid tithing that way. And I'm not professing that it's a magic solution that will always result in financial blessings. God's blessings come in myriad ways, but that time, all those years ago, it was how we chose to demonstrate our faith. Travis made more money that month at that job than he had before or did after. And we learned that God really can provide miracles in our lives, even seemingly impossible ones.

—Krista

"[The] 'covenant confidence through Jesus Christ' . . . is the quiet yet certain assurance of receiving the blessings that God promises for those who keep their covenants."

Ulisses S. Soares

"Covenant Confidence Through Jesus Christ," Apr. 2024

Genesis 13:10–11

And Lot lifted up his eyes, and beheld all the plain of Jordan, that it was well watered every where . . . even as the garden of the Lord. . . . Then Lot chose him all the plain of Jordan.

The Largest Backpack

Before Aesop wrote his fables, he was a lowly slave in ancient Greece. One day, his master laid out backpacks for his many slaves to carry on a long journey. Aesop ran the fastest and took the largest one. All the other slaves laughed at him. But at midday, he opened his sack, which was filled with bread, and distributed half his load. At dinner, he handed out the other half. The next day, while his fellow slaves struggled, he had nothing to carry but the empty sack. What looked like the worst choice was indeed the best.

When Abraham realized Lot and his family had to separate, he gave Lot the choice of where to go. Lot saw the well-watered plains of Jordan and the dry land of Hebron. He chose the side he thought was easiest. At that moment, Abraham may have felt stuck with the largest backpack. But the land of Hebron became a blessed place. While in Jordan, Lot and his family had lived in Sodom and Gomorrah. In the end, Lot's wife was even turned into salt. Abraham, instead, stayed faithful.

Recently I met a sweet sister with a huge backpack. Her life has been fraught with trials both physical and emotional. But it was those very trials that helped her find the gospel of Christ. So, when you are handed a large backpack, look for the blessings in disguise.

—Christine

"All that is unfair about life can be made right through the Atonement of Jesus Christ."

Quentin L. Cook

"Personal Peace in Challenging Times," Oct. 2021

Genesis 15:5–6

And he brought him forth abroad, and said, Look now toward heaven, and tell the stars, if thou be able to number them: and he said unto him, So shall thy seed be. And he believed in the Lord; and he counted it to him for righteousness.

Keeping Count

Whenever I take my children (and now grandchildren) to the pool, I do not swim myself. Instead, I sit on the side of the pool, keeping count of each child and making sure they are safe and no one is drowning. Keeping count is a tedious but necessary task with children. I know many women who would love to have the blessing of keeping count of even one child.

Abraham's promise of uncountable posterity is for *all* righteous women, whether or not they currently have children. Watching over His children is not limited to women who have already borne children. President Nelson charged all women to watch over and mother all of Heavenly Father's children: "We need women who are devoted to shepherding God's children along the covenant path toward exaltation" ("A Plea to My Sisters," Oct. 2015). Every righteous woman can mother others and look forward to the day when she will be keeping count of her own uncountable posterity.

—Marianna

"For reasons known to the Lord, some women are required to wait to have children. This delay is not easy for any righteous woman. But the Lord's timetable for each of us does not negate our nature. Some of us, then, must simply find other ways to mother. And all around us are those who need to be loved and led."

Sheri L. Dew

"Are We Not All Mothers?," Oct. 2001

Genesis 17:1

The Lord appeared to Abram, and said unto him, I am the Almighty God; walk before me, and be thou perfect.

Let the Water Do the Work

One summer morning years ago, I stood next to my grandma as we washed dinner dishes together. I wanted to show her I was a big kid now, that I could clean just as well as my older siblings and cousins. However, it seemed the crusted food on the plate in my hand had a different plan.

Upon seeing my struggle to scrub the plate clean, my grandma gently put her hand on mine, filled up the sink with hot, soapy water, then slid the plate under the suds.

"Let the water do the work," she said.

A few minutes later, I was able to wipe the now-moist food off easily and provide my grandma with a perfectly clean plate.

So often we try our hardest to be the best, to be perfect, even. But perfection is the work of the Savior, not ours.

We simply need to submit our hopes, faith, and efforts to Him and let Him do the work of perfection.

—Michelle

> "As we accept the Savior's invitation to come unto Him, we soon realize that our best is good enough and that the grace of a loving Savior will make up the difference in ways we cannot imagine."
>
> Vern P. Stanfill
>
> "The Imperfect Harvest," Apr. 2023

Genesis 18:14

Is any thing too hard for the Lord?

Level Infinite!

I recently taught my young daughter to embroider. While she sewed a simple flower on the pocket of a sweatshirt, I sat close by, working on a more complex stitching project of my own. Suddenly, my daughter tossed her sewing to the floor and huffed, "I can't do it! Mine looks so bad compared to yours!"

I put my arm around her and asked, "How long have you known how to embroider?"

"Only today," she answered.

"That makes you a level-one embroiderer. I've been learning and practicing since I was your age, so I'm a level-thirty-seven embroiderer!" She laughed. "It just means I know things and can do things you can't yet. But if you let me teach you, you'll get better."

I'm often overwhelmed by my own shortcomings. There are burdens and frustrations I can't overcome. But that's because I'm only a level-fifty human being. There's so much I haven't learned to do or be yet. Luckily, we have a Brother who is a Level-Infinite Savior! There is nothing too hard for Him. And if we trust Him, He will teach us to do and be better.

–Krista

"He will save us from our fallen state, beyond our challenges, infirmities, and needs in this temporal life, and give us the greatest of all gifts, which is eternal life."

Juan Pablo Villar

"His Hand Ready to Help Us," Oct. 2024

Genesis 19:16

And while he lingered, the men laid hold upon his hand, and upon the hand of his wife, and upon the hand of his two daughters; the Lord being merciful unto him: and they brought him forth, and set him without the city.

Sometimes He Holds Our Hand

I've read the story of Sodom and Gomorrah many times, but I never noticed that after Lot and his family were warned to leave, they still lingered. At last, the messengers of God had to take them by the hand and guide them away from the city. They just didn't have the emotional strength to leave on their own. But with help, they were able to do it.

Elder Craig Zwick shared a similar story a number of years ago. He told of his daughter running a marathon. She heard someone call behind her, "Blind man on your left!" She turned and saw a blind man running with a friend on either side, each holding his hand so he could run the race. The blind man could never have run the race alone, but with the help of his devoted friends, he was able to do it well.

Just as the blind runner had to be willing to ask and then take the hand of his friends to run the race, Lot let the messengers of God into his house and tried to protect them. As we hold to our covenants and put our hands in the Lord's, we too can accomplish more than we ever could alone.

—Christine

> "If we will keep the commandments of God and walk hand in hand with Him in His paths, we will go forward in faith and never feel alone."
>
> W. Craig Zwick
>
> "The Lord Thy God Will Hold Thee by the Hand," Oct. 2003

Genesis 21:18–19

Arise, lift up the lad, and hold him in thine hand; for I will make him a great nation. And God opened her eyes, and she saw a well of water; and she went, and filled the bottle with water, and gave the lad drink.

Opening Our Eyes

It was a cold, snowy winter in upstate New York, and our family had one car. My husband had been working overtime for many months, and would leave before all the children were awake and often came home just as they were getting ready for bed. One night, I sat on the old worn-out sofa in our family room, completely drained. I felt like I could not go on. I prayed for strength. After the prayer, I opened my eyes and saw my situation in a different light. I had a husband who worked hard and had a great job; I had three beautiful, healthy children; and I had a warm, comfortable home that protected us from winter storms. I saw blessings that gave me strength.

I could relate to Hagar, who felt rejected and alone wandering in the wilderness with her son. At the moment of her deepest suffering, the Lord sent an angel who told her that her son would become a great nation. Her eyes were opened, and she saw a well of water that quenched their thirst.

When you are on the brink of despair, turn to the Lord. He will open your eyes to your current and future blessings and help you find a well of living water that will bring you to Him.

—Marianna

> "If we will look to Christ and open our eyes and our ears, the Holy Ghost will bless us to see the Lord Jesus Christ working in our lives."
>
> Kim B. Clark
>
> "Eyes to See and Ears to Hear," Oct. 2015

Genesis 22:18

And in thy seed shall all the nations of the earth be blessed; because thou hast obeyed my voice.

Blessing Others

I didn't want to do it. I told myself I wasn't going to serve a mission just because I wasn't married by the age of twenty-one. And yet, there I was, taking up my bishop's invitation to pray about serving and receiving the answer that it was God's will. Didn't He know I had other plans, other hopes?

Yes, He did know that. But *He* plans not only for me, but for others He could bless through me.

Sometimes there are other things we want to do rather than blessing the families of the earth by serving them or sharing the gospel. We have other plans, other hopes. But God has a plan for us. He loves all of His children and has given some of us the opportunity—the *gift*—to bring His love to others through exposure to the gospel.

As you plan your day today, share with Him your hopes and plans, but ask Him what *His* hopes and plans are for you, and how you can help bless others by bringing His love and light to those around in small, and perhaps even big, ways.

—Michelle

"As the seed and children of Abraham, we participate in blessing all the families of the earth 'with the blessings of the Gospel, which are the blessings of salvation, even of life eternal.'"

D. Todd Christofferson

"The Joy of the Saints," Oct. 2019

Genesis 24:58

And she said, I will go.

Let Me Know if You Need Anything

Like Rebekah, my mother-in-law, Kathy, was an "I will go" woman. Not long after my husband and I were married, Kathy invited me to accompany her to the home of a widowed neighbor whom she felt prompted to serve. This sister was stubborn about accepting help, so Kathy decided we wouldn't ask permission. We were just going to show up.

With much trepidation, I agreed to tag along, certain that this sister was going to slam the door in our faces. But I was wrong. When Kathy explained we were there to visit, clean, and help in any other way she needed, the widow opened the door wide and welcomed us in.

I worked at my mother-in-law's side that entire day. We had the best time chatting with the widow while we cleaned out cupboards, washed dishes, and mopped floors. Most importantly, I was blessed with a new perspective. Kathy taught me I shouldn't wait for someone to "let me know if you need anything." If the Lord prompts, tell Him, "I will go." And then . . . do.

—Krista

> "With sufficient faith, we will ask for direction with the intent to go and do whatever He asks."
>
> Henry B. Eyring
>
> "The Faith to Ask and Then to Act," Oct. 2021

Genesis 25: 32–34

And Esau said, Behold, I am at the point to die: and what profit shall this birthright do to me . . . and he sold his birthright unto Jacob. . . . Thus Esau despised his birthright.

What Do You Value Most?

As a teenager, I went on a date with a boy who was gifted a new car by his parents. He was so proud of it and thought I should be impressed too. If a car worked, that was enough for me. I could not comprehend why he was so pleased by a silly car. Later, I found out it was an extremely expensive BMW.

The birthright Esau was to receive from his father held the keys to the Abrahamic covenant. It was more than simply being the head of his family; he was to become the head of God's covenant people on the earth—a legacy that would continue until Christ's birth in Bethlehem. But like me and the BMW, he was clueless as to its value and sold it for a mess of pottage.

Do we realize what is of real value? Do we spend our efforts and our time focused on what is most important—strengthening our faith in the Lord and doing our part in His kingdom on earth? If not, we, like Esau, could give away that which is of the most value for almost nothing.

Hold fast to that which is good!

–Christine

"Let me reemphasize: if the pull of the world is stronger than the faith and trust we have in the Savior, then the pull of the world will prevail every time."

Joy D. Jones

"Value Beyond Measure," Oct. 2017

Genesis 28:12

And he dreamed, and beheld a ladder set up on the earth, and the top of it reached to heaven: and behold the angels of God ascending and descending on it.

A Heavenly Ladder

Jacob went through a difficult time with his family. Jacob's mother disguised him as his brother, Esau, so he could receive the birthright from his father. Esau said he would kill Jacob for his subterfuge. Now, Jacob has left his home to find a wife in a place he's never been before and to find safety from his family troubles. He wonders how this will end happily. He falls asleep and sees the interconnection of the heavenly with the worldly. He describes it as a ladder with angels climbing up and down with the Lord overseeing the angels' work. The Lord speaks to Jacob and promises him that he will find a righteous wife and have an eternal family.

Jacob is having a type of temple experience. He makes a covenant with the Lord to always worship Him and to pay tithing as a sign of his devotion and consecration.

Every time I enter the temple, I see the heavenly ladder at work as the Lord oversees His work on this earth. In the temple, the Lord teaches His Saints eternal truths and gives them sacred covenants and promises, such as eternal families and numerous posterity. These covenantal promises are the same ones Jacob made with the Lord at Bethel—his temple or house of God.

—Marianna

"Ultimately, our destinies are changed because the covenant path leads to exaltation and eternal life."

Dale G. Renlund

"I Love to See the Temple," Apr. 2023

Gen 30:22

And God remembered Rachel.

God Remembers You

When my youngest daughter, Grace, was in elementary school, she participated in a school-wide musical. A few days each week, she would skip her bus ride home and stay after school for practice. Everything was going wonderfully until one day, when I was at home, I suddenly realized it was a musical practice day and I had forgotten to pick Grace up.

I raced (legally) to the school, which was six miles from our home, and pulled up to see a very sad daughter. Grace climbed into the car and, through wet eyes, said, "I didn't see you. I thought you forgot me." I felt awful because, for a moment, I had. And that hurt my daughter.

Sometimes we look around and don't "see" God. This can make us think He has forgotten our hurt or hopes, our pain and plans—that He has forgotten *us*. And we feel hurt.

But I testify to you that He has not forgotten you. He sees you. He knows you. He loves you. He isn't "late" to bless you, or annoyed to hear you pray one more time. You are on His mind and heart right now, and always. He remembers you, and you are His.

—Michelle

> "I testify that our Heavenly Father remembers His suffering Saints, loves you, and is intimately aware of you."
>
> Anthony D. Perkins
>
> "Remember Thy Suffering Saints, O Our God," Oct. 2021

Genesis 32:28

And he said, Thy name shall be called no more Jacob, but Israel: for as a prince hast thou power with God and with men, and hast prevailed.

Let God Prevail

When my parents dropped me off at college, I was petrified. The pressure of navigating life on my own was overwhelming. I'd never felt such stress and anxiety, and my body responded by forming nine giant ulcers on the inside of my bottom lip.

After three weeks of agony, I was desperate for relief for both my lip and my soul. In sacrament meeting that week, the talks were all about peace, exactly what my heart yearned to find. I dove into my scriptures, scouring the pages for help. When I discovered a verse that soothed my heart, I wrote it on a slip of paper and hung it on the wall above my bed. After a couple of weeks, the wall was covered, my lip was healing, and my heart had discovered the source of peace. I had let go of trying to do it all on my own, placed my hand in Christ's, and embraced walking confidently into the unknown with Him.

It is in Christ that we find peace.

—Krista

"Jacob proved what was most important to him. He demonstrated that he was willing to let God prevail in his life. In response, God changed Jacob's name to *Israel*, meaning 'let God prevail.' God then promised *Israel* that *all* the blessings that had been pronounced upon Abraham's head would also be his."

Russell M. Nelson

"Let God Prevail," Oct. 2020

Genesis 35:4

And they gave unto Jacob all the strange gods which were in their hand, and all their earrings which were in their ears: and Jacob hid them under the oak which was by Shechem.

Our Oak of Shechem

My husband spent some time working as a financial adviser, helping people get out of debt. When people struggled with credit card abuse but were unwilling to destroy their cards, he encouraged them to put their credit cards in a metal can filled with water in the freezer. If they felt they really needed to use them, they could wait a few days for the ice to melt. This gave them time to reconsider. Because the can was metal, they couldn't microwave it to make the ice melt faster.

Jacob used the same approach with his wife Rachel, who had brought idols from their time with Laban. For whatever reason, Rachel was not willing to destroy them, so the idols were buried under the Oak at Shechem. Jacob and his family settled in Hebron, about a fifty-mile trip to the Oak through hill country. There is no record that these items were ever retrieved.

If we have habits we are struggling to change or items that play to our personal weaknesses, utilizing our own Oak of Shechem may be a good strategy. Putting those things far from us and creating a barrier—either through a friend, a password, or just distance—may give us the strength to overcome.

—Christine

> "Burying our weapons of rebellion leads to a unique joy. With all who have ever become converted to the Lord, we are 'brought to sing the song of redeeming love.'"
>
> D. Todd Christofferson
>
> "Burying Our Weapons of Rebellion," Oct. 2024

Genesis 38:26

And Judah acknowledged them, and said, She hath been more righteous than I.

Judging Tamar

As a young single adult in college, I was grocery shopping and noticed a young mom with two toddlers fighting in the shopping cart while the baby in the carrier was crying. *Why wasn't this mother taking better care of her children?* Five years later, I was in the same situation as that young mom, with two fighting toddlers and a newborn crying in a carrier. My previous judgmental thoughts came vividly back into my mind. Instead of judging her, I should have helped her. It's easy to make judgments about someone when we only see their outward actions. We cannot judge their hearts, their situation, or the way the Lord sees them.

It might be easy to judge Tamar. As a widow, she was at the whim of her father-in-law, Judah, who had essentially abandoned her. The only way for a widow to find independence in the Old Testament world was to have a son who would inherit his father's goods. Because she was the widow of Judah's firstborn son, Tamar's child would also inherit the birthright. Tamar was favored by God to continue the line of Judah, revealing God's love for women, especially women who are abused by society and by adulterous men. Tamar's story teaches us to not be judgmental, but to view others the way the Savior sees them—with charity and mercy.

—Marianna

> "The expression of compassion for others is, in fact, the essence of the gospel of Jesus Christ and a marked evidence of our spiritual and emotional closeness to the Savior."
>
> Ulisses S. Soares
>
> "The Savior's Abiding Compassion," Oct. 2021

Genesis 39:21

But the Lord was with Joseph.

You Are Not Alone

When my son was in fifth grade, he had a fall bad enough to send him to the emergency room. The doctors suspected a broken arm but were more concerned about a possible head injury. They ordered a CT scan. I stood next to Spencer as they strapped him onto the cold platform so he wouldn't be able to move. He was scared and in pain.

The technician told me that I could stay in the room but had to stand behind a partition for my safety. I could still see Spencer, but he couldn't see me. It was heart-wrenching.

From behind the partition, I called out to my son, "Are you okay?" Unable to move, he simply said, "As long as I can hear you, I'll be okay." He didn't have to see me to know I was still with him. And this gave him the strength to do what needed to be done.

Sometimes you might not be able to see the Lord easily, but He is with you. He knows you and wants to help you. He loves you. Call out to Him today and know you are not alone.

—Michelle

> "Jesus Christ is your personal Messiah, your loving Redeemer and Savior, who knows the pleadings of your heart. He desires your healing and happiness. He loves you. He weeps with you in your sorrows and rejoices to make you whole."
>
> Kristin M. Yee
>
> "Beauty for Ashes: The Healing Path of Forgiveness," Oct. 2022

Genesis 41:39–40

And Pharaoh said unto Joseph, . . . Thou shalt be over my house, and according unto thy word shall all my people be ruled.

Good Things to Come

When his brothers sold him to a passing company of Ishmaelites, Joseph surely had no idea how God could turn his misfortune into a blessing. One minute he was a prisoner; the next, Pharaoh poured out riches upon him and appointed him ruler over all the land. Through all of those tough years, God had led Joseph to an opportunity to save Egypt from starvation and miraculously reunite with his family.

At my house, we like to say that God is infinitely resourceful. He knows every trial and trouble that will come into our lives and how to turn our misfortunes into opportunities that can become our greatest blessings. It's hard to be patient when our lives are dark, or when we feel stuck, abandoned, or alone. But no matter how rocky the road, God can see bright days on our horizon. We can trust that our Heavenly Father is always aware of us and that He is working miracles in our lives at this very moment. It's up to us to trust Him to lead us to them.

–Krista

"Don't you quit. You keep walking. You keep trying. There is help and happiness ahead—a lot of it . . . . It will be all right in the end. Trust God and believe in good things to come."

Jeffrey R. Holland

"An High Priest of Good Things to Come," Oct. 1999

Genesis 42:24

And he turned himself about from them, and wept.

It's Okay to Weep

When the Lord asks something hard of me, I like to think of Joseph. After being sold into Egypt by his jealous brothers, he met many trials. By keeping his faith in times of struggle, he became second to Pharaoh and prepared the land for a great famine. Then his brothers came to Egypt looking for food.

The verses where Joseph stays incognito while scaring his brothers into bringing back Benjamin seem like he is following an inspired script that proves successful. All his brothers return and move to Egypt permanently so they can be saved. During this time, Joseph must hide from his brothers so that he can weep. It was that emotionally hard for him! Yet, without Joseph in Egypt, there would have been no Moses.

Recently, my husband and I felt inspired to go on a full-time senior mission. Though I knew it was what the Lord wanted, like Joseph, I have often gone off and wept. I had to give up my dog and will miss my grandbabies *so* much! But I have faith it is what the Lord wants me to do, and I look forward to the miracles that will come as a result. I know following inspiration can be hard, but it matters. And it's okay to weep now and then.

—Christine

"I have learned that Heavenly Father's plan for us is fabulous, and that what we do in this life really matters."

Russell M. Nelson

"Think Celestial," Oct. 2023

Genesis 45:5

Now therefore be not grieved, nor angry with yourselves, that ye sold me hither: for God did send me before you to preserve life.

All Is Forgiven

As a teenager, I shared a closet with two of my sisters, and we would borrow each other's clothes. One of my sisters had bought a special outfit with money she had earned by babysitting for hours. She had asked us not to wear it, but I did anyway. Not only did I wear her outfit, but I also stained it by spilling an entire strawberry milkshake down the front of it. The stain never came out.

Joseph's ability to see the betrayal of his brothers in an eternal view is remarkable and illustrates his righteousness. He puts his trials of being almost killed, sold as a slave, and cast into prison into the larger context of saving his entire family from starvation. He even goes so far as to tell his brothers to stop being angry at themselves for what they did.

I felt bad for what I'd done to my sister's dress. Eventually, my sister did forgive me, because she now saw my betrayal—ruining her outfit—in an eternal view. Just like Joseph, she knows that family relationships are more important than past mistakes.

—Marianna

"The fact that we can repent is the good news of the gospel! Guilt can be 'swept away.' We can be filled with joy, receive a remission of our sins, and have 'peace of conscience.'"

Dale G. Renlund

"Repentance: A Joyful Choice," Oct. 2016

Genesis 46:2

And [Jacob] said, Here am I.

Showing Up

One of my husband's mantras is "eighty percent of success is just showing up."

It's so true. Yes, we need grit, talent, skills, humility, knowledge, and more to take on the tasks of life. But it all starts with showing up.

I love showing up for God like Jacob does here. God calls him by his name, "Jacob, Jacob," and Jacob simply says, "Here am I."

This is the kind of person we hope to be—the kind that shows up for God.

I love how the Lord directs us and invites us into His work! We aren't perfect. We will mess up. But if we simply choose to show up, God will do amazing things with and through us.

What will you do today to show up for God? When the Spirit whispers to text a friend, to hug a child, to reach out to a ministering sister, you have the chance to respond, "Here am I."

—Michelle

"When your love of God consumes your service, interests, priorities and affections, you are blessed and joy attends those blessings."

Ronald A. Rasband

"What's Not to Love," Feb. 2022

Genesis 48:9

And Joseph said unto his father, They are my sons, whom God hath given me in this place. And he said, Bring them, I pray thee, unto me, and I will bless them.

My Father's Daughter

As a child, I looked forward to the first day of school: new teachers, new friends, new clothes, and a new father's blessing. I loved how my dad would smooth my hair while he pondered what the Spirit was directing him to say. When he was ready, he would place his strong hands gently on my head and give me a blessing from both him and my Heavenly Father.

Our loving Father in Heaven has gifted us many opportunities to receive personalized blessings of guidance, comfort, and healing from Him: baby blessings, confirmations, priesthood ordinations, patriarchal blessings, blessings when we're sick or hurt, being set apart for a new calling, and blessings of comfort and counsel from a father, husband, or other worthy priesthood holder.

These blessings are a precious personal glimpse into His will and love for us. Few experiences have reminded me so profoundly that He knows me perfectly because I am His—my Father's precious daughter.

—Krista

"If, through our priesthood blessings, we could perceive only a small part of the person God intends us to be, we would lose our fear and never doubt again."

James E. Faust

"Priesthood Blessings," Oct. 1995

Genesis 49:10, 27

The sceptre shall not depart from Judah, nor a lawgiver from between his feet. . . . Benjamin shall ravin as a wolf: in the morning he shall devour the prey.

The Wolf and the Lion

While preparing to write this devotional, I kept getting interrupted by phone calls. Leaving the phone behind, I headed to the library to work. In the parking lot, an impression hit me: I should go watch *The House of David* with my granddaughters—right then. I fought against the idea. I prayed, but only felt it stronger. Despite being behind, I went. Twenty minutes later, I was sitting with my three beautiful granddaughters in their basement. We clicked on the TV. I was supposed to be writing about Jacob's blessings to the sons of Israel. Imagine my surprise when the episode was on exactly that—"The Wolf and the Lion," names given to those two tribes in Jacob's blessing. What followed was a lovely discussion with my girls about how patriarchal blessings work.

When Saul was made king, the tribe of Judah must have scratched their heads. Weren't they promised "the sceptre," or to rule? Then came David, who was from the tribe of Judah, and the fulfillment of the promise was amazing! When we are given blessings that don't make sense, it doesn't mean they won't come to pass. We need to prepare and have faith. Then we can watch the miracles unfold.

—Christine

"The meaning and significance of a patriarchal blessing will be taught line upon line in the course of time by the power of the same Spirit that inspired [it]."

Kazuhiko Yamashita, quoting Dallin H. Oaks

"When to Receive Your Patriarchal Blessing," Apr. 2023

Genesis 50:16, 28 (JST)

A seer shall the Lord my God raise up, who shall be a choice seer unto the fruit of my loins. . . . And he shall bring them to the knowledge of the covenants which I have made with thy fathers; and he shall do whatsoever work I shall command him.

The Seer That God Raised Up

In the Joseph Smith translation of the Bible, a large section of Genesis 50 is added (Genesis 50:24–38). In these additional verses, we learn about the prophecies of Joseph just before his death. Joseph truly saw the future of the tribes of Israel. He prophesied of Moses leading the Israelites away from the bondage of Egypt (v. 24, 34), the Messiah (v. 24–25), and how the branch of Israel that should be broken off and carried off into a far country, referring to the Nephites (v. 25). On Joseph's deathbed, the Lord promised that the Israelites would return to righteousness, and the covenants of the Lord would be restored to them.

He also prophesied of our day (v. 24–34). He saw a choice seer that God would raise up from his descendants. Joseph saw his namesake, Joseph Smith, who would be named after his father, Joseph Smith Sr. He talked about the Prophet's great latter-day work of restoring the covenants made to Joseph of Egypt's ancestors, Abraham, Isaac, and Jacob. He saw the translation of Book of Mormon, which would confound the false doctrines that had crept into the Bible.

We are fulfilling the prophecy of Joseph of Egypt through our latter-day missionary and temple service.

—Marianna

> "We need not be timid about testifying of Joseph's mission as a prophet, seer, and revelator."
>
> Craig C. Christensen
>
> "A Choice Seer Will I Raise Up," Oct. 2016

Exodus 2:24

And God heard their groaning, and God remembered his covenant with Abraham, with Isaac, and with Jacob.

Help

One day, my twenty-two–month-old grandson pulled a plastic straw from the lid of my disposable water cup and carefully inserted the bulky rubber end of his child's plastic fork in its place. He was quite pleased with his ingenuity . . . until he attempted, and failed, at removing the now-lodged fork. I watched as he grew increasingly frustrated. Finally, he looked up at me. "Help," he said.

I knew he could do it, so I smiled and shook my head. "You can do it. Try again." With a determined sigh and a few more pulls, he was successful. He looked up, beaming. "Fork!"

Life is full of struggles—some big, some little, some self-inflicted, some not. Oftentimes, when struggles come, we look to God and ask for help. When it doesn't come when and how we think it should, we might doubt God.

But God knows what we can do. He loves us. He knows who we are, what we feel, and who we can become. And He will always respond to our pleas in the way that is best for us.

—Michelle

"I testify that our Heavenly Father hears your tearful pleadings and will always respond in perfect wisdom."

Brian K. Taylor

"Swallowed up in the Joy of Christ," Apr. 2024

Exodus 3:5

And he said, Draw not nigh hither: put off thy shoes from off thy feet, for the place whereon thou standest is holy ground.

Don't Drop Your Shoes!

While traveling in Thailand, my husband and I visited the temple that houses the Emerald Buddha. Because the temple is considered holy ground, we were required to remove our shoes before ascending the stairs to the entrance. At the top of the stairs, we left our shoes in cubbies. The attendants explained that when we exited the temple, we should retrieve our shoes but hold them until we had walked back down the stairs.

But I forgot. On my way out, I pulled my shoes from the cubby and plunked them right down on the floor. The attendants immediately rushed to me with reminders to respect the ground where I stood.

We, too, believe in the principle of "holy ground"—places, doctrines, practices, and experiences where our Father invites us to be near Him. Now, when I encounter a holy space, I tell myself, "Don't drop your shoes!"—a reminder to respect sacred things and show proper reverence to my Heavenly Father.

—Krista

> "The principal purposes of sacred time and holy places are . . . to repeatedly focus our attention upon Heavenly Father and His plan, the Lord Jesus Christ and His Atonement, the edifying power of the Holy Ghost, and the promises associated with the sacred ordinances and covenants of the Savior's restored gospel."
>
> David A. Bednar
>
> "Be Still, and Know That I Am God," Apr. 2024

Exodus 4:26 (JST)

And the Lord spared Moses and let him go, because Zipporah, his wife, circumcised the child.

A Full Partnership

My husband and I always joke that together we make a whole person. He is very technical but hates writing. In complete contrast, I love writing but don't have a technical bone in my body. By working together, we get much more done than working alone.

The beauty of the partnership of marriage, with a wife lifting her husband to better things, is expressed multiple times in the scriptures. It starts with the Fall where Eve takes the fruit so Adam and all mankind can progress. Later, Rebekah helps her son Jacob get the birthright from Isaac. In 1 Kings, Abigail saves her family, despite her husband's poor choices, by pleading with David. My favorite is Aquila and Priscilla, who are always mentioned together as though they are one unit. They provide a haven for Paul and powerful missionary opportunities in the New Testament.

With Moses, his wife's intervention saves his life. Zipporah circumcised her son when Moses was too weak to do it. The scriptures say that the Lord's "hand was about to fall upon [Moses] and to kill him" (JST, Exodus 4:24). As a husband-and-wife team works together, we can lift each other in our times of weakness so we can both survive the day.

—Christine

"The restored gospel of Jesus Christ proclaims the principle of full partnership between woman and man, both in mortal life and in the eternities."

Ulisses S. Soares

"In Partnership with the Lord," Oct. 2022

Exodus 6:30, 7:1

Moses said before the Lord, Behold, I am of uncircumcised lips, and how shall Pharaoh hearken unto me? And the Lord said . . . I have made thee a god to Pharaoh; and Aaron thy brother shall be thy prophet.

The Power of a Calling

Have you ever had a church calling where you felt you did not have the skills to be successful? I have had many: Relief Society president, mission president's wife, and nursery leader. With each calling, I prayed to the Lord and asked Him for support. In each instance, the Lord sent me unexpected helpers, and I began to realize, through His help, that I had greater abilities than I thought. I could do His work because of my faith in Him. He would make up for my inadequacies.

Moses's "uncircumcised lips" meant that he stammered and was slow of speech (JST, Exodus 6:29). He felt that he did not have the communication skills needed to talk with Pharaoh and free the Israelites from bondage. The Lord sent Aaron to be his mouthpiece. Moses was in charge, but Aaron became his voice so that Moses could perform the important work the Lord asked him to do.

When we feel unable to fulfill whatever calling we have been asked to do in the Church, we can talk with the Lord—as Moses did—and ask for His support. The Lord will always help us when we accept His call to serve.

—Marianna

> "What is the most important calling in the Church? It is the one you currently have."
>
> Dieter F. Uchtdorf
>
> "The Greatest Among You," Apr. 2017

Exodus 10:1 (JST)

And the Lord said unto Moses, Go in unto Pharaoh: for he hath hardened his heart, and the hearts of his servants, therefore I will show these my signs before him.

He Did It

While I was driving on I-15, a red sports car cut me off and sped ahead in front of me. I was upset. How could this driver be so thoughtless? I had a right to be angry. He was the one in the wrong, not me. It's easy to blame someone else—another person or even the Lord—for our negative reactions when life takes a frustrating turn, especially when our actions were not the cause of the problem.

The King James Version of the Bible translates Exodus 10:1 as "And the Lord said unto Moses, Go in unto Pharaoh: for I have hardened his heart." But in Joseph Smith's translation of the same verse, the Lord inspired Joseph to clarify who really hardened Pharaoh's heart: "for he hath hardened his heart." Pharaoh did it to himself! He hardened his own heart against the plagues of Egypt, Moses, and the Lord. The plagues that the Lord sent were signs to the unbelievers that He is the Lord, the true God of Israel and Egypt (Exodus 10:2). Because *Pharaoh* decided to harden his heart against the Lord, he did not learn the valuable lesson the Lord was trying to teach him.

Even though we may blame other people or the Lord for what happens to us, we are responsible for how we respond to life's challenges.

—Marianna

> "To be able to exercise our agency, we need to have opposing options to consider."
>
> Mathias Held
>
> "Opposition in All Things," Apr. 2024

Exodus 12:31

And [the Lord] called for Moses and Aaron by night, and said, Rise up . . . and go, serve the Lord.

One of Those Girls

I stared at my bishop and shook my head. I was twenty years old, trying to find peace and direction after my recent failed engagement. Instead of telling me my former fiancé was a horrible person for breaking up with me (which he was not), my bishop suggested I pray about serving a full-time mission.

"I'm not going to be one of those girls who serve a mission because they can't get married," I told him. I wanted to serve because *I* wanted to, not because I didn't have other options.

He smiled and invited me to read my patriarchal blessing and pray. Hesitantly, I did. And received no confirmation. Later, while my mind was on other things, I heard the call to serve. I *felt* it. And I answered because, I realized, the girl I wanted to be was the kind who listened and followed the Lord. I'm so glad I did because my mission changed my life.

As you strive to hear Him and follow, the Lord can lead you to places of healing, growth, and understanding. He can lead you to Him.

—Michelle

> "In those two words—'Hear Him'—God gives us the pattern for success, happiness, and joy in this life. We are to *hear* the words of the Lord, *hearken* to them, and *heed* what He has told us!"
>
> Russell M. Nelson
>
> "Hear Him," Apr. 2020

Exodus 14:13

Fear ye not, stand still, and see the salvation of the Lord.

Dry Ground

Like the people of Israel who stood on the shore of the Red Sea, I, too, have stood in a place of despair with no logical means of escape. When my two-year-old daughter had an unexpected seizure that left her unresponsive, we rushed her to the emergency room, where she was diagnosed with a cancerous brain tumor. Doctors and nurses worked tirelessly to save her, but she died the next day, only thirty short hours later.

I could not see a way through my grief. It was an impassable sea of darkness and pain. But as I turned to the Lord, He opened a miraculous path to help and healing. Salvation for the Israelites was the parting of the water so they could walk across on dry ground. Salvation for me is a Savior who walks beside me, helping me carry the burdens of my daughter's death that are too heavy for me to bear alone. He truly has become my Savior.

The Lord's salvation is available to all who believe that He can provide a way. He is all-powerful and all-loving, and He can part the sea for every soul to walk with Him on dry ground.

—Krista

"I testify that you are not beneath the Master's reach. The Savior 'descended below all things' and is in a divine position to lift you and claim you from the darkest abyss and bring you into 'his marvellous light.'"

Kristin M. Yee

"The Joy of Our Redemption," Oct. 2024

Exodus 15:20–21

And Miriam the prophetess . . . took a timbrel in her hand; and all the women went out after her with timbrels and with dances.

Dancing to the Prophet's Words

I could never be in a marching band. When I watch dozens of musicians walking in perfect step, it is amazing to behold. Not only do I have a bit of a limp, but I also have a wild heart that would want to dance to my own tune rather than stick to the choreography. Luckily, walking the covenant path is not like being in a marching band. We each get to choose how best to walk or limp, run, or crawl down the path . . . or to dance!

Miriam, the sister of Moses, embodies this perfectly. After the Israelites crossed the Red Sea to safety, Moses sang a song. Part of it may be familiar: "The Lord is my strength and my song, and he is become my salvation: he is my God . . . and I will exalt him" (Exodus 15:2). Miriam hears these words and gathers the women together with musical instruments and dancing. And guess what she sings . . .

Not her own song, but the words of the prophet exactly as he said them. Still, the music and dance were her own. She also led the other women to join in. May we each dance to the prophet's words and add our own music, so others may hear our joy in the Lord and follow Him.

—Christine

"If we seek joy—if we look for reasons to rejoice and to happily follow the Savior, we will find them."

Dieter F. Uchtdorf

"A Higher Joy," Apr. 2024

Exodus 16:14–15

And when the dew that lay was gone up, behold, upon the face of the wilderness there lay a small round thing, as small as the hoar frost on the ground. And when the children of Israel saw it, they said one to another, It is manna: for they wist not what it was.

What Is It?

The children of Israel had been released from bondage. They had witnessed the miracle of the parting of the Red Sea. Now, they were murmuring about food. In response to their need, the Lord sent them another miracle—manna from heaven. This miracle would sustain them throughout their journey in the wilderness. When they first saw the white round globs of goodness, they asked, "What is it?" The children of Israel did not recognize the blessing for what it was—bread from heaven.

At first, I struggled to see the blessing of being called as a nursery leader in a ward with over thirty nursery-age children. My question was: Why me? I soon began to see how this calling blessed my life. I gained eternal friends who served with me on Sundays. I learned to love these children as the Savior loves them, and I was sad when I was released. The Lord continuously sends me blessings from heaven, but I need to recognize them. The greatest blessing of all is that He sent His Only Begotten Son—the true bread from heaven (John 6:33).

—Marianna

> "May the remembrance of what our eyes have seen and our hearts have felt increase our amazement at the Savior's atoning sacrifice."
>
> Ulisses S. Soares
>
> "In Awe of Christ and His Gospel," Apr. 2023

Exodus 19:5

Now therefore, if ye will obey my voice indeed, and keep my covenant, then ye shall be a peculiar treasure unto me.

Who's Your Favorite?

When I was pregnant with my second child, I was excited yet nervous. I wanted to add to my family, but I worried I wouldn't be able to love another child the way I love my first. I knew and adored the sweet person he was. Until then, he'd been my favorite child.

As soon as I held my new daughter in my arms, that fear dissipated as the love I felt for her filled every space in my soul. I stroked her cheek and realized that she was *also* my favorite! I knew her and adored the little person she was, too.

When we think of *favorite*, we often see it as exclusionary, as if one is more loved than another. But I love this meaning of favored—noticed, known, appreciated, and loved for who we are. And that love takes on a deeper meaning when we are connected through covenants.

Dear friend, God sees you. He knows you. He loves *you*. Every part of you. And yes, you are very much His favorite.

—Michelle

> "Isn't it wonderful that there are times when we can feel so fully and personally noticed and loved. . . . Divine love never runs dry, and we are each a cherished favourite."
>
> Karl D. Hirst
>
> "God's Favourite," Oct. 2024

Exodus 20:8–10

Remember the sabbath day, to keep it holy. Six days shalt thou labour, and do all thy work: But the seventh day is the sabbath of the Lord thy God: in it thou shalt not do any work.

Six Days Shalt Thou Labour

Sometimes the work Father asks me to do can seem tedious and mundane (laundry, I'm looking at you!), but I've learned to never discount that even the most menial tasks are preparing me to work in higher and holier ways. Work has taught me valuable principles, including patience, perseverance, organization, and grit. Work has strengthened my body and challenged my mind. Work has provided opportunities for growth, service, and unexpected fulfillment. I know that our Father asks us to work because that is one vital way that we become like Him, and learn to appreciate all He does for us.

The Lord rested on the seventh day after six days of labor building the heavens and the earth. He has explained that His glory is tied to His work (see Moses 1:39). To become like our heavenly parents, to dwell with them in the celestial kingdom, means learning to work in the same way they do.

Our Father is a loving mentor who invites us to join Him in all types of work, such as caring and providing for ourselves and our families, improving and beautifying the earth, contributing creatively, mentally, and physically to society, serving in our wards and stakes, and ministering to those in need.

Sometimes our work can seem tedious and mundane, but we should never discount the fact that even the smallest or most menial tasks are preparing us to work in even higher and holier ways.

—Krista

"His work is our work."

Alan T. Phillips

"God Knows and Loves You," Oct. 2023

Exodus 21:24–25

Eye for eye, tooth for tooth, hand for hand, foot for foot. Burning for burning, wound for wound, stripe for stripe.

Fist Fights or Forgiveness

After presenting the Ten Commandments, Moses continues to explain the law of Moses for three more chapters. It is here he teaches if someone knocks your tooth out, their tooth will get pulled. If someone smacks you in the face, they get smacked.

Having five sons, I've seen this law in action more times than I can count. It often begins with one boy bumping into another. In response, his brother hits him. Because the first altercation was unintentional and the second wasn't, the first brother hits him back. The anger makes him punch harder, so the other brother returns the punch with all he's got. Then a full-out brawl ensues. That's why someone once said, "An eye for an eye, a tooth for a tooth leaves everyone blind and toothless."

At the Sermon on the Mount, Christ taught the higher law. "Ye have heard it hath been said, An eye for an eye, and tooth for a tooth: But I say unto you, that ye resist not evil: but whosoever shall smite thee on thy right cheek, turn to him the other also" (Matthew 5:38–39). Not taking offense and forgiving others for their weaknesses leaves us free of all that negative emotion which only escalates. It may even diffuse the other person's anger. If nothing else, as we forgive, the Lord will forgive us—which is enough.

—Christine

"I repeat my call to end the conflicts in your life. Exercise the humility, courage, and strength required both to forgive and to seek forgiveness."

Russell M. Nelson

"The Power of Spiritual Momentum," Apr. 2022

Exodus 23:4–5

If thou meet thine enemy's ox or his ass going astray, thou shalt surely bring it back to him again. If thou see the ass of him that hateth thee lying under his burden, . . . thou shalt surely help with him.

Care for My Enemy?

My husband, Travis, served his mission in Russia. During one especially freezing winter, he was assigned a difficult companion. Travis tried to be patient and motivational, but nothing helped. The work became agonizingly slow. Travis felt stuck.

After a frustrating and bitterly cold day, the two Elders returned home in low spirits. Travis retreated to the bedroom to pray. "Heavenly Father, I'm so angry. I don't know what to do." A thought came into his mind. "Go put his boots on the heater." His companion had left his snowy boots by the door. Without the heater, the shoes would be wet and freezing cold the next morning. Travis pushed off the thought. He would take care of them later. He started his prayer over. Again, he thought about the boots. Again, he pushed off the thought.

By the third prompting, Travis got the message. The moment he took care of his companion's shoes, something happened in his heart. That simple act of service turned frustration into compassion. That was the day things began to improve.

—Krista

"I testify that as we strive to incorporate the Savior's compassionate example into our lives, our capacity to compliment the virtues of our neighbors will increase and our natural instinct to judge their imperfections will decrease."

Ulisses S. Soares

"The Savior's Abiding Compassion," Oct. 2021

Exodus 25:8

And let them make me a sanctuary; that I may dwell among them.

I Feel God in My Heart

In 2011, we adopted our youngest child. She was seven years old. She'd come from a complicated background of love, neglect, change, and difficulty. A month after the legal adoption, our family knelt together in the sealing room of the Sacramento temple as my father, an ordained sealer, sealed us together.

As we sat on the couch in the sealing room, I looked down at my daughter and asked how she felt. She said, "I feel God in my heart."

This is part of the sacred power of the temple—amid the internal and external chaos, we can find the Lord there.

How wonderful that we are so loved that Heavenly Father and Jesus Christ want us to have a place we can dwell together now! Regardless of where we've been, or what's going on around us, inside or out, we can come to the temple and feel God there.

—Michelle

> The temple is the Lord's house and a sanctuary from the world. His Spirit envelops those who worship within those sacred walls."
>
> Ronald A. Rasband
>
> "Recommended to the Lord," Oct. 2020

Exodus 27:20

And thou shalt command the children of Israel, that they bring thee pure oil olive beaten for the light, to cause the lamp to burn always.

Temple Light

I remember the first time I saw the Washington DC Temple. I was visiting a friend who lived in the area, and though the temple was closed for cleaning that week, I still wanted to see it. My friend convinced me it would be best to wait until dark. "Trust me," she said.

We drove along the Capital Beltway when suddenly the temple appeared as if rising from the ground, shining bright and glorious, a heavenly call to come and worship. The sight was breathtaking!

As in days of old, our temples are always lit—a reminder that this is the house of the Lord, and He is always home. As we serve in the temple, we can receive inspiration, comfort, and direction from the Lord—heavenly light. He hears us. He knows our hearts. We can always find light at the temple.

—Krista

> "I testify that Jesus Christ is the everlasting light that 'shineth in darkness.' There is no darkness that can ever suppress, extinguish, overpower, or defeat that light. Our Heavenly Father freely offers that light to you. You are never alone."
>
> Timothy J. Dyches
>
> "Light Cleaveth unto Light," Apr. 2021

Exodus 29:4

And Aaron and his sons thou shalt bring unto the door of the tabernacle of the congregation, and shalt wash them with water.

I Will Meet You

As with the ancient temple, the first ordinance we receive when entering into our temple covenants is washing and anointing. If you turn to Exodus 29 and read about it, parts are similar to our current ordinance. But there is also a lot of complex animal sacrifice. It includes sin offerings, an atonement offering, wave offerings, and heave offerings (which are similar to weightlifting because the meat offerings were lifted up and presented to the priests). Although there is beautiful symbolism in the sacrifices we make to get to the temple, these Old Testament sacrifices can be hard to understand.

However, near the end of the chapter, the Lord clearly states the purpose and gift of temple covenants. He says it is at the temple "where I will meet you, to speak there unto thee . . . And I will dwell among the children of Israel, and will be their God" (Exodus 29:43, 45).

Making and keeping sacred covenants turns us into God's covenant people. But more than that, it is essential for us to truly hear everything He wants us to know.

I personally know there are some messages we can only receive from God within the temple walls.

—Christine

"Sacred temple covenants and ordinances can strengthen us and purify our hearts as we 'Hear Him!'"

David A. Bednar

"Let This House Be Built unto My Name," Apr. 2020

Exodus 30:30

And thou shalt anoint Aaron and his sons, and consecrate them, that they may minister unto me in the priest's office.

Ministering

As ministering sisters, we are to live a higher law. Rather than checking off every month a visit to an assigned person's home, we are supposed to minister to them. But what does it mean to minister to another person?

When I was pregnant with my tenth child, our family moved to the Northwest, far away from family and friends. We were all trying to navigate our new life. At this crucial time, I developed a serious medical problem that required me to be confined to bed rest for the rest of my pregnancy. I could not drive, and I was limited in the amount of time I could be out of bed. I had nine active children to take care of, and my husband's new job would not allow him to take time off. That is when I learned what it meant to minister to another person. Sisters whom I had never met before would drive my children to games and lessons, clean my house, and make meals. I really needed a friend to talk to, so sisters in the ward would come and visit. Through this experience, I learned that connecting with someone is the best way to minister.

Ministering is not a new concept. Aaron and his sons were commanded to minister to the children of Israel through their consecrated priestly offices. Their ministering connected the Israelites with the Lord. When we minister, we connect ourselves and our sisters with the love of the Lord through our service to them.

—Marianna

"Let us reach out and care as our Savior would."

Gerrit W. Gong

"Ministering," Apr. 2023

Exodus 32:34

Behold, mine angels shall go before thee.

Thank You for Taking Care of My Daughter

Toward the end of Mom's life, she experienced a minor stroke. I flew down to California to spend some time with her and Dad, and to help them pack and move into a new home. Seeing Mom in this new state wasn't easy for me, and the work around the house was tiring. I was emotionally and physically strained. I prayed earnestly for help, support, and strength.

Late one night, I was packing the kitchen and listening to music when I heard these words: "Thank you for taking care of my daughter."

I turned, expecting to see my grandma there. The voice had been so loud. So clear. Except no one was there. My grandma had passed away ten years before.

As I stared into the empty dining room, I felt warm. Somehow I knew I wasn't alone. I was being taken care of while I was taking care of Mom.

I believe in angels. Someday, when the veil is pulled back, I think we will be surprised at how many were sent to help us, comfort us, and do the Lord's work with us, even when we don't see them.

—Michelle

"I believe in angels . . . [The Lord] knows who needs angelic help, and He will put them in our path."

Carlos A. Godoy

"I Believe in Angels," Oct. 2020

Exodus 33:11

And the Lord spake unto Moses face to face, as a man speaketh unto his friend.

My Savior, My Friend

I treasure the knowledge that the mighty God of the universe, who has all power and wisdom, would descend from His throne to talk to and spend time with me as a friend. When I think about a perfect friend, I imagine someone who is always there, celebrating my successes, crying with me over my losses, interested in all the things I love, and cheering me on even when I come in last. A perfect friend is patient, kind, and a superb listener. Jesus is all of these things and more.

I need my friend Jesus constantly. It's not enough for me to just check in with Him in the morning and evening during formal prayer, so I've decided to take Him with me in the hours between. I picture Him at my side, included in every moment of my day, like a best friend should be. We chat and work together over every task, joy, and trouble that comes my way. This exercise helps me view the Lord as approachable and accessible. With Him at my side, I am more confident in asking for His help. He teaches me how to work, serve, repent, and see others like He does. I strive to become the type of friend that He is to me.

—Krista

"Nowhere in holy writ do we hear Him say, 'Ye are just my friends.' Rather, He taught that 'greater love hath no man than this, that a man lay down his life for his friends.' And 'ye are they whom my Father hath given me; ye are my friends.'"

David L. Buckner

"Ye Are My Friends," Oct. 2024

Exodus 34:1–2 (JST)

Hew thee two other tables of stone . . . but it shall not be according to the first, for I will take away the priesthood out of their midst . . . that they shall not enter into my presence, into my rest, in the days of their pilgrimage.

Turning the Chainsaw On

There was once a lumberjack who could cut down fifty trees a day with a simple ax. A chainsaw salesman asked him to try his product. "It will triple your production." The next day, the lumberjack looked sweaty and exhausted. "I tried my hardest," he said, "but I only cut down forty trees." Flabbergasted, the chainsaw salesman took the saw back. "Only forty? It must be broken." He pulled the cord, and the engine roared to life. "What's that?" asked the surprised lumberjack. He hadn't known of the chainsaw's full capacity.

After forty days on Mount Sinai, Moses found the Israelites worshipping a golden calf. His "anger waxed hot" (Exodus 32:19), and he broke the first set of tablets that held the fulness of the law. Moses was instructed to make new tablets. On them, the Lord wrote the lesser law. The Israelites could still find Christ, but it would be more challenging. They were only given a simple ax.

Today the fulness of the gospel has been restored. We have access to all priesthood ordinances and blessings. But are we using our covenants to the fullest, or, like the lumberjack, have we not turned the chainsaw on? The way we do that is by focusing on Jesus Christ and doing His will.

—Christine

"Just as we are today, God's ancient people were invited to see their lives through Him in order to see more of Him in their lives."

Tracy Y. Browning

"Seeing More of Jesus Christ in Our Lives," Oct. 2022

Exodus 35:2

Six days shall work be done, but on the seventh day there shall be to you an holy day, a sabbath of rest to the Lord: whosoever doeth work therein shall be put to death.

Staying Alive

The children of Israel were told to keep the Sabbath as a day of holiness and rest or they would be put to death. The Lord was giving them a physical law to protect their families from a world of physical labor and spiritual trials.

His law has not changed today. I may not be put to death physically, but spiritually, my soul feels starved and malnourished as I deal with work issues, people problems, and world news during the week. Even though I take bites of spiritual food on weekdays through scripture reading and prayer, my spiritual feast happens on Sunday. I gain the nourishment and rest I need to stay spiritually alive for the next week.

Wherever I am in the world on Sunday, I try to find a ward or branch to visit. This practice has brought incredible spiritual experiences into my life! Whether I am in Pune, India; Pretoria, South Africa; or Dayton, Ohio, being with the Saints strengthens my testimony.

I need to keep a holy and restful Sabbath day to stay spiritually alive in today's world.

—Marianna

"Let your family be filled with love as you honor the Sabbath all day long and experience its spiritual blessings throughout the week."

L. Tom Perry

"The Sabbath and the Sacrament," Apr. 2024

Exodus 39:30

And they made the plate of the holy crown of pure gold, and wrote upon it a writing, like to the engravings of a signet, HOLINESS TO THE LORD.

Holiness to the Lord

I've heard "holiness to the Lord" in reference to the temple being holy in place and purpose. I completely agree. But I also love another layer of possible meaning. What if "holiness" could refer to us?

The scriptures teach us that we can become more sanctified and holy through our faith. Worshipping in the house of the Lord *is* an act of faith. We have faith that the gospel is real, that the temple is His house, that angels will attend us there, that we can learn and grow and change and be helped along the way.

This is God's purpose in a sense—our holiness. And this is what we bring: our current level of holiness and our desire to become more holy. We bring our "holiness" to the Lord, not to say we are perfect, but so that He can perfect us. To me, this is a beautiful phrase and example of a covenant relationship. We bring what we have to Him, and He makes it more. What a holy place and experience indeed.

—Michelle

"'Holiness to the Lord.' These inspired words are a clear invitation that when we enter the Lord's house, we embark on a sacred journey of learning to become higher and holier disciples of Jesus Christ."

Ulisses S. Soares

"Covenant Confidence Through Jesus Christ," Apr. 2024

Exodus 40:13

And thou shalt put upon Aaron the holy garments, and anoint him, and sanctify him; that he may minister unto me in the priest's office.

A Symbol of Discipleship

At baptism, I took upon myself the name of Jesus Christ. Every Sunday, I partake of the bread and water to help me remember this baptismal covenant that I have made with Him. But that reminder comes only once a week.

When I went to the temple to receive my endowment, the initiatory ordinance clothed me in the garment of the holy priesthood. These garments also symbolize that I am taking upon myself His name. But this outward symbol is one I have the privilege of wearing twenty-four hours a day, every day. Even though they may, at times, be hot and uncomfortable, or prevent me from wearing the latest fashions, I am blessed to wear them as a symbol of my constant devotion to Him.

I remember the first day I wore garments after going through the temple for the first time. They made me feel safe, covered, and protected from the world. I have been wearing garments for forty-eight years, and my garments still make me feel that way. I am thankful for their reminder of the covenants I have made.

—Marianna

> "I believe that my willingness to wear the holy garment becomes *my* symbol to Him. It is my own personal sign to God, not a sign to others."
>
> J. Anette Davis
>
> "Put Ye On the Lord Jesus Christ," Apr. 2024

Leviticus 1:3–4

He shall offer it of his own voluntary will at the door of the tabernacle . . . and it shall be accepted for him to make atonement for him.

The Atonement Offering

When I served in the Rexburg temple, I was often put on hall duty by the stairs where a lovely painting depicts the ancient sacrifices of the law of Moses. It encouraged me to ponder how we live those sacrifices today. My favorite sacrifice is the Atonement Offering.

Unlike many ancient temple sacrifices done as payment for sin or in preparations for holy feasts, the Atonement Offering could be done any time and as often as one chose. The only requirements were that a person offered it of their "own voluntary will" and that the animal be without blemish. Finally, the animal was killed, washed, and completely burned. Every bit was given to the Lord.

I realized my temple service follows a similar pattern. First, temple attendance isn't scheduled by the Lord. I can go as often as I choose. No one compels me to serve. I do so of "my own voluntary will." And, I must be without blemish, which is why I have a temple recommend.

Lastly, while I'm in the temple, every bit of myself is given to the Lord. I leave behind my clothes, my purse, even my cell phone. But as I worship, oh, the blessings I get in return! The veil thins, I can feel Christ's atoning power, and my heart becomes one with Him.

—Christine

> "The Savior's Atonement, which makes available both His redeeming and His enabling power, is the ultimate blessing that Jesus Christ offers to all."
>
> Brent H. Nielson
>
> "Is There No Balm in Gilead?," Oct. 2021

Leviticus 3:1

And if his oblation be a sacrifice of peace offering . . . he shall offer it without blemish before the Lord.

Offering Gratitude

When Lehi's sons returned safely from their trip to Jerusalem to retrieve the brass plates, the family offered "sacrifice and burnt offerings unto the Lord; and they gave thanks unto the God of Israel" (1 Nephi 5:9). Under the law of Moses, there were three types of altar sacrifices: sin offerings, burnt offerings, and peace offerings. The third type, peace offerings, was the most common, offered during occasions of rejoicing and gratitude to God for His blessings.

When I'm in pain or troubled, my natural inclination is to seek help from the Lord. But when things are going right, how often do I think to run to Him in thanksgiving? Our baptismal covenants include the promise that His Spirit may *always* be with us, which means that He accompanies us through our hardest days *and* He is also there to celebrate our best and most cherished moments. Our happiness is made possible because of and through Jesus Christ, and we can strive to be more intentional in celebrating our joy *with* Him.

—Krista

> "Each new morning is a gift from God. Even the air we breathe is a loving loan from him. He preserves us from day to day and supports us from one moment to another. Therefore, our first noble deed of the morning should be a humble prayer of gratitude."
>
> Russell M. Nelson
>
> "Joy Cometh in the Morning," Oct. 1986

Leviticus 6:6–7

And he shall bring his trespass offering unto the Lord . . . and it shall be forgiven him.

She Felt Peace

One Sunday years ago, I stepped out of a Relief Society lesson for a few minutes. When I returned, the sisters were engaged in a gospel discussion. I raised my hand and contributed some thoughts I felt good about. Afterward, a sister approached me and told me my comment had hurt her deeply. I felt awful! I would never intentionally hurt her.

As we talked, we realized that while I was out, she'd made a comment I hadn't heard and that my comment had been completely unrelated to hers. Though the pain my words caused was unintentional, I still apologized. I didn't want to be the source of her pain. I prayed for her, and eventually, she felt peace.

Part of being human means we often leave a wake of hurt behind our mistakes, choices, and even good intentions. I love that we have the gift to repent of them and to make amends.

I love even more that the same Atonement that mends our pain can also mend what we've hurt in others. We can't fix everything, but we can try to trust the Lord's power to do the rest.

—Michelle

> "Although the Savior has power to mend what we cannot fix, He commands us to do all we can to make restitution as part of our repentance."
>
> James A. Rasband
>
> "Ensuring a Righteous Judgment," Apr. 2020

Leviticus 11:44

For I am the Lord your God: ye shall therefore sanctify yourselves, and ye shall be holy; for I am holy.

Twenty-Two Miles on a Wooden Leg

I live near the historical homesite of John R. Moyle, a master stonemason for the Salt Lake City Temple. For years, John would wake up early Monday morning and walk twenty-two miles over the hills from his home in Alpine to the temple site. He worked on the temple all week, then returned home late Friday night.

One weekend at home, John was milking a stubborn cow who kicked him in the leg. The bone shattered, and his leg was amputated. But that didn't stop him. He carved a wooden leg and slowly, painfully relearned to walk. When he had the strength to walk the perimeter of his property, he knew he could return to the temple. John strapped on his wooden leg, hiked twenty-two miles, climbed the temple scaffolding, and carved the words "Holiness to the Lord, The House of the Lord."

When I see those words above the entrance to the temple, I think of John's dedication to the Lord and reflect on what it means to be holy. Holiness is to be like God—spiritually and morally pure. If John could walk twenty-two miles on a wooden leg, what sacrifice can I make to show the Lord my dedication to becoming more like Him?

—Krista

> "As we observe our covenants by sacrifice, we are made holy through the grace of Jesus Christ; and at the altars of the holy temple, with broken hearts and contrite spirits, we give our holiness to the Lord."
>
> L. Todd Budge
>
> "Giving Holiness to the Lord," Oct. 2021

Leviticus 13:3

It is a plague of leprosy: and the priest shall look on him, and pronounce him unclean.

Incurable

In Old Testament times, leprosy was the only illness that could label a person permanently unclean. Anciently, it was incurable. If a priest branded you a leper, you were most often shunned for life—even by the Church.

Today, some may feel that same way. Conditions like anxiety, depression, difficulty reading, forgetfulness, addictive personalities, issues from past trauma, or physical disabilities can last our entire lives and don't have a cure. It is easy to feel like because we are not healed of these burdens, we don't belong to those who seem so perfect in the church. But this is one of Satan's big lies.

During His lifetime, Christ healed the lepers of their incurable illness, but He made only the grateful leper whole. The greater miracle is when He makes us whole without healing our burdens. Though we may have to carry them until the resurrection, our difficult conditions will not lessen the blessings and love we can feel as we reach out to the Lord. In fact, our physical burdens may help others feel both understood and accepted as they struggle with their own weaknesses.

—Christine

"Wholeness does not necessarily mean physical and emotional restoration in this life."

Camille N. Johnson

"Spiritually Whole in Him," Apr. 2025

Leviticus 15:1

And if a woman have an issue, and her issue in her flesh be blood, she shall be put apart seven days: and whosoever toucheth her shall be unclean until the even. And every thing that she lieth upon in her separation shall be unclean.

Healing Unclean Women

Whenever I read these verses in the Old Testament, I think of the woman in the New Testament who had an issue of blood for twelve years. I think about how lonely she must have been. Everybody and everything she touched would be considered unclean. No one could touch her. No one could live with her.

When I am in pain, no one can live with me either. I find myself seeking the comfort of my bed and just wanting to be alone. A few years ago, my hip was hurting me so much that I was having a hard time walking. When the woman in the New Testament was in pain, she reached out to the Savior and touched Him. The Savior turned to her and said: "Daughter, be of good comfort: thy faith hath made thee whole; go in peace" (Luke 8:48). Like this good woman, I, too, needed to reach out to the Savior for His healing, not just for my hip, but for the way I was handling my pain.

We are all unclean women in some aspect of our lives. We need to reach out to the Savior in faith for our cleansing. Then, we will find the healing and peace we seek.

—Marianna

> "Through the Atonement of Jesus Christ, all that is broken can be healed."
>
> S. Mark Palmer
>
> "Return unto Me . . . That I May Heal You," Apr. 2025

Leviticus 19:18

Thou shalt not . . . bear any grudge against the children of thy people, but thou shalt love thy neighbour as thyself.

Be Nice to My Friend

Last year I was having an awful day. Things were bad, externally and internally. Typically, I cope pretty well, but on this particular day, I was angry. Angry at the world, but more so with myself. I was texting a friend about how I was so . . . (insert long list of very negative things here).

She sent me one simple text back: *Be nice to my friend. I love her.*

Sometimes loving ourselves is hard. We can be so critical and unkind. But, loving ourselves is the foundation of how we love our our heavenly parents as well as our Brother, Jesus Christ. We truly are loved by Them. As we strive to see ourselves as They do, we will be able to see the good in us They love so much. We can also see our weaknesses, faults, and negative traits through Their eyes.

You are wonderful. Faults and all. Today, I hope you are kind to my friend—to you. You deserve God's love, my love, and your own love.

—Michelle

> "Have you ever thought of loving yourself as a commandment? Our Heavenly Father wants us to love ourselves—not to become prideful or self-centered, but to see ourselves as He sees us: we are His cherished children."
>
> S. Gifford Nielson
>
> "This Is Our Time!," Apr. 2021

Leviticus 20:1–2

And the Lord spake unto Moses, saying,
Again thou shalt say to the children of Israel . . .

Higher and Holier

Can I be honest? Reading Leviticus makes me exhausted for the ancient Israelites. The law of Moses had so many rules to learn and follow! After Christ's death fulfilled the law, I wonder if it was challenging for them to move away from this prescriptive set of rules they had abided by for generations.

The Lord constantly moves His people toward higher and holier ways of living His gospel. In my lifetime, the focus of many Church programs, policies, and procedures has shifted away from merely checking boxes to providing opportunities for each of us to discover God's will.

While discussing some recent changes, my daughter said, "Mom, I don't want to do something just because I can. I want to understand what God wants me to do." So wise.

Following a set list of rules might make us behave well, but discovering God's will transforms us. It's not about how well we follow the rules, but about developing a relationship with Him and following His will because we love and trust Him.

—Krista

> "He is pleading with us to 'increase [our] spiritual capacity to receive revelation.' He is inviting us to 'hear Him.' He is calling us to follow Him in higher and holier ways."
>
> Dieter F. Uchtdorf
>
> "Jesus Christ Is the Strength of Youth," Oct. 2022

Leviticus 23:2

Speak unto the children of Israel, and say unto them, Concerning the feasts of the Lord, which ye shall proclaim to be holy convocations even these are my feasts.

The Same Yesterday, Today, and Forever

The first time I presented the three great feasts of Israel to my early-morning seminary class, I learned something new.

The first feast, Passover, lasted a week in April and was also the new year. The Jews would gather at the temple, sacrifice a lamb, bring a portion home, and feast with their families while retelling the miracle of being freed from Egypt.

The second feast was Pentecost, which is only two days long. Fifty days after Passover, the Israelites celebrated receiving the law at Mount Sinai. It was at this feast that the early disciples of Christ received the Holy Ghost.

Finally, the Festival of Tabernacles was in October. Five days after the Day of Atonement, the only time the high priest could enter the temple, the people would gather and listen to the inspiration of the high priest while in the holy of holies.

After I told my students about these three days, one of them asked why we don't celebrate them anymore. I looked at the dates—April and October. We still gather, listen to the words of the high priests, and celebrate with our families. God is the same yesterday, today, and forever. But what of Pentecost? What do you think?

—Christine

> "So please, please, stay for the whole feast even if you aren't sure about the broccoli."
>
> Jeffrey R. Holland
>
> "Fear Not: Believe Only!," Apr. 2022

Leviticus 26:1

Ye shall make you no idols nor graven image, neither rear you up a standing image, neither shall ye set up any image of stone in your land to bow down unto it: for I am the Lord your God.

Idols of the Internet

We are a society who looks down at our phones—a lot! When I walk down the hallway at work, people run into me because they are looking at their phones rather than watching where they are going. They are so busy scrolling, they do not even realize that others are having to step out of their way.

When entering an elevator, people look at their screens rather than at the face of the person next to them. A smile, a nod, a simple greeting would be sufficient to brighten someone else's day. But screens seem to be more enticing.

God warned us about worshipping idols. We do not have graven images that we bow down to or pray to, but we do have phones and screens that we bow our heads over and even lie down with at night.

The idols we worship may be different from the ones the Lord was originally warning about in the Old Testament, but our new gods are just as deadly to our faith. Ask yourself, What am I looking at today?

—Marianna

> "Mortality is a master class in learning to choose the things of greatest eternal import."
>
> Russell M. Nelson
>
> "Think Celestial," Oct. 2023

Numbers 1:19

As the Lord commanded Moses, so he numbered them in the wilderness of Sinai.

Kevin!

In the classic holiday movie *Home Alone*, eight-year-old Kevin is left behind when a cousin miscounts the family members as they rush to the airport to catch their flight. A head was counted, but it wasn't Kevin's. His euphoria of being alone fades quickly as reality sinks in—his family had forgotten about him.

When his mother realizes on the plane what has happened, she sits up and yells, "Kevin!" Then, she spends the rest of the movie getting back to her lone boy.

It's a fun movie with a lovely message—family is important. But I love the deeper truth it makes me think of: *You are not forgotten.*

God has not miscounted or ignored you. He knows exactly where and who you are right now. He knows your hopes, your struggles, your efforts, and your heart. And He is doing all He can to help and care for you. You are seen. You are numbered. And you are loved.

—Michelle

"When we feel insignificant, cast off, and forgotten, we learn that we may be assured that God has not forgotten us."

Dieter F. Uchtdorf

"God Among Us," Apr. 2021

Numbers 4:49

According to the commandment of the Lord they were numbered by the hand of Moses, every one according to his service, and according to his burden.

From the Nursery, With Love

The tribe of Levi was set apart for a special service: taking down and setting up the tabernacle. Each family in the tribe had a specific assignment. The family of Gershon cared for the coverings of the tabernacle and the hangings of the courtyard. The family of Kohath was responsible for the ark of the covenant and other sacred items. The family of Merari attended to the walls, bars, pillars, and bases of the tabernacle. Each responsibility was vital to the sacredness of and worship in the tabernacle, and yet, is it possible that there was some comparison about which job was more important?

As we serve in Church assignments and callings, we may feel tempted to compare ourselves to others. Do we say we're *only* serving in the nursery? Are we disappointed by a less exotic mission call? We have all committed to serve the Lord. The application of where and how doesn't matter; only that we serve Him with all our heart, might, mind, and strength in whatever assignment we are given.

—Krista

"We do not 'step down' when we are released, and we do not 'step up' when we are called. . . . I once presided at the release of a young stake president who had given fine service for nine years. . . . [He and his wife] were called to be the nursery leaders in their ward. Only in this Church would that be seen as equally honorable!"

Dallin H. Oaks

"The Keys and Authority of the Priesthood," Apr. 2014

Numbers 6:2, 5

When either man or woman shall separate themselves to vow a vow of a Nazarite, to separate themselves unto the Lord . . . there shall no razor come upon his head . . . until the days be fulfilled. . . . He shall be holy.

Nazarites Today

My husband and I are serving as missionaries in the London area. Yesterday we visited Arundel Castle. Greg was ahead of me, and as I hurried to catch up, I heard a guard say to his coworker, "You know, I'm related to Joseph Smith." I turned and smiled at him. "Really?" He explained how he saw my husband's badge and tie and knew who we were, though he was not a member.

The concept of missionaries being recognizably different from others began with the law of Moses. Nazarites were those who chose to fulfill a full-time calling to serve God. They vowed not to cut their hair, abstained from certain foods, and even wore different clothing from common people, mostly skins. Samson, Samuel the prophet who called King David, and John the Baptist were all Nazarites. We know that because of their physical descriptions.

Today men and women who serve missions follow a similar pattern. Men cut their hair short. All missionaries abstain from dating, and their clothing choices reflect their calling. The gift of these rules is that people can recognize full-time elders and sisters from across the street, the same way my husband sparked a discussion about family history. In this way, missionaries become a light shining to all nations. Even a light in the darkness, easily seen.

—Christine

"All missionaries teach and testify of the Savior. The spiritual darkness in the world makes the light of Jesus Christ needed more than ever."

Russell M. Nelson

"Preaching the Gospel of Peace," Apr. 2022

Numbers 11:1

And when the people complained, it displeased the Lord: and the Lord heard it; and his anger was kindled; and the fire of the Lord burnt among them, and consumed them that were in the uttermost parts of the camp.

Consumed by Complaining

Jenny recently returned from her mission. After coming home, everything seemed to go wrong. She hoped to get a job at a nearby store as a cashier, but they did not have any openings. She applied at the local university, but she received a rejection letter instead. She played on a community volleyball team, but during a game, she fell and tore her meniscus.

After she shared her list of problems, which were significant, I asked her, "Since coming home from your mission, how many times do you pray each day?" She was taken aback. She thought for a moment and said, "Well, maybe once or twice." I then asked, "How often did you pray on your mission every day?" She soon realized that acknowledging her dependence on the Lord and praying for His help could change her heart and her situation.

When we forget to talk with the Lord about our problems and become consumed with complaints, we will find ourselves consumed with misery. The Lord can help us understand that we need to be patient because He will help us in His own time and in His own way. Jenny's situation did not change immediately, but her heart did, which brought her strength to deal with the problems she was facing.

—Marianna

> "The joy we feel has little to do with the circumstances of our lives and everything to do with the focus of our lives."
>
> Russell M. Nelson
>
> "Joy and Spiritual Survival," Oct. 2016

Numbers 12:6

And [the Lord] said, Hear now my words: If there be a prophet among you, I the Lord will make myself known unto him.

The Room Wasn't Empty

Years ago, as my cousin and I walked around Temple Square while my older brother and his wife were being sealed, I had an idea: I wanted to meet President Ezra Taft Benson.

The empty foyer of the small Church Office Building seemed to be a sign. So, we climbed the stairs to where I assumed President Benson would be. We were stopped halfway up by a security guard who was so amused at my gumption that, even though President Benson was traveling that day, he offered to give us a tour.

Then we came to the room where all the prophets meet each week. A long table ran down the center, surrounded by chairs. It was empty . . . but it wasn't.

The Spirit in that room was palpable, like a rush of warm air on a snowy winter day. It was rich and powerful, and testified of who prays in that room and who answers. Prophets truly are called of God. They commune with the Lord, leading and loving us for Him. Of this I know to be true.

—Michelle

"I promise you that no leaders on earth are more honest with you than prophets are. And no leaders care more about you and your future."

Sheri L. Dew

"Prophets Can See Around Corners," BYU devotional, Nov. 2022

Numbers 15:38–39

Bid them that they make them fringes in the borders of their garments . . . that ye may look upon it, and remember all the commandments of the Lord, and do them.

Outward Expressions, Inner Commitment

Let's admit it: Our mortal memories are fallible, prone to forgetfulness and lapses in attention. (Daydreamers, raise your hands!) Our Heavenly Father knows this about us, so He gives us visual reminders, observances, and rituals to help keep us on track. It's one reason we attend church and partake of the sacrament every week.

The fringes that the Lord commanded ancient Israelites to wear on the borders of their garments, and which are still worn by some Jewish men, are called "tzitzis." These tassels or fringes are worn on the four corners of the outer garments, each made with one blue strand. They serve as visual reminders to observe all of God's commandments.

Similarly, those who have been endowed in the temple wear the temple garment as a reminder of the covenants made in the house of the Lord, an outward expression of an inner commitment to follow Him (see *General Handbook*, 26.3.3.2).

But even if we haven't yet made those covenants in the temple, our thoughts and actions can still be a sign to the Lord that we are committed to obeying His commandments and following Him.

—Krista

"What sign do I want to give to God?"

David A. Bednar, quoting Russell M. Nelson

"The Principles of My Gospel," Apr. 2021

Numbers 19:2, 19

Speak unto the children of Israel, that they bring thee a red heifer without spot. . . . And the clean person shall sprinkle upon the unclean on the third day, and on the seventh day; . . . and [he] shall be clean at even.

The Red Heifer

On a tour bus in Israel ten years ago, I was talking to another woman about biblical symbols when she asked, "Have you heard of the red heifer?" I hadn't. She smiled and said to study it. I did, and was so grateful for this reminder of all the Savior does and will do on our behalf.

The red heifer was a sacrifice made outside the temple walls. (Christ was crucified outside the city walls.) The animal was sacrificed with cedar (for cleansing), hyssop (for healing) and scarlet (for blood). Then the ashes were mixed with water (emblems of the sacrament). For those exposed to death, the holy water was sprinkled on the third day (dispensation of Moses) and the seventh day (the Millennium). By the end of the seventh day, they were made clean. (Through Christ we are healed, made pure, and will overcome death.)

Nine red heifers have been sacrificed, but covenant Jews are still waiting and watching for the tenth red heifer to come. As are we. Surprisingly, I recently ran into the "red heifer" lady again, and it was a moment of joy. We are both serving together in Britian and both looking forward to that happy day when the tenth red heifer, our Savior, is revealed.

—Christine

> "Jesus Christ, the Redeemer of Israel, leads this, His Church. He is preparing to come again. May we likewise prepare to receive Him."
>
> Russell M. Nelson
>
> "Confidence in the Presence of God," Apr. 2025

Numbers 20:12

And the Lord spake unto Moses and Aaron, because ye believed me not, to sanctify me in the eyes of the children of Israel, therefore ye shall not bring this congregation into the land which I have given them.

Acknowledge the Lord

Moses had performed many miracles for the complaining children of Israel on their journey in the wilderness. Three days after crossing the Red Sea, the Israelites were thirsty, and the only water to drink was bitter. Moses cried unto the Lord and was told how to fix the water with a tree branch. When performing this miracle, Moses acknowledged the Lord's power in providing it and reminded the people to "diligently hearken to the voice of the Lord thy God, and . . . keep all his statutes" (Exodus 15:26).

In Numbers 20, the Lord provided another water miracle for the thirsty Israelites. But this time, Moses did not sanctify the Lord in the eyes of the people by acknowledging Him in this miracle. Because of this, the Lord would not allow Moses and Aaron to enter into the promised land.

President Russell M. Nelson told us to seek for miracles. Because of the prophet's counsel, I try to find miracles in my life. A phone call from a friend when I'm having a bad day, helping a temple patron who is lost finding the sealing office, being impressed to send a note to a grandchild who is struggling become miracles to me rather than coincidences. I begin to see the daily miracles that the Lord sends to me every day.

—Marianna

> "Miracles, signs, and wonders abound among followers of Jesus Christ today, in your lives and mine."
>
> Ronald A. Rasband
>
> "Behold! I Am a God of Miracles," Apr. 2021

Numbers 24:11

I thought to promote thee unto great honour; but, lo, the Lord hath kept thee back from honour.

Thank You for Trying

I had known since I was a young girl that I was destined for fame. Then everyone would love me and know I mattered.

When I was nineteen or twenty, I auditioned for the lead in a band. As my voice rose higher and louder, so did the twitch in the band manager's eye. Afterward, he shook my hand and, with a kind smile, said, "Thank you for trying."

This, plus a handful of other special moments, helped me to understand that God had a different path for me. One that didn't involve my worth being dictated by the people around me. I began to see myself differently—through God's eyes. I took the power I'd given others to define me, reclaimed it, and gave it to God.

As you ponder where your value comes from, let God—not the world—tell you who you are and who you can become. You just might love what He has to say, even (or maybe especially) if it's different from what you or the world thinks.

—Michelle

"Our focus is on the Savior. . . . We go out of our way to avoid any perception that our actions may be influenced by the honors of men, to receive personal recognition, generate more likes, be quoted, or published."

Jack N. Derard

"Integrity: A Christlike Attribute," Apr. 2024

Numbers 26:2

Take the sum of all the congregation of the children of Israel.

Counted

My husband walked in the door that night to find me on the couch, still in my pajamas, surrounded by a mountain of laundry taller than my head. I'd burned the macaroni and cheese dinner, and the kids were running wild, half-naked, through the house. My husband brought me my car keys and scriptures. "Why don't you drive to the temple and take a break?" I changed into a pair of jeans and got in the car.

On the back lawn of the temple grounds, I sat on a secluded bench and cried. I felt so small. The night sky was filled with millions of stars, and I couldn't fathom that among all of God's incredible creations, He could know *me*. I flipped through my scriptures and landed on Alma 26:37: "We see that God is mindful of every people . . . ; yea, he numbereth his people, and his bowels of mercy are over all the earth." The most delicious warmth spread through me. My Father in Heaven knows exactly who I am. Just as I know the precise birth order of each of my children, He has known and numbered me from the moment of my premortal creation. I am His. You are His. We are counted.

—Krista

"Do not misunderstand or devalue how important you are to your Father in Heaven. You are not an accidental by-product of nature . . . or the result of matter plus time plus chance. . . . Your life has meaning and purpose. . . . You are a beloved child of Heavenly Father."

Alan T. Phillips

"God Knows and Loves You," Oct. 2023

Numbers 27:18, 23

And he laid his hands upon him, and gave him a charge, as the Lord commanded by the hand of Moses.

Given a Charge

When Moses called Joshua, he laid his hands on his head and "gave him a charge." A charge is an order or command. I've never thought of the blessings I've received when priesthood hands are laid on my head as a charge. I always looked on them as gifts that would float down from heaven if I was worthy, but my granddaughter taught me differently.

My son was blessing his first child, and all my other children wanted to be there. My daughter drove from Arkansas to Idaho for the event with four children and unintentionally brought the flu with her. Adelaide, age six, and her mother got the worst of it. We were up all night at a hotel on the night they arrived with sick tummies. The day before the baby blessing, my husband anointed my daughter and three of her children with consecrated oil and gave them blessings. Most were simply words of comfort, but when he got to Adelaide, my husband blessed her that she would be well enough to attend the baby blessing. I thought that would be impossible.

The next morning Adelaide's fever had broken, and she begged to go to church with us. She was the only one in attendance from her whole family for the baby blessing. Though she was weak, she took her charge seriously. As a result, we got to watch the miracle of healing from an inspired blessing and a valiant child.

—Christine

"The Lord will bless you with miracles if you believe in Him, 'doubting nothing.'"

Russell M. Nelson

"The Power of Spiritual Momentum," Apr. 2022

Numbers 29:8

But ye shall offer a burnt offering unto the Lord for a sweet savour; one young bullock, one ram, and seven lambs of the first year; they shall be unto you without blemish.

A Sacrifice Without Blemish

Modern readers often find these Old Testament descriptions of sacrifices boring and wonder why they are relevant to our gospel study today. Reading them with an eye to recognize the symbols of the Savior can make these passages faith-affirming.

These sacred solemnities (described in Numbers 29) are meant to focus Israel on the Lord. The seventh month is the space between harvest and seedtime. *Matthew Henry's Concise Commentary on the Bible* explains: "The more leisure we have from the pressing occupations of this life, the more time we should spend in the immediate service of God" (https://www.ccel.org/ccel/henry/mhcc.html).

The bullock, the ram, and the lambs to be sacrificed are to be without blemish. The Savior's sacrifice was without blemish because He lived a perfect life and was perfectly obedient to His Father.

I blemish my life's sacrifices when I complain, murmur, or become angry or bitter. But through His Atonement and my repentance, my sacrifices become without blemish and turn into blessings. Serving as a mission leader was initially a sacrifice but became a blessing of eternal significance.

—Marianna

> "Through His sacrifice, the Atonement, Jesus Christ made it possible for us to be redeemed from our sins and be resurrected and receive eternal life."
>
> Takashi Wada
>
> "The Words of Christ and the Holy Ghost Will Lead Us to the Truth," Oct. 2024

Numbers 32:13

[The Lord] made them wander in the wilderness forty years.

The Miracle Will Come

I had always wanted a big family, but fertility issues led to a hysterectomy when I was twenty-nine after having birthed two children. The night before the surgery, I received a blessing in which the Lord told me I wasn't finished adding to my family. I reminded Him I wasn't going in for a tonsillectomy, but the Spirit confirmed what the Lord had said.

My son and daughter had brought me so much joy, but there was always the shadow of that promise. For ten years, I waited upon the Lord. Then, one random day, we got a call from a social worker about a little girl who needed a home. A year later, we adopted her.

If you feel like you're wandering in the desert right now, hold on. I know it's hard. But God is keenly aware of you and will bring you the miracle you seek in His perfect timing.

—Michelle

"Waiting upon the Lord can be a sacred place—a place of polishing and refining where we can come to know the Savior in a deeply personal way. Waiting upon the Lord may also be a place where we find ourselves asking, 'O God, where art thou?'—a place where spiritual perseverance requires us to exercise faith in Christ by intentionally choosing Him again and again and again."

Amy A. Wright

Christ Heals That Which Is Broken, Apr. 2022

Numbers 34:2

This is the land that shall fall unto you for an inheritance.

Inheritance

After forty years of wandering in the desert, the children of Israel were finally ready to receive the inheritance the Lord had prepared for them. Canaan, the promised land, was a beautiful place where they could grow crops, raise herds, and build homes. It had been there for them all that time, but they hadn't claimed this gift because they were afraid to fight for it. They didn't trust that the Lord would help them win.

Through our heavenly parents, we've already inherited many wonderful gifts: qualities, traits, and talents that come from Them, and a beautiful world to enjoy. I wonder if the reason I love fall, and reading books, and playing my guitar, and laughing with friends is because they do too!

But the plan of happiness also includes a glorious inheritance that our Father has prepared for us in the next life. He longs to lead us home to live with Him, where we can inherit all the Father has. All. This is the incomprehensible gift He wants to give us. It's up to us to decide whether we will fight to be worthy to receive it, trusting that He can help us claim our eternal destiny. He is a perfect Father who has already given us incomprehensibly wonderful gifts, and that's why I know that He can and will help us to inherit all the gifts of eternity.

—Krista

"The Savior would declare, in no uncertain terms, that you are a daughter or son of the Almighty God. Your Heavenly Father is the most glorious being in the universe, full of love, joy, purity, holiness, light, grace, and truth. And one day He wants you to inherit all He has."

Dieter F. Uchtdorf

"Jesus Is the Strength of Youth," Oct. 2022

Deuteronomy 1:1

These be the words which Moses spake unto all Israel on this side Jordan in the wilderness.

The Retelling

My grandfather's father died some months before he was born. Grandpa always felt a connection to his cowboy father, but I never understood why. One Sunday afternoon, I was browsing through Family Search and came across a story about Grandfather Edwards that I had never heard before. At a time of weakness, he almost picked up a lit cigar to try it. He heard the voice of his father telling him not to go down that road. This was especially poignant to me. At a time of great stress in my life, my angel grandfather whispered to me in the temple. His words lifted me and kept me going.

The word *Deuteronomy* literally means "the retelling." Right before Israel crossed Jordan into the promised land, Moses retold the miracles and tragedies that brought them there. Remember, it had been forty years, so these were the children of the people that had experienced it.

How I would have loved to hear that story from my grandpa's own lips. Have we retold the miracles and tragedies of our lives? Do our children know the first time we felt the Spirit, received inspiration that saved us, or were healed in a time of distress? Perhaps we each have some retelling of our own to do.

—Christine

"In their moments of crisis, [Alma the Younger, the sons of Mosiah, and Enos] remembered the words of their parents, words of the doctrine of Jesus Christ. Remembering saved them."

Henry B. Eyring

"Simple Is the Doctrine of Jesus Christ," Oct. 2024

Deuteronomy 3:11

For only Og king of Bashan remained of the remnant of giants; behold, his bedstead was a bedstead of iron; . . . Nine cubits was the length thereof, and four cubits the breadth of it, after the cubit of a man.

Giant Problems

Og, king of Bashan, was huge. His bed was about 13.5 feet long and 6 feet wide. In comparison, today's king-size bed is about 6 feet, 4 inches wide and 6 feet, 8 inches long. He was big, and just seeing him caused the Israelites to fear.

Giant problems are also big, overwhelming, daunting, and larger than normal-size problems. Fear limits our faith and makes us vulnerable to Satan's whispering. The only way to conquer a giant, as King David will later show us, is through the help of someone more powerful than anyone or anything: the Lord.

When I experienced a problem with my health, I could not physically fight this giant in my life alone. I could not move and had to stay in bed. Servants of the Lord became my hands and my feet. The Lord was by my side, and helped me conquer my giant problem, while His Saints fought alongside me.

—Marianna

> "Whatever questions or problems you have, the answer is always found in the life and teachings of Jesus Christ."
>
> Russell M. Nelson
>
> "The Answer Is Always Jesus Christ," Apr. 2023

Deuteronomy 4:1, 9

Hearken, O Israel, unto the statutes and unto the judgments, which I teach you, for to do them, that ye may live. . . . Teach them thy sons, and thy sons' sons.

The Seeds of Truth

When we testify of truth, we plant seeds in the hearts of our children that, in the Lord's timing, will sprout when they are ready.

I am not much of a gardener. I'm patient when I need to be, but the thrill of waiting for months to pick a tomato from my backyard hasn't captured me yet. Still, I know there is beauty in seeing something wonderful grow from a hidden seed planted months ago.

Though I grew up in the Church, as a teen I began to have questions, followed by a rebellious streak. I stopped doing many of the things that nurtured my testimony in my youth. My little seeds I had planted seemed to struggle. But, one thing remained consistent—I remembered what my parents had taught me. The seeds they sowed stretched through my questions and fear, and gave strength and life to my own budding testimony.

—Michelle

"[We have an] individual responsibility to seek to learn and to teach our families that there is a Father in Heaven who loves us and who has developed a divine plan of happiness for His children; that Jesus Christ, His Son, is the Redeemer of the world, and that salvation comes from faith in His name."

Ulisses S. Soares

"How Can I Understand?," Apr. 2019

Deuteronomy 6:5

And thou shalt love the Lord thy God with all thine heart, and with all thy soul, and with all thy might.

One Small Word

When my kids were young, I read this verse during a morning gospel study and nearly cried. I was barely keeping up with the dishes, laundry, and everything else. How could I even begin to love God with *all* my heart, soul, and might? I felt utterly overwhelmed. But instead of slamming the book shut, I felt drawn to reread the verse, and this time, one small word stood out—a word I'd never paid much attention to, but which changed my perspective: *Thy*.

Thy—as in *my*.

My heart, *my* soul, *my* might. The Spirit helped me see that God wasn't comparing my efforts against anyone else's. He was only asking me to give what I have, to the best of my personal capacity. As I learn and grow, I'll have more to offer, but as long as I offer Him my personal all, it will always be enough.

–Krista

> "I testify of Christ, who has the power to perfect even our most humble offering. Let us do our best, bring what we can, and, with faith, lay our imperfect offering at His feet."
>
> Vern P. Stanfill
>
> "The Imperfect Harvest," Apr. 2023

Deuteronomy 7:6

For thou art an holy people unto the Lord thy God; the Lord thy God hath chosen thee to be a special people unto himself, above all people that are upon the face of the earth.

God Hath Chosen Thee

One of my worst childhood traumas happened in gym class. Almost weekly, my fourth-grade teacher would have two team captains choose their players one by one. I was big for my age and not very coordinated. To make matters worse, we had just moved to the area. Almost every time, I was chosen last.

But there is another team I have been chosen to be part of. Instead of being last, I'm one of the first. If you are a member of Christ's restored gospel, then you are part of that team as well. We are a little more than 1 percent of the world's population. If you were born in a member family as I was, that was a gift directly from the Lord. If missionaries found you, the Lord chose you at that moment and may have put numerous spiritual awakenings in your path so you would be ready. And, if you have stayed faithful, I'm sure you can see the Lord's hand constantly blessing you and strengthening you to stay true.

On His team, we are all captains. We need to invite everyone to join, because we are in the last inning, and the game is heating up.

—Christine

> "My dear brothers and sisters, do you see what is happening right before our very eyes? I pray that we will not miss the majesty of this moment! The Lord is indeed hastening His work."
>
> Russell M. Nelson
>
> "The Lord Jesus Christ Will Come Again," Oct. 2024

Deuteronomy 11:22–23

For if ye shall diligently keep all these commandments which I command you, to do them, to love the Lord your God, to walk in all his ways, and to cleave unto him; Then will the Lord drive out all these nations from before you.

Cleaving unto Obedience

In Genesis 2, the Lord told Adam and Eve to cleave to each other and no one else. Now, the children of Israel are also told to cleave to the Lord and no other gods. By cleaving unto our spouse, we become one in our marriage covenant. By cleaving to our God, we also become one with Him through the covenants He asks us to enter into with Him.

I cleave to my spouse and to the Lord because I love them. Stephen Ricks taught that the focus of Deuteronomy is to teach about the love the Lord has for His people and the love we should have for Him. He wrote: "The Israelites, as the children of God and the recipients of his blessings are expected to return his love. Love (Hebrew *'ahab*) and reverence (Hebrew *yare'*), translated in the King James Version as *fear,* are to be the motivating factors in Israel's relationship with God" (*Ensign*, April 1990).

I am obedient because of my love and reverence for God. Going to the temple regularly helps me understand the covenant of obedience. In return for my obedience to Him, the Lord drives out worldly problems in my mind and heart, substituting in their place joy and peace.

—Marianna

> "Obedience paves the way for a joyful life for you today and a grand, eternal reward tomorrow."
>
> Russell M. Nelson
>
> "Think Celestial!," Oct. 2023

Deuteronomy 12:11–12

Then there shall be a place which the Lord your God shall choose to cause his name to dwell there. . . . And ye shall rejoice before the Lord your God.

This Not Church!

Years ago, our extended family spent the weekend camping in the Northwest woods. Having received prior permission, we held a short sacrament meeting. As we shared our testimonies, suddenly, my toddler niece began to cry. "This not church!" she yelled. We explained to her that "church" is more than a building, but the sacred things we do inside the building as covenant brothers and sisters. She didn't buy it. She wanted *her* church.

I love that God's business is bigger than a building. But I love even more that He has provided us chapels and temples to gather as friends and families, places where His Spirit is, even in the spaces between ordinances. Buildings don't make a church, but God can make His buildings a place of familiarity, peace, and rest for us. A place we can be healed, come to Him, practice love, and rejoice.

—Michelle

"From the beginning, God has sought to gather and organize His children. . . . With that purpose in mind, He has instructed us to build places of worship where we receive knowledge and the ordinances of salvation . . . and gather together often to remember Jesus and strengthen each other in Him."

Reyna Aburto

"We Are The Church of Jesus Christ of Latter-day Saints," Apr. 2022

Deuteronomy 15:1

At the end of every seven years thou shalt make a release.

Forgiveness Festival

I have an idea. Let's start a forgiveness festival! Every seven years, we'll throw a giant party and everyone's debts will be forgiven! Who's in? Imagine it—a dedicated day when we willingly free ourselves from any hard feelings we've harbored toward someone else. It's a lovely idea—one we have the personal power to enact in our lives—and yet, forgiveness isn't always so straightforward.

When I'm having difficulty forgiving, I think of a parable I once read about two monks on a journey. They came across a woman who needed help crossing a muddy street. The older monk carried her to the other side, but she treated him rudely in return. Several miles later, the younger monk asked the older one why he wasn't offended by the woman's behavior. The older monk replied, "I set the woman down miles ago. Why are you still carrying her?"

Forgiveness is an act of faith, acknowledging that Christ has already suffered for every person. As we let Him carry those burdens, it brings relief and freedom to our souls. With His help, we can learn to live joyfully unburdened.

–Krista

> "Extending forgiveness can take tremendous courage and humility. It can also take time. It requires us to put our faith and trust in the Lord as we assume accountability for the condition of our hearts."
>
> Amy A. Wright
>
> "Christ Heals That Which Is Broken," Apr. 2022

Deuteronomy 18:18–19

I will raise them up a Prophet from among their brethren like unto thee, and will put my words in his mouth; . . . whosoever will not hearken unto my words which he shall speak in my name, I will require it of him.

Now or Later

My brilliant and kind nephew Miles is going to BYU–Idaho this semester. We've always lived on the other side of the country, but since I live in Rexburg now, we get the privilege of seeing him more often. Somehow, we got on the topic of parenting. When it came to chores, I'd often say, "You can choose to do it now or be forced to do it later while the rest of us go get ice cream." Miles smiled and asked, "Is that really giving them their free will? Really?"

I will readily admit that for some children that approach may not be effective. For my boys, it worked. A similar principle is expressed in Deuteronomy. The prophet Moses declared that the words the Savior speaks will be obeyed either in this mortal life or later: "I will require it of him." Sin is primarily limited to mortality, as is repentance.

Funny. Now that my children are mostly grown, I'm parenting myself. So when I grow weak and am putting off something I know I should do, I often say to myself, "I can do it now by choice or be forced to do it later." I'd rather do it now—and then go get ice cream.

—Christine

"I testify to you that following the Lord's will in our life will enable us to find the most precious pearl in the world–the kingdom of heaven."

Ulisses S. Soares

"Aligning Our Will with His," Oct. 2024

Deuteronomy 19:15

One witness shall not rise up against a man for any iniquity, or for any sin, in any sin that he sinneth; at the mouth of two witnesses or at the mouth of three witnesses shall the matter be established.

The Law of Witnesses

The law of witnesses was a protection for the children of Israel against false witnesses. One person could not pin iniquity on another. Instead, two or three witnesses had to be found for the wrong doing. After the judge's diligent questioning, if it was found that the witness was lying, then the false witness would have done to him the punishment he was trying to get for his brother: "Life shall go for life, eye for eye, tooth for tooth, hand for hand, foot for foot" (Deuteronomy 19:21).

In the book of Deuteronomy, the Lord seems to be repeating Himself, but the repetition is a second witness of all that the children of Israel learned during their sojourn in the wilderness.

The law of witnesses has continued today. The Lord chose three witnesses, and for emphasis, another eight witnesses to bear testimony to the world of the reality of the translated gold plates. After every general conference, I send an email to family and friends sharing my impressions and bearing testimony of the truthfulness of the gospel of Jesus Christ. I can be a witness of Jesus Christ in my actions and in my words.

—Marianna

> "You and I are witnesses who testify. It is with the power of this united witness that we continue to move forward with faith in the Lord Jesus Christ and His gospel."
>
> Brent H. Nielson
>
> "A Record of What I Have Both Seen and Heard," Apr. 2024

Deuteronomy 23:14

For the Lord thy God walketh in the midst of thy camp, to deliver thee, and to give up thine enemies before thee; therefore shall thy camp be holy.

He's Here

Can an emergency room be a holy place? A few years ago, while my brother was out of cell phone reach at girls' camp, my sister-in-law needed urgent attention. Through several calls, we were able to reach my brother, who immediately started his one-hour journey to the hospital.

I sat by my sister-in-law's side in the ER waiting room, trying to calm and distract her. Every time the automatic doors slid open, she would look up, hoping to see her husband. After a while, she was in so much pain, she stopped looking. Then the doors opened, and he walked through. "He's here," I said.

Everything changed. Her countenance, her pain, her hope—the room. His presence in that loud waiting room steadied her. His faith and love helped make that room holy.

It is the same with you, wherever you are right now. Your faith helps make that place holy.

God is among you. Now. Whatever pain, frustration, fear, or struggle you're going through. Look up. He's here. You're not alone.

—Michelle

> "Open your hearts to our Savior and Redeemer, no matter your circumstances, trials, sufferings, or mistakes; you can know that He lives, that He loves you, and that because of Him, you will never be alone. God is among us."
>
> Dieter F. Uchtdorf
>
> "God Among Us," Apr. 2021

Deuteronomy 26:8

The Lord brought us forth out of Egypt with a mighty hand, and with an outstretched arm, and with great terribleness, and with signs, and with wonders.

His Fingerprints

After my daughter's funeral, I was desperate to hold on to every memory of her. I spent days writing down everything I could remember about her life and her brief fight with cancer.

Writing about Elora required the courage to examine the darkest, most painful moments surrounding her death. I was afraid to take those memories out of my heart because I believed I would only find grief, pain, and guilt. But what I found was Jesus. His fingerprints covered each painful moment, and I discovered He had been with me every step of the way.

There are still days when I grieve my daughter's loss, but in the same way the Lord often reminded the children of Israel how He had delivered them from Egypt, my Savior reminds me that He has delivered me and is still working to deliver me now. He will never leave me to face my trials alone.

—Krista

> "Regardless of the causes of our worst hurts and heartaches, the ultimate source of relief is the same: Jesus Christ. He alone holds the full power and healing balm to correct every mistake, right every wrong, adjust every imperfection, mend every wound, and deliver every delayed blessing."
>
> Matthew S. Holland
>
> "The Exquisite Gift of the Son," Oct. 2020

Deuteronomy 28:1–2, 15

If thou shalt hearken diligently unto the voice of the Lord thy God . . . all these blessings shall come on thee, and overtake thee. But . . . if thou wilt not hearken . . . all these curses shall come upon thee, and overtake thee.

Blessings, Cursings, and the Fence

I heard the following story once. In a dream a person was shown two fields divided by a wide stone wall. The field on the right had people working on a beautiful garden that was in full bloom. The field on the left had people partying and playing around. They looked like they were having fun. An angel came to the dreamer and said, "One field is the Lord's and the other Satan's. Choose the one where you wish to dwell."

The person didn't really want to work that hard but knew that joining the party would have bitter consequences. Then, he looked at the fence. It was wide and comfortable to sit on. If he sat on the fence, he could be close to the Lord's side but still watch the partiers. Soon, Jesus and the devil arrived. The person hoped to jump onto the Lord's side. But before he could, the devil grabbed him. "No!" the person shouted. "I was on the fence!" The devil smiled. "The fence is on my side."

When Moses took his people to Mount Ebal and Mount Gerizim, he had six tribes stand on one mount and six on the other. Then, he pronounced blessings to the obedient on Gerizim and cursings to all others on Ebal. There was no middle ground. Today, we must also choose happiness or sorrow. May we see clearly and choose wisely.

—Christine

> "The intent of the Father's great plan of happiness is your happiness, right here, right now, and in the eternities."
>
> Patrick Kearon
>
> "God's Intent Is to Bring You Home," Apr. 2024

Deuteronomy 31:12

Gather the people together, men, and women, and children, and thy stranger that is within thy gates, that they may hear, and that they may learn, and fear the Lord your God, and observe to do all the words of this law.

Family Home Evening

In Deuteronomy 31, Moses is 120 years old and knows he will soon leave his people. In preparing them to enter the promised land, Moses gathers the people and reviews the covenants they have made with God. To make sure they won't forget these teachings, the Israelites are commanded to gather every seven years when the law shall be read for all to hear.

While raising my children, I did not wait for seven years to read the scriptures to them. We tried to read the scriptures every morning. And Monday night was a sacred time for family home evening. Each week, a different child would prepare a lesson and another child would be in charge of refreshments (the coveted job). *The Family Home Evening Resource Manual* was a wonderful help with lessons, games, and illustrations that made family home evening easy and fun.

Now, we are blessed with the Come, Follow Me program. Each week, we gather our families together to study the scriptures so that we will remember Him throughout the week. We may even invite the "stranger"—a neighbor or friend—to join us. What a wonderful way to prepare us for His promised land.

—Marianna

> "Each week when I open my *Come, Follow Me* manual, I write this question at the top of the page: 'What is the Holy Ghost teaching me?'"
>
> Mark L. Pace
>
> "Conversion Is Our Goal," Apr. 2022

Deuteronomy 32:2

My doctrine shall drop as rain, my speech shall distill as the dew, as the small rain upon the tender herb, and as the showers upon the grass.

Drop by Drop

I killed Matt. Well, almost. I didn't mean to. I cared for him. I put him by the window and watered him every day. But Matt, my tall money tree plant, was nearly dead. Why? Because I gave him too much sun and too much water. He wasn't built to receive that much at one time. He couldn't process it. And so, he began to die. Once I realized not only what he needed, but *how* he needed it given to him to be effective—a little here and there—he came back to life and thrived.

Sometimes we pray for a massive download of information, direction, and revelation. We think having all the things right now would help our faith, our peace, and our spirits. But God knows how to give us what we need. He knows our capacity to learn, process, and change. And so, He gives us His doctrine, wisdom, direction, peace, strength, gifts, and more drop by drop because He loves us and wants us to thrive.

—Michelle

"As we incrementally learn to do what He asks of us . . . His love will flow through us and make all that He asks not only possible but eventually much easier and lighter and more joyful than we could ever imagine."

J. Anette Dennis

"His Yoke Is Easy and His Burden Is Light," Oct. 2022

Deuteronomy 34:4

This is the land which I sware unto Abraham, unto Isaac, and unto Jacob. . . . I have caused thee to see it with thine eyes, but thou shalt not go over thither.

Regrets

Moses lost his temper. The Israelites were complaining because there was no water where they were camped. The Lord told Moses to *speak* to the rock in front of him and it would give water, but in frustration, he *struck* the rock with his rod instead. The Lord is a God of justice, so Moses's actions had consequences. Because of his disobedience and for drawing attention away from God, the Lord told Moses he would not be permitted to enter the promised land.

We've all done things we regret. And while we can always be forgiven, the God of justice can't always shield us from the consequences of our actions. After my daughter passed away from cancer, I felt this keenly. There were so many things I regretted, things I wished I could do over, or take back. But time doesn't work like that. Thankfully, our Father is also a God of mercy. At the end of His life, the Lord led Moses up to a high mountain to look out over the promised land and see it with his own eyes. And Father has led me step by step to a place of healing where I've learned to see with my own eyes a more realistic and gentle view of my efforts as a mother. If we keep our hand in His, the God of mercy can turn even our worst mistakes into opportunities for healing, growth, service, and joy.

—Krista

> "If we have made choices that we now regret . . . there is the precious gift of Christ's Atonement. . . . His Atonement allows us to leave the past behind and move forward with clean hands, a pure heart, and a determination to do better and especially to become better."
>
> Dieter F. Uchtdorf
>
> "Of Regrets and Resolutions," Oct. 2012

Joshua 1:6–7

Be strong and of a good courage . . . that thou mayest observe to do according to all the law. . . . Turn not from it to the right hand or to the left, that thou mayest prosper whithersoever thou goest.

Stay On the Path

The Sound of Thunder is a short story written by Ray Bradbury that reflects the importance of staying on the path. A great hunter named Eckels pays a company to take him back in time to kill a T-Rex. The only rule is that he must stay on the path. He agrees and goes to the prehistoric era. As a dinosaur emerges, Eckels fears for his life and chickens out. He makes a beeline for the time machine. It is only after the T-Rex has been shot that the guide notices the mud on Eckels's shoe and chides him for leaving the path. "By stepping on one single mouse . . . So the caveman starves . . . From his loins would have sprung ten sons. From their loins one hundred sons . . . Destroy this one man, and you destroy a race, a people, an entire history of life."

In the end, Eckels finds a dead butterfly stuck to his shoe. When he returns to his time, everything has changed.

Looking back at Joshua's valiant life, we can see the huge part he played in establishing Israel which lasts even to this day. Each of us also has the ability to change the world. But a little step off the path—either to the right or left—could not only affect ourselves, but many others connected to us. Let us stay on the covenant path so we and those around us can prosper.

–Christine

"Loving the Lord is often measured in small daily deeds, footsteps on the covenant path."

Gary E. Stevenson

"Bridging the Two Great Commandments," Apr. 2024

Joshua 3:7

And the Lord said unto Joshua, This day will I begin to magnify thee in the sight of all Israel that they may know that, as I was with Moses, so I will be with thee.

Magnified by the Lord

After Moses's leadership for an entire generation, Joshua must have felt overwhelmed. I felt the same way when I was called as a mission leader. The previous mission leaders were people I loved and admired. How could I follow their leadership? There was only one answer to that question: through the Lord's magnification of my abilities.

Joshua and the children of Israel had come to the River Jordan. The Lord spoke to Joshua that He would magnify Joshua in the eyes of His people, just as He did with Moses. As soon as the priests who carried the ark of the covenant set the soles of their feet into the waters of the Jordan River, the waters divided and the priests walked on dry ground (Joshua 3:11). The miracle was similar to the parting of the Red Sea. All the Israelites passed over the Jordan on dry ground. This was a generation who had only heard about the previous miracle with Moses. Now, they were able to experience a similar miracle through the priesthood power of Joshua. The Lord showed the people that He was with Joshua, just as He had been with Moses.

We can have the same confidence—that the Lord will magnify our efforts—when we are given a new Church assignment.

—Marianna

"Magnify your callings."

Russell M. Nelson

"A New Normal," Oct. 2020

Joshua 5:6

For the children of Israel walked forty years in the wilderness.

The Waiting Wilderness

"You're not finished adding to your family." This is a lovely sentiment, unless you're told this in a blessing the night before having a hysterectomy. And yet, I fell asleep that night with the promise of "adding" in my heart and no way of knowing how in my head.

I fell asleep every night for the next nine years waiting. Sometimes it was easy; other times, heartbreaking. Then, out of the blue, God brought a little six-year-old girl into my life. She was the daughter I couldn't have birthed—the one He knew would complete my family. He'd known all along, and worked His work to bring us together, all while I waited.

God really does have a plan for me and for you. Trust that sometimes when you're asked to wander in the waiting wilderness, He is actively working to bless you. He is good. He will keep His promises. You are not forgotten.

—Michelle

> "Wait and trust in God and in His timing, because you can trust His heart with all of yours."
>
> Michelle Craig
>
> "Eyes to See," Oct. 2020

Joshua 7:11–12

Israel hath sinned . . . for they have even taken of the accursed thing. . . . Neither will I be with you any more, except ye destroy the accursed from among you.

Spiritual Realignment

As I arrived at work, my sweat-soaked coworker informed me that the air conditioning was broken. She'd called the boss many times with no success but decided to try again. The call went to voicemail. She left a polite message, then ended the call . . . or so she thought. But she'd pushed the wrong button, and the boss's voicemail recorded my co-worker's angry opinion of him. We were both horrified. Though I hadn't spoken during the recording, the owner would know I had listened and hadn't stood up for him.

My coworker went home, and I worried and stewed for hours. I told myself I had done nothing wrong, but the more I tried to justify and ignore the pit in my stomach, the worse I felt. There was only one path to relief. I had to admit what I'd done wrong and apologize. Terrified, I called my boss. He was very understanding and forgave me. The guilt and dread immediately faded. I could feel the peace of realigning with God.

—Krista

> "Just as minor deviations can draw us out of the Savior's Way, so too can small and simple acts of realignment assuredly lead us back."
>
> Dieter F. Uchtdorf
>
> "Daily Restoration," Oct. 2021

Joshua 9:8–9

And Joshua said unto them, Who are you? And from whence do you come? And they said unto him, from a very far country thy servants come because of the name of the Lord thy God.

Almost There

Wendy was an organist who was paid to accompany various congregations each Sunday. She probably approached the missionaries because we met early enough she could add us to her list. Wendy pleasantly listened to the discussions, read the Book of Mormon, and believed it. When asked about baptism, she declined, worried that it would require her to find a new career. She said, "When I die, you can do the work for me. I'll accept it then. I know it's true."

Similarly, the Gibeonites heard about the Israelites' crossing of the Red Sea and their initial victories at Jericho and Ai. In fear of the true God, they deceived Joshua into making a promise not to destroy them. They claimed to be from a distant land, rather than from the region God had commanded Israel to cleanse and inhabit. As a result of this vow, the Gibeonites became servants to God's chosen people instead of being driven out or destroyed. Eventually, they joined with the Israelites and even helped rebuild the temple.

Many who recognize truth or have been prompted by the Spirit may not choose to enjoy the full blessings of the gospel now. But as we love and include them, like the Gibeonites, in time they may get there.

—Christine

> "The Savior's job is to heal. Our job is to love—to love and minister in such a way that others are drawn to Jesus Christ."
>
> Dale G. Renlund
>
> "The Powerful, Virtuous Cycle of the Doctrine of Christ," Apr. 2024

Joshua 11:6

And the Lord said unto Joshua, Be not afraid because of them: for tomorrow about this time will I deliver them up all slain before Israel.

God Will Prevail!

Joshua and the children of Israel were in a scary situation. All of the kings residing in the promised land were gathered to fight at the waters of Merom. The sight would have made anyone afraid. But the Lord reminded Joshua that they need not fear because He would deliver them.

And He did.

The Lord gave the Israelites direction that was difficult both physically and emotionally. In faith, they followed His counsel, which removed the advantage of the kings' armies and ensured this battle would be won by Israel. Because of the Lord's commands, neither horses nor chariots could be used in future battles as a weapon of war against Israel.

Our prophet reminds us that "it takes both faith and courage to let God prevail" (Russell M. Nelson, "Let God Prevail," Oct. 2020). The Israelites used their courage and faith in the Lord to win their insurmountable battles. As a covenantal woman, I can prevail against life's challenges by following Israel's example.

—Marianna

> "When your greatest desire is to let God prevail, to be part of Israel, so many decisions become easier. So many issues become nonissues!"
>
> Russell M. Nelson
>
> "Let God Prevail," Oct. 2020

Joshua 14:12

Now therefore give me this mountain.

Give Me This Mountain

I love those pivotal moments in stories where the protagonist is faced with a challenge—usually one that can result in saving himself or others—and steps up to the plate with bold and brave statements like "I can do this," "Let me try," or even "Let's do this." There is something so beautiful and sacred about not only stepping up to a challenge of purpose, but welcoming it.

The quote below is a classic. President Kimball was a man who did just that—he welcomed his mountain of challenges because he knew the climb was the opportunity to spend time with and become like God.

Rather than shying away or even resenting challenges, see them as an invitation to climb with God, to see His faith in you, to see His love for you, and to see His support of you. See them as opportunities to prove yourself to yourself, to grow, to learn, and to become. Yes, it will be hard (they are called "challenges" because they are challenging), but as you lace up your shoes of determination and optimism, you'll find an unexpected excitement and ability to overcome and become.

—Michelle

> "There are great challenges ahead of us, giant opportunities to be met. I welcome that exciting prospect and feel to say to the Lord, humbly, 'Give me this mountain,' give me these challenges."
>
> Spencer W. Kimball
>
> "Give Me This Mountain," Oct. 1979

Joshua 21:45

There failed not ought of any good thing which the Lord had spoken unto the house of Israel; all came to pass.

The Lord Keeps His Promises

My two-year-old daughter, Elora, had just been diagnosed with a cancerous brain tumor. She was in a coma, unresponsive, and I was in agony. My husband offered to give me a priesthood blessing and spoke a promise from God: "All will be well."

When the blessing ended, I jumped out of my chair. "Do you know what this means?! God is saying that Elora will recover and we'll get to take her home!" But my husband was skeptical. "What if He means that no matter what happens, *eventually* all will be well?" As much as I wanted my interpretation to be right, I had to admit there was peace in knowing that whatever happened, God could see sunny days on my horizon.

Elora died the next morning. And though my path through grief has been long and arduous, Christ has also led me to countless moments of joy, peace, and gratitude. I will always mourn Elora, but with Christ's love and grace, I can honestly say that I have arrived at "all is well."

–Krista

> "God will indeed honor His covenants and promises to each of us."
>
> D. Todd Christofferson
>
> "Our Relationship with God," Apr. 2022

Joshua 23:8

But cleave unto the Lord your God, as ye have done unto this day.

Super Glue

My son was working on a project and super-glued his fingers together. He came to me, horrified that they would be stuck together forever. We tried vinegar, nail polish remover, and paint thinner. Nothing worked. But the next day, when he woke up, his fingers were free. Apparently, the outer layer of human skin constantly sheds, so the glue only adhered to the surface and naturally came off within a day.

The Israelites were told to *cleave* unto God. The word *cleave* means to attach or adhere firmly, like supergluing yourself to Him. That is the point of our covenants—they bind us to the Lord. But, human nature is similar to our skin. We cannot make covenants to God once and think they will last forever. While we sleep, that bond will pull away unless we constantly strengthen it by applying more glue.

The act of daily worship is the only way to keep our relationship with the Savior strong enough to last through these difficult times. Starting the morning with prayer allows us to face the day knowing our connection is sure.

—Christine

> "Our faith in Jesus Christ needs to be nourished daily. It is nourished as we pray daily, study the scriptures daily, reflect on the goodness of God daily, repent daily, and follow the promptings of the Holy Ghost daily."
>
> Dale G. Renlund
>
> "The Powerful, Virtuous Cycle of the Doctrine of Christ," Apr. 2024

Joshua 24:15

And if it seem evil unto you to serve the Lord, choose you this day whom ye will serve; . . . but as for me and my house, we will serve the Lord.

Our Family Scripture

When my children were younger, we decided to choose a family scripture. This verse would become our family mantra—a slogan we would all memorize and dedicate our lives to doing. The process of selecting the scripture took a while. Each person spent time deciding on which verses they liked the best. Finally, the family unitedly chose Joshua 24:15.

At this point in the scriptures, Joshua was nearing the end of his life. He reminded the people that he and his family would always serve the Lord and no other god. He asked the people if they would covenant to do the same. The people responded, "God forbid that we should forsake the Lord, to serve other gods" (Joshua 24:16). Joshua used a stone as a physical reminder of Israel's covenant with the Lord.

This verse became our family theme. I had it painted on the beam supporting our kitchen ceiling as a daily visible reminder of our covenant to serve Him.

I continually reflect to ensure that I am not serving other gods and that I do not forsake the Lord. Worldly pursuits can lead me away from worshipping Him alone if I am not watchful.

—Marianna

> "Each of us should evaluate our temporal and spiritual priorities sincerely and prayerfully."
>
> David A. Bednar
>
> "Put On Thy Strength, O Zion," Oct. 2020

Judges 2:10

There arose another generation . . . which knew not the Lord, nor yet the works which he had done for Israel.

No Dead Ends

I wasn't paying attention to my GPS and ended up at a dead end. No more road ahead. Just a barricade. I was stuck, but only for a moment. With a few taps on my phone, my GPS now showed me the way home.

Sometimes we, or those we love, find ourselves at a dead end spiritually. We face a barricade of doubts, fears, anger, and even resentment. But this dead end doesn't have to be *the* end.

God has a plan for us, even when we go off track. There is always a way back for us and those we love. Always. This is the great hope of the gospel. It only takes a few small things to change direction again—and, if you ask, God will show you how. There are no dead ends, just chances to turn around.

—Michelle

"We are all susceptible. No matter how strong our spiritual experiences have been in the past, as human beings, we wander . . . but we can get back on course. We can navigate through the darkness and trials of this life and find our way back to our loving Heavenly Father if we seek and accept [the things] He has provided, embrace personal revelation, and strive for daily restoration."

Dieter F. Uchtdorf

"Daily Restoration," Oct. 2021

Judges 3:9

When the children of Israel cried unto the Lord, the Lord raised up a deliverer.

Our Deliverer

Three times in this chapter, the children of Israel, realizing they had drifted from their faith and distanced themselves from God, cried out to Him for help. Each time, the Lord heard their cries and raised up a deliverer—a strong, faithful man willing to fight for his people and bring them out of captivity, physically and spiritually. Othniel went to war with the Spirit of the Lord upon him, defeated a wicked king, and there was peace in the land for forty years. Ehud freed his people from another wicked king, which gave them the courage to follow him into battle and gain peace for another eighty years. Shamgar battled with a simple ox goad, a pole with a sharp tool on the end, and delivered Israel. These men are what we call types of Christ; examples to help the people then, and us now, understand how Jesus can and will save His people.

As in times of old, our Father actively listens for our cries for help. He has heard mine countless times, and I know He hears yours. He has raised up and sent us a Deliverer, Jesus Christ, who is perfectly prepared to bring us out of captivity and offer relief. Whatever difficulties you or I face, if mortal afflictions hold us captive, with Christ fighting at our side, every problem can be transformed into peace. He is my Deliverer in every way. And He is yours.

—Krista

"I know that our Lord and Savior, Jesus Christ, is mighty to save."

Kristin M. Yee

"The Joy of Our Redemption," Oct. 2024

Judges 4:8

And Barak said unto [Deborah], If thou wilt go with me, then I will go: but if thou wilt not go with me, then I will not go.

Training Wheels

For my sixth birthday I got a brand-new bicycle with training wheels. I was thrilled because I could ride it right away. After a time, my father took the training wheels off. He said he'd hold up the bike and run beside me for as long as I needed him. At first, I was very wobbly, but my father was right there, panting in my ear. A few runs later, I got my balance down and was pedaling great until I realized I couldn't hear my father. I turned my head to find he was gone and crashed big time. Though I had the skills, I didn't have the confidence to do it on my own.

The story of Deborah is not about women ruling and men drooling, as some supposed. It is more about Barrack, who wanted to keep using training wheels, and a righteous woman who encouraged him to increase his faith. Barrack insisted Deborah come to the battle with him, and the consequence was that he would not win the battle alone. Jael, another woman, hammered a tent stake in the opposing captain's temple, ending the conflict and gaining the glory.

Each of us has our own training wheels. There may be callings we're not willing to accept or activities we choose not to do alone. The only way for us to build our confidence in the Lord is to be willing to act—no matter the challenge. Our faith will increase as we sincerely try doing hard things for the Lord.

—Christine

> "I invite you to take intentional steps to grow in your confidence before the Lord.
>
> Russell M. Nelson
>
> "Confidence in the Presence of God," Apr. 2025

Judges 7:7

And the Lord said unto Gideon, By the three hundred men that lapped will I save you, and deliver the Midianites into thine hand: and let all the other people go every man unto his place.

How Do You Drink Water?

The Lord wanted Israel to know that their victory over the Midianites was a miracle of His doing—not by their own hand. Originally, Israel's army was twenty-two thousand men. But the Lord told Gideon that there were too many. Then, the Lord said that anyone who was afraid could go home. More than half of the men left.

Now, there were only ten thousand men left to fight. The Lord told Gideon this was still too many. He had all the men go to the water (though they didn't know this was a test). If a man knelt down on his knees to drink water, he was sent home. Only a small number brought the water to their mouths with their hands. These three hundred men were the ones chosen to be part of the Lord's miracle to save Israel.

After reading this story, I thought about how I would drink water from a stream. Would I kneel—or bring the water up with my hand? The Lord had a work for those three hundred men to do. He chose them to perform His miracle, but all twenty-two thousand had prepared themselves and were ready to serve. Am I prepared to be a part of the Lord's miraculous victories?

—Marianna

> "When we say yes to serving, we are saying yes to Jesus Christ."
>
> Steven D. Shumway
>
> "Participate to Prepare for Christ's Return," Apr. 2025

Judges 8:23

I will not rule over you. . . .
The Lord shall rule over you.

Who Is Your King?

The above verse was spoken by Gideon, an Israelite judge and military leader who had been chosen by God to deliver his people from Midianite oppression. After their victory, they looked to Gideon to be their protector, leader, and king.

It was a flattering offer, I'm sure—and perhaps tempting—to be exalted to a king. But, Gideon was aware of the Israelites' pattern of apostasy by looking beyond the mark, and, with this simple rejection, he made it clear where they should be focused—on the Lord.

We might see people around us whom we admire and even love. We might even be tempted to let them lead and guide us in our beliefs, thoughts, and actions. But ultimately it's the Lord we should turn to for guidance, support, power, and peace.

We can gather Israel now—today—by choosing to look to the Lord. As we focus on Him as our King, we can have covenant confidence, powerful peace, genuine guidance, and spiritual strength.

—Michelle

> "The Lord knows you and loves you. He is your Savior and your Redeemer. He leads and guides His Church. He will lead and guide *you* in your personal life."
>
> Russell M. Nelson
>
> "Make Time for the Lord," Oct. 2021

Judges 11:39

She returned unto her father, who did with her according to his vow which he had vowed.

Lament for a Christ-like Daughter

The devastating story of Jephthah sacrificing his only daughter teaches us several important truths: First, Heavenly Father doesn't expect us to bargain in order to secure blessings. He asks us to form a relationship with Him, align ourselves with His will, and trust His plan.

Second, it is hard to accept that suffering sometimes results from the actions of others. The plan of salvation requires that each person be endowed with agency, and the Lord honors that gift seriously. There are consequences for the abuse of agency, but because it is a vital principle for our learning and progress, the Lord cannot always intervene.

Third, Jephthah's daughter is a humble example of Christ-like submission. With maturity and grace, she placed herself in the Lord's hands. I haven't always found this easy to do. But I know that if I hold on to anger, hatred, or revenge, I damage my soul even further. It takes much faith and courage to place those hurts in Christ's hands and trust Him to deal with them fairly. But when I do, the peace to my heart is immediate.

When we find ourselves in situations that don't seem fair, we can follow this faithful daughter's example and place ourselves in the Lord's hands, knowing He will care for us and lead us home to Him, where all will be made right.

—Krista

"Submit[ting] our will to God's is an act of faith. . . . In making that choice, we discover that our agency is not diminished; rather, it is magnified and rewarded by the presence of the Holy Ghost, who brings purpose, joy, peace, and hope we can find nowhere else."

David P. Homer

"Trusting Our Father," Oct. 2024

Judges 13:8

Then Manoah intreated the Lord . . . teach us what we shall do unto the child that shall be born.

The Child that Shall Be Born

I believe one of the most sacred responsibilities parents are given is to decide about their future family. The choice of when to bring children into the world is a partnership between a mother, her husband, and the Lord. Samson's mother, Manoah, was told she was to have a son and raise him a certain way. Sariah was ninety-nine when she had her only son, and Mary wasn't married when she conceived. But both were warned of their blessed pregnancies.

After having my fifth child, I hoped my family was complete and set a doctor's appointment to be sure. That day, a friend said she had a babysitter that we could share if I wanted to go to the temple. With three preschoolers, I jumped at the chance. During the session, I began crying. My friend whispered, "What's wrong?" I was going to say nothing, but something else came out. "I need to have another baby," I said, a little surprised. I knew the Lord had a plan for me. For us.

I realize others may receive a different answer. Health issues—either physical or mental—may affect what some feel is right. But I know that the Lord cares about our families. If you ask, He will direct you. That next baby was a sweet girl who brought me great joy. I can't imagine our family without her.

—Christine

"I invite you to have faith in the message Nephi taught us—that the words of Christ and the Holy Ghost will direct you to 'all things what [you] should do.' Everything!"

Takashi Wada

"The Words of Christ and the Holy Ghost Will Lead Us to the Truth," Oct. 2024

Judges 16:28

And Samson called unto the Lord, and said, O Lord God, remember me, I pray thee, and strengthen me, I pray thee, only this once, O God, that I may be at once avenged of the Philistines for my two eyes.

Praying for Strength

An angel told Samson's mom that Samson was to be raised as a Nazarite. He was not to drink wine nor to touch any unclean thing. And he was not supposed to cut his hair.

Living as a Nazarite, Samson received super-human strength. His weakness, however, was the women he chose. His first wife betrayed his trust and left him for another man. Then Samson fell in love with Delilah, who discovered, through cunning and deceit, the source of his strength—his hair—and she cut it. In reality, Samson's strength was not his hair but in the covenant he had made with God to live a higher and holier life as a Nazarite—a covenant which he broke.

Samson was now powerless in the face of his enemies, taken prisoner, and tortured. During a feast, Samson was brought out for display. In weakness and humility, Samson cried out to God and pleaded for a final act of strength to pull down the walls on his wicked oppressors.

I, too, have cried out to the Lord in my weakest moments, even when I maybe didn't completely deserve His help. He heard my cries and gave me strength to vanquish my foes.

—Marianna

"Although we are imperfect at remembering Him, our loving Heavenly Father never fails to remember us."

Joaquin E. Costa

"The Power of Jesus Christ in Our Lives Every Day," Oct. 2023

Judges 17:6

In those days there was no king in Israel, but every man did that which was right in his own eyes.

Follow Him

During this time, the Israelites were kingless and faithless, knee-deep in idolatry and betrayal. It's a heartbreaking part of their story, but one we can avoid in our own lives.

Years ago I watched a movie about a new young teacher who took a job at a riotous inner-city school. The students had no regard for authority and were violent, disrespectful, unhappy, and unlearned. They made their own rules, resulting in chaos that drove even seasoned teachers away. But this new teacher stayed, believed in them, held them accountable, and loved them.

At first, the students rebelled, but as they learned to respect her, they followed her, and eventually, they loved her back. They looked at her as a leader who cared, someone they could follow. They obeyed not simply to obey, but they obeyed because of the *relationship* they had with her. Living within the culture of expectation, rules, and love, they learned, they prospered, and even excelled.

God sees us. He knows us. He knows what is right. And He loves us enough to make it known to us. As we choose to follow, obey, and love Him, we, too, can learn, prosper, and excel.

—Michelle

"This is the beauty of the covenant path—the path of worship, love, and loyalty to God."

D. Todd Christofferson

"Worship," Apr. 2025

Judges 21:3

O, Lord God of Israel, why is this come to pass in Israel, that there should be to day one tribe lacking in Israel?

Never Lost

A friend of mine has been struggling through some complicated family challenges and recently stepped away from her membership in the Church. Her decision left me saddened and confused. For weeks, I worried about her and her family. I didn't understand her reasoning, but I wanted to. So, I finally decided to call.

She was excited that I wanted to talk and graciously answered my questions. We laughed and cried together as she explained her struggles. When I hung up the phone, the most delicious warmth spread over me from head to toe, a sample of Father's love for my friend, His daughter. Though she may wander spiritually for a time, she will never be lost to Him. He will always know exactly where she is.

–Krista

> "From before the world was, a loving Father in Heaven and His Beloved Son loved and worked with those who They knew would wander. God will love them forever."
>
> Henry B. Eyring
>
> "To My Grandchildren," Oct. 2013

Ruth 1:16

And Ruth said, Intreat me not to leave thee, or to return from following after thee: for whither thou goest, I will go . . . thy people shall be my people, and thy God my God.

The Violin

When I was eight, my mother found a violin at a thrift shop and decided I was the child who'd learn to play it. It hurt my collar bone, and even if I did hit the right notes, the tone sounded like nails on a chalkboard. I faithfully practiced for over a year but didn't see improvement. One day, my brother grabbed my violin and started strumming it like a rockstar's guitar. I tried to take it back, but in the scuffle, it was dropped and cracked. High repair costs coupled with my lack of interest ended my instrumental career. I joined the choir instead.

A few months later, a new woman moved into our ward. She was a lovely mother of three and played the violin in our sacrament meeting. The dynamics and tone of her playing were mesmerizing. I grieved that I hadn't heard her before. If I had realized the violin could be that beautiful, I would have wanted to reach for that. It could have made all the difference.

Most women need someone to aspire to. They need to hear life beautifully played, and see the joy of righteous choices. Ruth found Naomi and could pattern her life and faith after her. Even in our struggles, we can share, love, and lift other women to see the options that lead to happiness.

—Christine

> "As we follow the example of the Savior and live as He lived . . . that light will burn within us and will light the way for others."
>
> Thomas S. Monson
>
> "Be an Example and a Light," Oct. 2015

Ruth 4:11

And all the people that were in the gate and the elders, said, We are witnesses. The Lord make the woman that is come into thine house like Rachel and like Leah, which two did build the house of Israel.

The Symbol of the Shoe

Boaz wanted to marry Ruth, but knew, under the law, that he needed to gain permission from the closest kin to her father-in-law, Naomi's deceased husband. Originally, the kinsman thought his responsibility was just to buy the land. He said, "I will redeem it" (Ruth 4:4). But Boaz quickly reminded him that if he bought the land, he must also marry Ruth and try to have a son with her. The kinsman said, "I cannot redeem it for myself, lest I mar mine own inheritance: . . . I cannot redeem it" (Ruth 4:6).

The man then plucked off his shoe and gave it to a third-party witness as a testimony of the transaction. (A shoe was a symbol of physical protection.) In this instance, the ceremony of the shoe was a confirmation that the closest kin had given up his right to protect Ruth and her husband's inheritance. After the ceremony of the shoe, Boaz said to all the men present, "Ye are witnesses this day, that I have bought all that was Naomi's husbands and sons' property" (Ruth 4:9). This included his right to marry Ruth, Naomi's oldest son's wife.

Boaz became the bridegroom of Ruth and the redeemer of both Ruth and Naomi, protecting them from the pains of poverty and starvation. The Savior's birth came through this lineage. The Savior is our Bridegroom and He redeems and protects us from the sting of sin and death.

—Marianna

"Jesus Christ is the . . . Redeemer of all mankind."

Kristin M. Yee

"The Joy of Our Redemption," Oct. 2024

1 Samuel 2:1

My heart rejoiceth in the Lord.

We Can Let Go

Hannah longed for a child. Deep in her grief, Hannah went to the temple to pray, to plead, for a child, promising that if the Lord would bless her, she would consecrate her child to Him. He did bless her. When her son was still just a toddler, Hannah took him to the temple, and "lent him to the Lord" (1 Samuel 1:28). She let go of his tiny hand and, in that moment of heart-wrenching sacrifice, exclaimed, "My heart rejoices in the Lord" (1 Samuel 2:1).

How could Hannah feel such joy when it seems she just sacrificed her only child? I mean, I struggled to feel joy when I let go of my adult son's hand so he could board the plane to the MTC. Like Hannah, I knew that sacrifice and consecration are different. We weren't giving up something (someone) we love for something better, but *to* Someone better. God has big plans for us, for those we love, for the talents we have, for the things He's given us. He's not asking us to give them up, but to give them to Him so He can make something wonderful in, through, for, and *with* us. We can trust His power, His vision, and His love. We can let go, because His arms are already extended to receive our sacrifices and us.

—Michelle

> "When we consecrate something . . . we put it to use in the Lord's service. We dedicate it to Him and His holy purpose."
>
> Dieter F. Uchtdorf
>
> "Our Heartfelt All," Apr. 2022

1 Samuel 3:10

Then Samuel answered, Speak; for thy servant heareth.

Is It Me? Or Is It the Spirit?

Yesterday, I was in the kitchen washing dishes when suddenly a thought flashed through my mind, accompanied by a feeling of urgency. It was my ministering sister's birthday, and I needed to deliver the gift I had bought her! I dropped the pot I was washing into the sink and told my husband I'd be right back.

My ministering sister wasn't home, so I visited with her mother for a few minutes before leaving the gift and a hug. As I stepped off the porch to walk home, I noticed a friend on the opposite sidewalk and called out to her. She turned, saw my face, and burst into tears. I ran across the street and embraced her until she could compose herself enough to explain. A family member had been in a car accident, resulting in some injuries. Her heart was in agony. She couldn't rest, so she'd gone for a walk, hoping it would help. I listened and hugged her as she cried and expressed all that was in her heart.

"How did you know to come find me?" she asked.

It wasn't until that moment that I understood: "The Lord told me I needed to run an errand, and He told me I needed to do it right now. I didn't know He meant *this* errand. But He knew."

—Krista

> "In His name, you will be sent on errands to serve others. He will give you experiences with promptings from the Holy Ghost. . . . You can show Him that He can trust you and can rely on you."
>
> M. Russell Ballard
>
> "Missionary Service Blessed My Life Forever," Apr. 2022

1 Samuel 5:12

And the men that died not were smitten with the emerods; and the cry of the city went up to heaven.

Emerods

While I was teaching seminary one year, we hit the war chapters in early Samuel. I knew that some of my class would be bored, so I gave them each modeling clay and told them to make something reflective of the chapters we were covering. During the reign of the judges, the people were held in captivity for a time and then, repented and were freed, only to be defeated again. At last, the Philistines stole the ark of the covenant, but it didn't bless them. Instead, when they put it in the temple of their idol God, the image kept falling over and at last fell apart. In every city the ark went to, the people got sick. In the end, the Philistines sent it back with five gold mice and five emerods.

When I turned to the back row, I saw that one student had made a man in armor. Another had sculpted a lovely mini ark of the covenant. The last student held up his creation, and we all scratched our heads. It looked like a little volcano. "It's an emerod!" the artist said, which is a boil or pustule. On closer look, I saw he had done a terrific job.

The best part of this Bible story is that the next battle, whether because of fear or emerods, the Philistines lost. When we turn to Him, the Lord really does help us to fight our battles.

—Christine

> "Fighting against temptation takes a lifetime of diligence and faithfulness. But please know that the Lord is ready to assist us."
>
> Ulisses S. Soares
>
> "Seek Christ in Every Thought," Oct. 2020

1 Samuel 10:24

And Samuel said to all the people, See ye him whom the Lord hath chosen, that there is none like him among all the people? And all the people shouted, and said, God save the king.

Keeping a New Heart

After an angry outburst one day, I asked God to help me become a new woman with a new heart. I humbled myself and asked my family to forgive me. But my new heart needed constant effort, or the old me would come back (Mosiah 3:19).

Samuel called Saul to be Israel's anointed king. Saul humbly answered: "Am not I a Benjamite, of the smallest of the tribes of Israel? and my family the least of all the families of the tribe of Benjamin?" (1 Samuel 9:21). Saul's submission to the will of the Lord allowed the Lord to turn him into another man (1 Samuel 10:6) and to give Saul a new heart (1 Samuel 10:9). Then, he was ready to be king. But, it wouldn't last.

At the beginning of Saul's reign, Saul acknowledged his limitations, and he followed the prophet's words. King Saul became adored by his people, but he had trouble keeping his new heart and eventually stopped keeping the commandments of the Lord (1 Samuel 13:14). His heart was no longer new.

The Lord can give us new hearts, but it's up to us to try to keep them. And with His help and divine commitment, we can.

—Marianna

> "If we sincerely repent, humble ourselves, and trust and rely on the Lord, our hearts will be softened."
>
> Christopher H. Kim
>
> "Harden Not Your Heart," Apr. 2025

1 Samuel 13:14

The Lord hath sought him a man after his own heart.

His Own Heart

During his reign over the people of Israel, Saul's heart changed, and not for the better. Through Samuel, he was told that the Lord was looking for a man and a heart like His to rule the kingdom. That man was David.

I think it's fascinating that the Lord wasn't looking for a man who was kind or brave or giving like Him. But a man that had a heart like Him. What does that even mean? I think of the times when someone tells me they enjoy something I enjoy or want something I want. "You're a person after my own heart!" I say.

We don't need to be the best, the prettiest, the thinnest, the richest, the most successful, or the most famous to have a heart like His. We simply need to want what He wants and enjoy what He enjoys.

I find such relief in this truth! I don't need to be perfect! As I choose love and meekness, faith and repentance, joy and charity, even in my imperfection, I can be a woman after His own heart. A woman He will seek after to bless and do His work.

—Michelle

> "As we rely upon the rock of salvation, the Savior of our souls . . . I can assure you that our spiritual maturity will grow at an increasing pace, changing our heart, making us more like Jesus Christ."
>
> Ulisses S. Soares
>
> "Seek Christ in Every Thought," Oct. 2020

1 Samuel 14:6

It may be that the Lord will work for us: for there is no restraint to the Lord to save by many or by few.

Unrestrained

Jonathan ventured into a Philistine garrison with only his armor-bearer, even though he was outnumbered and outmatched. His faith was not in his own strength but in God's power to save through even the smallest means. I love Jonathan's testimony that the Lord has no restraints. He has all power to save, whether it be "by many or by few." And yet, do we sometimes limit the Lord's saving power in our lives because we don't think it extends to us?

We believe in His forgiveness . . . except I'm too far gone.

We see the inherent value in each person . . . but my value must be earned.

We trust He can heal . . . everyone except me.

We know He hears and answers prayers . . . but is certainly too busy to notice mine.

What if the ten lepers or the woman with the issue of blood had doubted the Lord? Their faith in an unrestrained God allowed Him to work unparalleled miracles in their lives. We can trust that He will work miracles in our lives, too.

—Krista

> "The Lord performs miracles to remind us of His power, His love for us, His reach from the heavens to our mortal experience, and His desire to teach of that which is of most worth."
>
> Ronald A. Rasband
>
> "Behold! I Am a God of Miracles," Apr. 2021

1 Samuel 16:7

For man looketh on the outward appearance, but the Lord Looketh on the heart.

A Makeover

My sister Carolyn is three years younger than me and one of the nicest people I know. She had long, long light brown hair for as long as I could remember. She went beyond the mermaid club. She could sit on it! She also lived in pants, except for church. Her first semester at BYU, she lived in the dorms, and I lived on the south side of campus. She was social and pretty busy, so we didn't see each other often.

One Saturday afternoon, I got a knock on my apartment door. A lovely girl in a flowy dress with a Farrah Fawcett light blonde hairstyle stood on my threshold. "Yes?" I asked, thinking she was lost. "Christine!" Carolyn pushed her bangs to the side. "It's me!" Her new haircut with highlights and her new dress made her completely unrecognizable to me. Although her makeover changed her appearance, her voice and spirit were as familiar and dear as ever. She was still my brilliant sister.

It was so brave of Carolyn to cut off years of hair growth, but the result was amazing. The Lord doesn't care that much what we look like, but He really cares about our hearts. Do we need a "heart" makeover? I hope I am willing to let go of what the Lord asks so that I may become the woman he wants me to be. As I do, my heart is broken and my spirit contrite.

—Christine

> "And He will not refuse you or those you love when you bring to Him your broken hearts and contrite spirits."
>
> Patrick Kearon
>
> "God's Intent Is to Bring You Home," Apr. 2022

1 Samuel 17:37

The Lord that delivered me out of the paw of the lion, and out of the paw of the bear, he will deliver me out of the hand of this Philistine. And Saul said unto David, Go, and the Lord be with thee.

The Lord Will Deliver Me

A young shepherd boy versus a giant. An obviously crazy, uneven match of strength. But David's strength did not come from himself—it came from the Lord.

David had previous experiences that prepared him to meet this challenge. He had slain a lion and a bear. In each of these encounters, he should have lost the battle, yet he became the victor because of his practiced skill and his faith that the Lord would deliver him. It only took David one stone, slung into Goliath's forehead, to knock the giant down. Even though David was skilled with the sling, his confidence that he would be victorious came from his faith in the Lord.

When I win life's battles, whether great or small, I try to acknowledge the Lord's hand in delivering me from my oppressors, even when my own skill helped in the victory. Preparing for the Utah Bar Exam took me months of daily study, but I also sought the Lord's help in prayer and temple attendance. When I passed the bar, I acknowledged the Lord's support and grace in conquering that test. The Lord will deliver you, even when you face giants, as you put your trust in Him.

—Marianna

"We have confidence that God will remember His covenants with us, visit us in our afflictions, and deliver us from bondage."

Benjamin M. Z. Tai

"The Love of God," Apr. 2025

1 Samuel 18:14

And David behaved himself wisely in all his ways; and the Lord was with Him.

The Lord Is with You

I love the phrase "God meets you where you are." I think there is so much beauty and truth to it. I also think, however, that the reciprocal nature of our relationship with God can get overlooked. Yes, God meets us where we are, but can He say the same about us? Do we meet *Him* where He is too? The Lord can be with us in our dark spaces and His light places.

This is how David lived. He called upon God in times of need, but he also met God where He was by behaving "wisely." He kept his eyes and heart focused on God. He kept the commandments and sought personal revelation. He invested in a relationship with God, and put Him first. When he struggled, he repented. And God was with Him.

Chances are, you're doing just that—behaving wisely. So, though you may feel alone and are waiting for God to meet you where you are, I suspect you've already come to Him. Take heart, my friend. You're not alone. The Lord is with you.

—Michelle

> "If you are waiting for Him to come, might He already be there and within reach?"
>
> Karl D. Hirst
>
> "God's Favourite," Oct. 2024

1 Samuel 20:16–17

So Jonathan made a covenant with the house of David. . . . And Jonathan caused David to swear again, because he loved him: for he loved him as he loved his own soul.

Be a Jonathan

Jonathan, the son of King Saul, was next in line for the throne, but because of his father's wickedness, the Lord instructed that David was to be anointed the next king. Jonathan had every reason to feel bitter toward David, but they had become friends, and he prioritized that relationship over his own self-interest. He made a covenant of friendship and loyalty with David, going to extreme lengths to protect his friend from being killed by his father. He supported David's rule when he became king. David repaid his friend's loyalty by protecting Jonathan's family, even after his death.

The Lord has given us a charge to be ministers among His people. This call may include assignments to care for someone we don't necessarily align with. There may be political differences, past offenses, or conflicts of personality. I have a friend who views nearly every aspect of life—from politics to religion—through a very different lens than mine. But we keep each other close because we know that our friendship, and striving to understand each other's points of view, deepens our understanding, lends our hearts compassion, and widens our perspectives. Like Jonathan, I've learned the value of setting aside differences and striving to be a loyal, proactive friend. Because this assignment comes from the Lord, I know He blesses our efforts.

—Krista

"I see the Savior's declaration 'ye are my friends' as a clarion call to build higher and holier relationships among all of God's children 'that we may be one.'"

David L. Buckner

"Ye Are My Friends," Oct. 2024

1 Samuel 24:5

And it came to pass afterward, that David's heart smote him, because he had cut off Saul's skirt.

Respecting God's Symbols

My husband and I volunteered to serve in the temple laundry so that all the full-time missionaries in London could attend a session. While there, I was so impressed by the tender care of those preparing the sacred temple clothing. It stood in sharp contrast to what David did to Saul.

The kings of Israel wore a mantle showing their royalty much like our temple priesthood robes. The mantle had four tassels which represent the four parts of Exodus 6:6: "I will bring you from under [your] burdens. . . . I will ride you out of bondage, and I will redeem you with stretched out arms. . . . And I will take you to me for a people." Through our temple covenants, this powerful promise is fulfilled, and we do become His.

When King Saul, out of jealousy, tried to kill David, the giant-killer went into hiding. David later found Saul asleep in a cave and cut off those sacred symbols on the king's mantle. That was when "David's heart smote him." Perhaps it was because he wasn't showing proper respect for the sacred symbols of the Lord. May we reverence the symbols that bind us to the Lord so we can truly become His.

—Christine

> "Our temple garment reminds us that the Savior and the blessings of His Atonement cover us throughout our lives."
>
> J. Anette Dennis
>
> "Put Ye On the Lord Jesus Christ," Apr. 2024

1 Samuel 25:32

And David said to Abigail, Blessed be the Lord God of Israel, which sent thee this day to meet me: And blessed be thy advice and blessed be thou, which hast kept me this day from coming to shed blood, and from avenging myself with mine own hand.

Be a Peacemaker, Not a War-maker

It had been a bad day. William missed the school bus, Adam forgot his lunch, Julia was late for her dancing lessons, and Deborah's soccer practice was half an hour longer than I expected. Dinner was not prepared. The first thing my husband said when he came home was, "Where's dinner?" I began to take my frustrations out on him, even though he did not deserve it. Before things escalated, I apologized for my behavior and explained about my no good, very bad day.

Nabal was a vulgar man who was always uncivil to others and never apologized for his rudeness. Ironically, the name "Nabal" translates as "fool." He was a fool for the way he treated David, the anointed king of Israel, and his army of men. David had four hundred men with him and was going to kill Nabal for his inhospitality.

Luckily for Nabal, his beautiful wife, Abigail, was a peacemaker. She understood how David, a man of war, might take offense at her husband's actions. She quickly took bread, wine, sheep, corn, raisins, and fig cakes to David and his men (without telling her husband) as a sign of peace and reconciliation. Abigail's offering to David and his men stopped the battle before it began and saved her husband's life.

Being a peacemaker is powerful. It can also stop battles from happening, mend hearts, and may even save a life or two.

—Marianna

> "You have your agency to choose contention or reconciliation."
>
> Russell M. Nelson
>
> "Peacemakers Needed," Apr. 2023

1 Samuel 26:23

The Lord render to every man his righteousness and his faithfulness.

The Perfect Judge

Years ago, I entered a writing contest. I submitted the first five hundred words of a short story I'd worked particularly hard on. Though I didn't win, I was eager to receive some positive feedback from the anonymous judges. I opened the email and read. One hundred points were possible. Three of the four judges gave me ninety-five or higher. The fourth judge gave me a thirty-one. Why? It was good writing, they said, but was entered into the wrong genre.

My writing was overlooked because the judge felt it didn't fit the genre. It did. But my approach to the genre was nuanced. Clear enough for the first two judges, but not the third. It was frustrating being judged on a perceived mistake rather than the quality of my writing.

Since then, I've often considered how grateful I am that the only judgment that really matters in life is the judgment of God because He doesn't make mistakes. He sees me perfectly. He judges me for what I create and who I am. He is the perfect judge. I trust Him completely. This brings me so much peace.

—Michelle

"Our agency and freedom have meaning because we are accountable before God and ourselves for who we are, for what we know and do. Thankfully, we can trust God's perfect justice and perfect mercy to judge perfectly our intents and actions."

Gerrit W. Gong

"Trust Again," Oct. 2021

1 Samuel 30:4

Then David and the people that were with him lifted up their voice and wept, until they had no more power to weep.

The Dark Night of the Soul

Have you ever wept like David and his people did in the verse above? Cried and cried until you have no more power or tears left to cry? I have. It hurts. It's hard, emotional work that leaves you with a massive headache and a severe case of hiccups. But even more significantly, weeping from this depth can leave you feeling spiritually and emotionally drained, and perhaps very alone.

If you're currently weeping over a loss, significant challenge, or major shift in your life plans, I send you all the love in my heart. I'm wrapping my arms around you from afar. But even more importantly, I know the Savior is wrapping His arms around you. You are not alone. My favorite of Christ's promises is "I will not leave you comfortless: I will come to you" (John 14:18). I have faith that He keeps His promises. He will help, comfort, carry, and heal, and in His time and His way, He will restore. This is the hope we have carried in Him even before we came to earth, and He will not fail us. Cling to Him.

—Krista

> "We can be spiritually whole, even while we wait for physical and emotional healing. . . . I am sure that all things will be restored and healing will come, in His time, because He lives."
>
> Camille N. Johnson
>
> "Spiritually Whole in Him," Apr. 2025

2 Samuel 1:24–25

Ye daughters of Israel, weep over Saul, who clothed you in scarlet, with other delights. . . . How are the mighty fallen in the midst of the battle!

Apple Cores

One autumn, we got a box of fresh apples. My young daughter took one and toddled outside to enjoy her first apple ever. She returned later with her nose scrunched up. "I don't like apples!" When she handed me the half-eaten fruit, I didn't even have to ask why. She had chewed her way right through the core and finished off half the seeds. I hadn't explained to her that part of the apple shouldn't be swallowed.

Some people are a lot like apples. They may have much good about them, but they have other parts that are hard to deal with. King Saul was like that with David. As king, Saul united the tribes of Israel, was victorious in many battles, and established them as a nation. But his jealousy toward David drove him to do some terrible things. After David married Saul's daughter, the king even took her back and gave her to another man. When Saul died and David became king, it would have been natural for him to publicly express his frustration at Saul's actions, but he didn't. He praised Saul's life at his funeral and even avenged his death.

As we forgive others by focusing on their strengths and letting their apple cores go, we receive the greater gift. Forgiveness frees us from negative thoughts and gives us peace.

—Christine

> "Forgiveness is a glorious, healing principle. We do not need to be a victim twice. We can forgive."
>
> Kevin R. Duncan
>
> "The Healing Ointment of Forgiveness," Apr. 2016

2 Samuel 4:11

How much more, when wicked men have slain a righteous person in his own house upon his bed? Shall I not therefore now require his blood of your hand, and take you away from the earth?

The Poison of Revenge

Revenge movies have become box office hits. A man's family is killed by evil men and no one will help him put them in jail. So the man takes the matter into his own hands and kills everyone who hurt his family.

This storyline might make a good action-packed movie, but revenge does not follow the principles of Christ's teachings. The Savior wants mankind to rise above the poison of revenge. He said, "Love your enemies, bless them that curse you, do good to them that hate you, and pray for them which despitefully use you and persecute you" (Matthew 5:44).

Now that David was serving as king, other men thought David should now seek revenge on Saul's family. These men thought they would curry favor with David by killing Ishbosheth, Saul's son who had reigned for two years after Saul's death.

When they brought news of what they had done (hoping for a reward), David responded to their evil act by sentencing them to death for killing an innocent man. David knew revenge would not bring peace to himself or to his country.

—Marianna

> "The poison of revenge, or of unforgiving thoughts or attitudes, unless removed, will destroy the soul in which it is harbored."
>
> H. Burke Peterson
>
> "Removing the Poison of an Unforgiving Spirit," Oct. 1983

2 Samuel 6:6–7

Uzzah put forth his hand to the ark of God, and took hold of it; for the oxen shook it. And the anger of the Lord was kindled against Uzzah; and God smote him there for his error.

Stumbles and Doubts

Reports of the war between Russia and Ukraine left me troubled. My husband served his mission in Russia and has rejoiced over the Church's growth among those wonderful Saints. But suddenly, it seemed like all that progress had been snatched away. We wondered whether either county would ever recover from this setback so that the work of salvation could continue. After hours of worry, I wondered what Heavenly Father thinks about the messes His children often make. For a comical second, I imagined God scratching His head over this war, saying, "Oh, no! I didn't see this coming! What am I going to do?" I burst out laughing. Ridiculous!

Like Uzzah, who reached out a well-intended hand to steady the ark, I sometimes forget that the Lord's work is not hindered by the stumbles of this world. Father is never surprised. He knows every detail of this world's history and people. He has all power to accomplish His work, and He will rise triumphant in the last days.

—Krista

"Our world today is often characterized by fear and anxiety—fear of what the future might bring for us. But Jesus has taught us to trust and 'look unto [Him] in every thought; doubt not, fear not.'"

Mathias Held

"Opposition in All Things," Apr. 2024

2 Samuel 7:16

And thine house and thy kingdom shall be established for ever before thee; thy throne shall be established for ever.

Establishing Thy Throne Forever

Now that I am an empty-nester mom, I often think about where I should spend my time and energy. I definitely have interests to pursue. But when my heart asked what the Lord wanted me to pursue, my thoughts turned to the temple. I became a temple worker and started serving as a patron more often.

King David finally found peace, and his thoughts went to the Lord. He looked at his palace of cedar and realized that the Lord's tabernacle still resided within curtains (2 Samuel 7:3). He offered to build a house for the Lord. In a revelation, the Lord told Nathan that David's son would be the one to build His temple, but David and his family would be blessed for David's willing heart.

When we regularly attend the temple, the Lord will bless us and our family. Even if we live far away from a temple but our heart yearns to attend, the Lord will bless us for the yearnings of our heart.

—Marianna

"Should distance, health challenges, or other constraints prohibit your temple attendance for a season, I invite you to set a regular time to rehearse in your mind the covenants you have made."

Russell M. Nelson

"The Temple and Your Spiritual Foundation," Oct. 2021

2 Samuel 11:15

Set ye Uriah in the forefront of the hottest battle, and retire ye from him, that he may be smitten, and die.

Mess Upon Mess

Upon learning we were expecting baby number four, we decided to finish our basement and add more bedrooms. Four-year-old Walker was fascinated by the work. Every day, he put on his overalls, hard hat, and plastic tool belt and went downstairs to "help" his father and grandfather. When it was time to add texture to the drywall, I explained to Walker that the walls were wet and he couldn't go downstairs that day. Soon after, I discovered him in the bathroom attempting to wash a suspicious white substance from his hands and arms. He promised he hadn't been downstairs, but obviously, he had. And in his attempt to cover up his mistake, he'd only made the problem worse, smearing a muddy mess all over the counter, mirror, hand towel, rug, and his favorite overalls.

We've all done things we wish we could hide from God. But our attempts to cover up what we've done wrong may lead to even bigger messes. It can be frightening to admit our mistakes and sins to Him, but the truth is He already knows. Hiding them from Him is miserable and messy. But repentance and leaning on His mercy are a balm to the soul.

—Krista

> "Through the matchless power of the Atonement of Jesus Christ, you can be made whole again. But if you hide from Him . . . you distance yourself from the very source that can and will give you the strength to overcome."
>
> Scott D. Whiting
>
> "Beware the Second Temptation," Apr. 2025

2 Samuel 13:15

Then Amnon hated her exceedingly; so that the hatred wherewith he hated her was greater than the love wherewith he had loved her. And Amnon said unto her, Arise, be gone.

Getting What You Want

When I was at BYU, I thought I was in love with the young man who managed our apartment complex. He was smart, good-looking, and polite. Whenever he came to the apartment to fix something, he was always kind. To spend time with him, I would ask him to fix things that really didn't need fixing. Soon, I realized that my interest in him was not reciprocated. I was devastated. But a couple years later, I met the man of my dreams who did love me back. He was worth the wait.

On a darker note, Amnon had feelings for his half-sister, Tamar. A friend gave him a sinister idea. Amnon pretended to be sick and had Tamar come to his bed to feed him. After taking advantage of her, rather than feeling the love he thought he would feel for her, Amnon hated Tamar. Amnon's intent and actions led to his death by the brother of Tamar, and negatively affected the rest of his family.

Trying to gain what we want through dishonest or evil means often brings disappointment, resentment, and worse for ourselves and others. Conversely, when we pursue righteous goals in righteous ways, we can find peace in unexpected outcomes and find joy in God's plan for us.

—Marianna

> "God wants for us a radical reorientation of our selfish and prideful impulses, the eviction of the natural man, for us to 'go, and sin no more.'"
>
> Patrick Kearon
>
> "God's Intent Is to Bring You Home," Apr. 2024

2 Samuel 16:18

Whom the Lord, and this people, and all the men of Israel, choose, his will I be, and with him will I abide.

You've Got a Friend in Me

To say that there was some familial dysfunction during David's time is a severe understatement. Perhaps some of you read snippets of his life and feel deep pain or sorrow for your own family situation. Many times, our families are not what we hoped they'd be. I'm sure David felt that keenly. But, I take heart that though we can't choose our family, we can choose our friends and our faith family.

Hushai was David's friend, more loyal than even some of David's family. He was a spy for David in Absalom's house. Though the quoted verse was spoken by Hushai to Absalom to gain his trust, the standalone truth of it remains: in his heart, Hushai chose the Lord and David—they were whom he was committed to.

I was born into a healthy and happy home. I was grateful for that. However, as I grew older, I realized it was up to me to choose to be a meaningful part of the family. To be not just a daughter or sister, but a friend.

Regardless of our family circumstances, we can all choose to have and be loyal friends. We can all choose the Lord. We can—and *deserve*—to have meaningful relationships that bring us peace, safety, and joy.

—Michelle

> "To divide and conquer is the adversary's plan to destroy friendships, families, and faith. It is the Savior who unites."
>
> David L. Buckner
>
> "Ye Are My Friends," Oct. 2024

2 Samuel 18:33

O my son Absalom, . . . would God I had died for thee, O Absalom, my son, my son!

Expressions of Compassion

Absalom was angry with his father, King David, and formed a military campaign to contest his rule. David was aware of Absalom's hostility, but he loved his son and did what he could to keep Absalom safe, instructing his generals, "Deal gently for my sake with the young man" (2 Samuel 18:5). But Joab did not obey David's instructions. During the battle, Joab discovered Absalom caught in a tree and killed him. Joab likely thought he was doing the king a service, ridding him of this threat, but he was tragically mistaken. When news of Absalom's death reached David, he was overcome with despair and wished he could have given his life for his son's.

Absalom's actions did not change his father's love.

My actions do not change *my* Father's love.

Father's love is infinite, and there is nothing I can do to change that. He is patient when I'm angry. He is compassionate when I feel sorrow. He is forgiving when I make mistakes. And I can show my gratitude for His endless charity to me by offering the same gift of love and compassion to my family and His.

—Krista

> "Your worth is constant; it never changes. It was given to you by God, and there's nothing you or anyone else can do to change it."
>
> Tamara W. Runia
>
> "Your Repentance Doesn't Burden Jesus Christ; It Brightens His Joy," Apr. 2025

2 Samuel 20:16–19

Then cried a wise woman out of the city, Hear, hear . . . thou seekest to destroy a city and a mother in Israel: why wilt thou swallow up the inheritance of the Lord?

A Wise Woman

Belle Spafford was general Relief Society president from 1945 to 1974. She told of a time when a priesthood leader wouldn't listen. She asked a wise woman in her ward for advice who said, "If someone came to you, Sister Spafford, and had a great but different gift in each hand—one was power and the other was influence. Which gift would you choose?" Sister Spafford thought about it and said she would choose influence. The woman nodded and said, "You probably did."

That sort of influence was shown by an unnamed woman in the city of Abel. Joab, one of David's captains, was chasing a man who had risen up from the tribe of Benjamin as a false king named Sheba and took refuge in Abel, a walled city. When Joab's men descended on the city to destroy it, this wise woman explained that she was faithful and asked Joab what he wanted. He said the head of Sheba, thrown over the wall.

We will never know how she did it, but that wise woman must have listened to the Spirit and talked to the right people because before too long, Sheba's head was thrown at Joab's feet. A wise woman, protecting her family and with the Lord on her side, can do almost anything.

—Christine

> "The righteous woman's strength and influence today can be tenfold what it might be in more tranquil times."
>
> Joy D. Jones, quoting Spencer W. Kimball
>
> "An Especially Noble Calling," Apr. 2020

2 Samuel 22:33–34

God is my strength and power: and he maketh my way perfect. He maketh my feet like hinds' feet: and sitteth me upon my high places.

Where Are Your High Places?

I live in the foothills of the Wasatch Mountains, and many wild deer live around me. When I walk in the mornings, I love watching the way the deer securely, swiftly, and surely manage climbing the nearby mountaintops.

The metaphor of our feet becoming like hinds' feet, or a female deer's feet, reminds me that feet propel us to our destination, whether it is up or down. Our feet keep us upright and stop us from falling.

Where are my feet taking me? Are they taking me swiftly and surely to high places or low places? My high places are my home, the Church, and the temple. Low places are destinations that take me away from the Lord. They are places I do not want to go.

David's psalm of praise to the God of Israel strengthens my testimony of the power of God to change my life and direct my paths. Even though David is an imperfect man, his understanding of God's redemptive power fortifies my faith and lifts me to higher places.

—Marianna

> "Everything about the Father's plan for His beloved children is designed to bring everyone home."
>
> Patrick Kearon
>
> "God's Intent Is to Bring You Home," Apr. 2024

2 Samuel 23:2

The Spirit of the Lord spake by me, and his word was in my tongue.

The Spirit Speaks

It's a moment I will never forget. My daughter told me she'd just tried to hurt herself. I was sitting on my bed when she handed me some sharp objects and asked me to take them from her. I said a thousand screaming prayers in a fraction of a second, and God heard them all.

I looked at my daughter, took the implements, and, with a calmness and strength that could only come from heaven, received the right words to say to her in that moment. The words came. The fear did not. I knew exactly what to say. We hugged. She cried. I prayed. She was okay. And it was over. I haven't felt such power before or since.

The Spirit doesn't always work this boldly, but it works. As we seek for the gifts of the Spirit, we *can* be given what to say when we need to say it—when God needs us to say it.

You are not alone. God, through the Holy Ghost, can lead and guide you, support and strengthen you. I promise you, He will give you what you need when you need it.

—Michelle

"What are the fruits of exercising spiritual gifts? They include promptings from the Spirit that help us face our daily needs and show us what to do and say."

Gary E. Stevenson

"Promptings of the Spirit," Oct. 2023

1 Kings 1:5

Adonijah . . . exalted himself, saying, I will be king.

Stay in Your Lane

I was thrilled to get to speak at a favorite conference until the opening keynote speaker began her address. She was radiant, articulate, and poised—a paragon of everything I wanted to be. I started comparing myself. Hard. I began wishing I could have her experiences, her skills, and yes, even her clothes! In an instant, my confidence evaporated, replaced by stomach-twisting panic. Why would anyone want to hear from me when they could learn from someone like her? I blinked back tears that threatened to run my mascara.

The temptation of comparison is hard to avoid. But it's damaging because it tempts us to take our eyes off Heavenly Father's plans for our lives and replace trust in Him with envy for something else. As I prayed for help that day, Father showed me that I was swerving into a lane that wasn't mine. The keynote speaker had a specific assignment that utilized her talents and abilities. And I did, too. We were different, but both skill sets and messages were needed by different people at the conference. When I trust Him and stay in my lane, He leads me to beautiful places I could not reach on my own. He knows me. And He will lead me on the best path for my life—the one that will bring me safely home.

–Krista

> "Knowing who we are and being true to our divine identity brings calm. Christlike poise requires that we avoid comparing ourselves to others or pretending to be someone we're not."
>
> Mark L. Bragg
>
> "Christlike Poise," Apr. 2023

1 Kings 2:2–3

I go the way of all the earth: be thou strong therefore . . . and keep the charge of the Lord thy God, to walk in his ways . . . that thou mayest prosper in all that thou doest.

What Does It Mean to Prosper?

King David's last words to his son were that if he walked in the ways of the Lord, he would prosper in all that he did. With Solomon's gift of wisdom, he was able to grow the kingdom and accumulate great wealth. But did he prosper? Upon his death, King Solomon's son was to take the throne, but one of his father's captains rebelled and split the kingdom in two. It would never reunite in biblical times. Some righteous people are blessed both physically and spiritually. Others are only given one talent. Yet they all prosper in different ways.

When I first married, we lived in an affluent part of Dallas. A woman in our ward was married to a member of the stake presidency. I loved sitting next to her during lessons because her comments were so deep. One Fourth of July, she invited everyone to come to her home for fireworks. I was shocked to find she lived in a run-down farmhouse on a couple of unkempt acres. Though the wallpaper hadn't been updated in years, she had raised her large, faithful family in that home. Her children were now raising righteous families of their own. My friend had indeed prospered, though the world might disagree.

—Christine

"The Lord has promised that those who keep the commandments of God 'prosper in the land.' God's prosperity is the power to press forward despite the problems of life."

L. Whitney Clayton

"The Finest Homes," Apr. 2020

1 Kings 3:9

Give therefore thy servant an understanding heart to judge thy people, that I may discern between good and bad: for who is able to judge this thy so great a people?

Wisdom

If the Lord came to you in a vision and asked, "What shall I give thee?" (1 Kings 3:5), how would you answer? Would you ask for wealth, a happy family, or a long life free from pain?

Solomon answered that he wanted an understanding heart. He knew he needed it to make the right decisions as a king. Because he did not ask for riches or the honors of men, the Lord blessed him with wisdom.

Solomon's wisdom would be put to the test when two mothers came to him both claiming that a newborn baby was theirs. Solomon asked for his servants to bring him a sword and declared that the baby be divided in half. The one mother said, "O my lord, give her the living child, and in no wise slay it" (3:26). The other mother did not care and told them to kill the child. Solomon gave the child to the mother who was willing to give the child up, rather than watch the child be split in two.

I think that it didn't matter whether the mother was the child's biological mother or not. Solomon's wisdom was that she was the one who deserved to raise the child because she protected the baby and cherished the child's worth.

—Marianna

> "Where is wisdom? It pulses and surges with the Lord's light of truth!"
>
> Russell M. Nelson
>
> "Where Is Wisdom?" Oct. 1992

1 Kings 6:13

I will dwell among the children of Israel, and will not forsake my people Israel.

To Be Connected

My first cell phone was seven inches tall, three inches thick, and weighed two pounds. And all it did was make and receive calls. It was a gift from my husband. I didn't love it because I felt so high-tech. I loved it because of what it represented—a way we could always stay connected.

For over four hundred years, the Israelites had carried the tabernacle with them, a portable place of worship that housed the ark of the covenant. Now, under the guidance of Solomon, the first fixed building dedicated as a temple would be built in the promised land—a physical place they could go to worship and receive the Lord's blessings. It represented the Lord's desire to be connected.

Today, we have almost four hundred temples dotting the earth—each with the same power and promise. Why? Because the Lord wants us in His house. He wants us to see Him, to feel Him, to connect with Him, and become like Him. He *wants* to spend time with us, to be connected with us. With *you*.

—Michelle

> "Jesus Christ declared that He had accepted the [Kirtland] temple as His house and made this stunning promise: 'I will manifest myself to my people in mercy in this house.' This significant promise applies to every dedicated temple today."
>
> Neil A. Andersen
>
> "Temples, Houses of the Lord Dotting the Earth," Apr. 2024

1 Kings 8:29

That thine eyes may open toward this house night and day, even toward the place of which thou hast said, My name shall be there.

The House of the Lord

Visiting my parents in their home is a joy. We spend long hours talking together, laughing, playing, and working. In their home, my parents teach me valuable skills and truths of the gospel. And after my visit, I return home to my house feeling loved and rejuvenated.

In King Solomon's dedicatory prayer for the temple he had built for the Lord, he reminded us that this is the Lord's house. Today, our temples have His name inscribed above the door. This is His address, His home on earth, and He invites us all to come and visit Him there. Inside the temple, we help our Father with His work to gather Israel and spend time visiting with Him in holy prayer. In His home, we are taught eternal truths and receive precious blessings. And after our visit, we return home to our houses feeling loved and rejuvenated.

—Krista

"The temple is literally the house of the Lord. I promise you as you come worthily and prayerfully to His holy house, you will be armed with His power, His name will be upon you, His angels will have charge over you, and you will grow up in the blessing of the Holy Ghost."

Neil L. Andersen

"Temples, Houses of the Lord Dotting the Earth," Apr. 2024

1 Kings 9:2–7

If thou wilt walk before me . . . in integrity of heart and in uprightness . . . then I will establish the throne of thy kingdom upon Israel forever. . . . But if ye shall at all turn from following me . . . then will I cut off Israel out of the land . . . and this house.

Expecting More

After King Solomon built the first temple in Jerusalem, the Lord appeared to him for the second time. The first time the Lord came to him, Solomon was given the gift of wisdom. Now that he had built the temple, I wonder if Solomon was expecting more. Some new gifts and instructions. Instead, God repeated the warning and promise given to David and Moses. If the people followed the Savior, they would be blessed. But if they turned from the Lord, they would lose those blessings and more.

As general conference approaches, I often wish for some great new message or announcement. I want more. Sometimes I become disappointed because it's the same old thing. Recently, Elder Dale G. Renlund told of a Primary child who worried about the Second Coming because bad things are going to happen. In response, this kind Apostle said, "The best advice for her, for you, and for me is to follow the Savior's teachings. His instructions are neither mysterious or complex." Sound familiar? It's the same message Solomon got.

The simple truth is that I only need to feel the Spirit and remember that doing as the Lord asks is all I need to feel peace and joy. I don't need more. That is enough.

—Christine

> "When we follow [the Savior's teachings], we do not need to fear or be anxious."
>
> Dale G. Renlund
>
> "Personal Preparation to Meet the Savior," Apr. 2025

1 Kings 11:7

And they spake unto him, saying, If thou wilt be a servant unto this people this day, and wilt serve them, and answer them, and speak good words to them, then they will be thy servants for ever.

Becoming a Servant-Leader

As a young mom, I tried to teach my children to clean the house. I started by laying down the law but soon found out that didn't work. The children revolted, and the day often ended in tears (usually, mine). Then, I decided that we would make it fun. We all worked together, played music while we worked, and finally, celebrated when we were all done! When I stopped being the tyrant and started making it fun, my home was a happier, cleaner place.

Rehoboam became king of Israel after the death of his father, Solomon. The people came to the new king and asked him for a reprieve from the heavy yoke his father had placed on them. Rehoboam asked his old advisers what to do. Their advice was to be kind to the people, serve with them, and lighten their load. They promised that if he did this, the people would serve him as their king forever. Then, Rehoboam asked his young friends, who told Rehoboam to warn the people that if they thought Solomon was hard on them, he would be much harder. He followed their advice, and the people revolted.

The Lord taught: "And whosoever of you will be the chiefest, shall be servant of all" (Mark 10:44). Rehoboam learned the importance of this statement the hard way.

—Marianna

"I testify of Jesus Christ, whose light and Spirit guide all of the children of God in helping the poor and distressed throughout the world."

Dallin H. Oaks

"Helping the Poor and Distressed," Oct. 2022

1 Kings 12:16

To your tents, O Israel.

To Your Tents

A rock hit the windshield, creating a small crack. It seemed harmless. Over time, it grew a bit here and there, but nothing seemed threatening—until one day, another rock hit the small crack and split the windshield in two.

Israel had finally been united under David and Solomon—solid and intact like the original windshield. Over time, tensions and political problems caused small fractures. Rehoboam's refusal to listen, and subsequent increase in the people's taxes, was like hitting the windshield in a weak spot, causing the crack to spread. The northern tribes had had enough, and with the powerful statement above, stood on the side of God. The Kingdom of Israel was split into two, and the scattering began.

It feels tragic. Broken. Permanent. But it's not. *With God, nothing tragic or broken needs to be permanent.* Through the restored priesthood, Israel is being gathered together again!

With the right help, a new windshield was replaced. With the Lord's help, the things we feel are tragic or broken in our lives can be fixed. We can be helped. We can be healed. To our tents, my friends. Stand on the side of God. He won't fail you.

—Michelle

> "There is nothing in your life that is broken that is beyond the curative, redeeming, and enabling power of Jesus Christ."
>
> Amy A. Wright
>
> "Christ Heals That Which Is Broken," Apr. 2022

1 Kings 15:26

And he did evil in the sight of the Lord, . . . and in his sin wherewith he made Israel to sin.

Exemplars and Defenders of the Faith

The moral and spiritual choices of leaders can shape the destiny of their people. For example, King Asa "did what was right in the eyes of the Lord" (1 Kings 15:11–14). He removed idols and even removed his mother from her position as queen because of her idolatry. The Lord was pleased with his efforts, and the nation improved. On the other hand, King Baasha "did evil in the sight of the Lord" (1 Kings 15:28–34). He murdered, started wars, and "provoked the Lord God of Israel to anger." His example led his people into sin.

Righteous leadership honors God and uplifts the people, while wicked leadership defies God and leads to a nation's decline. Leadership is a sacred trust that carries great responsibility and has a lasting impact. We have a moral duty to help elect and appoint good men and women into leadership roles in our governments and places of influence. But equally vital, we need to be good leaders in our homes and communities, influencing the circles directly around us, and having a positive, lasting impact on our families and neighborhoods.

–Krista

"It would be impossible to measure the influence that such women have, not only on families, but also on the Lord's Church, as wives, mothers, and grandmothers; as sisters and aunts; as teachers and leaders; and especially as exemplars and devout defenders of the faith."

Russell M. Nelson

"A Plea to My Sisters," Oct. 2015

1 Kings 17:6

And the ravens brought him bread and flesh in the morning, and . . . in the evening; and he drank of the brook.

The Grocery Store Miracle

When I was a young mother of five, my finances were tight. When another family asked to move in with us, I didn't know how I could afford to feed everyone. Still, I felt it was the right thing to do, so I agreed. Soon after, I went grocery shopping. The cereal box I got was dented, and the checkout lady replaced it. I asked what she was going to do with the old one. She said they usually gave damaged goods to the food pantry, but they were full. I asked if I could take it and give the extra to others in need. She was thrilled and brought me to the manager. It was a grocery store miracle!

For the next few months while that family lived with me, I didn't have to buy groceries at all. Everything, and more, was provided. I knew of some other struggling families and would often deliver care packages of extra food to them. Once the family staying with us returned to their home, the food pantry opened again. And we were back to penny pinching.

The Lord really does care for our needs. Sometimes we get a grocery store miracle. Other times, we may need to have the humility to share our circumstances with the bishop and ask for help, or we may discover opportunities that alleviate our want. Either way, the Lord will take care of His own. Just remember, it's not as bad as eating bird droppings like Elijah did.

—Christine

> "Jesus Christ lives and stands there at every moment, waiting for us to choose to call upon Him to provide succor, strength, and salvation."
>
> Mathias Held
>
> "Opposition in All Things," Apr. 2024

1 Kings 18:39

And when all the people saw it, they fell on their faces: and they said, The Lord, he is the God; the Lord, he is the God.

The Lord Is the God!

The Israelites had a problem figuring out who or what they should worship. Too often, the Israelites were persuaded to leave the one, true God and worship the more popular gods of their neighbors. Jezebel, the queen of Israel, was not originally from Israel. She was Phoenician and brought with her the worship of Baal. The Israelites began to follow her faith and to forget the God of Israel.

Elijah wanted to prove to the people which god they should worship. He challenged Jezebel's priests to a contest. They were to prepare a sacrifice and call down the power of their god to light it with fire and he would do the same with the Lord. The priests tried hard—crying and cutting themselves—to no avail. No fire came. Then, Elijah prepared his sacrifice with an altar of twelve stones and buckets of water applied three times to make it even harder to burn. After Elijah's prayer, the fire of the Lord consumed the sacrifice, the stones, the water—everything! The people fell on their faces proclaiming that the Lord is the God of Israel.

Sometimes, we might be persuaded to worship the gods of the world. When we return to God, the Atonement cleanses us so that we can proclaim the Lord is the only God in our lives.

—Marianna

> "True worship means loving God and yielding our will to Him—the most precious gift we can offer."
>
> D. Todd Christofferson
>
> "Worship," Apr. 2025

1 Kings 20:13

And, behold, there came a prophet unto Ahab king of Israel, saying, Thus saith the Lord.

Our Choice Is Our Chance

Ahab was in a tight spot. He was afraid, under a lot of pressure, facing a powerful enemy, and unsure how to respond. The Lord sent a prophet to help—three times.

Ahab listened to and followed the prophet when it benefited him militarily, but when it came to justice and obedience, he ignored the words of the prophet to his detriment.

Did God know Ahab would listen twice? I believe so. He knows everything. So, then, did God know Ahab wouldn't listen the third time? Yes. So, why did He send a prophet to someone who wasn't going to listen?

Because He loves us enough to let us *choose* to listen.

Prophets don't force us to believe or follow. They receive truth and share it with us so we can have the choice. We can choose truth. We can choose God. That choice is our chance to become like Him.

—Michelle

> "Prophets receive truth from God and share that truth with us."
>
> John C. Pingree Jr.
>
> "Eternal Truth," Oct. 2023

1 Kings 22:7–8

Is there not here a prophet of the Lord besides, that we might inquire of him? And the king of Israel said . . . there is yet one man, Micaiah . . . but I hate him; for he doth not prophesy good concerning me, but evil.

We Listen to a Prophet's Voice

Imagine a powerful CEO planning a risky merger that will give him wealth and power. In his mind, there is no way he can fail. He gathers his board of directors, who are all on his payroll, to approve his plans. They know the risks are enormous and that failure is likely, but the boss expects them to agree with him. They want to stay in the boss's good graces, so they all lie and tell the CEO, "It's a great plan!"

But then, one lone financial analyst enters the room. He has run the numbers and values truth over popularity, so he speaks up. "The data shows this merger will fail and bankrupt the company." The CEO is furious and tries to suppress the analyst's voice. Despite all his manipulation, bullying, and lying, when the merger goes through, it ends in disaster, just as the analyst predicted.

Like this CEO, King Ahab learned that ignoring the truth cannot prevent consequences, especially when that counsel comes from God through His prophets. Even if we surround ourselves with millions of voices telling us what we want to hear, God's plan and His truth will always prevail.

—Krista

> "Seek guidance from voices you can trust—from prophets, seers, and revelators and from the whisperings of the Holy Ghost."
>
> Russell M. Nelson
>
> "Think Celestial!," Oct. 2023

2 Kings 2:23–25

There came forth little children out of the city, and mocked him, and said unto him, Go up, thou bald head. . . . And he . . . cursed them in the name of the Lord. And there came two she bears out of the wood, and tare forty and two children of them.

Truth and Consequences

Sometimes we are told the truth but not in context. Once my four-year-old rushed to my side in tears. "Marcus took my new sword!" he screamed. I ran into the family room to find Marcus with the sword, kneeling by the baby.

"Marcus, give your brother back his sword!" I said, thinking I understood the truth.

Marcus got to his feet. "But he was hitting the baby with it." Looking to my preschooler, I could tell that was also telling the truth. In context, the sword should have been taken away.

So, when I read that Elisha cursed forty-two "little children" who were killed by two she-bears for calling him bald, I knew there had to be more to the story. After some research, I learned that the children were older teenagers who had just witnessed Elijah ascending into heaven on a chariot of fire. Instead of allowing this miraculous event to increase their faith, they chose to mock Elisha, the new prophet, who had shaved his head in mourning of Elijah's passing. In consequence of this disrespect, the prophet cursed them. And the she-bear? That was the Lord's idea.

—Christine

"We are free to choose and act, but we do not control the consequences."

Quentin L. Cook

"Be One with Christ," Apr. 2024

2 Kings 4:2

And Elisha said unto her, What shall I do for thee? Tell me, what hast thou in the house? And she said, Thine handmaid hath not anything in the house, save a pot of oil.

Multiplying What We Have

We were very poor when Steve and I started our family. Yet, the Lord always made sure we had enough food and money for rent. I felt this was, in part, because we paid our tithing, prayed and worshiped regularly, and sought His guidance. The Lord multiplied what little we had by making things last longer and by sending miraculous help when we needed it.

A widow was destitute after the death of her righteous husband who had been part of the sons of the prophets. She cried to the prophet Elisha for help, saying that creditors were going to take her sons as payment. Elisha asked her what she had in her home. She said she only had a pot of oil. Elisha counseled the widow to gather as many empty vessels as she could find from friends and family. Then, the miracle happened. Using her original vessel, she was able to fill all the other empty vessels with oil.

The prophet Elisha did not give the widow gold or silver to pay her debts. Instead, the prophet prayed to God that He would multiply what she already had. We may feel we have little to offer, but when we trust and consecrate it to the Lord, He can multiply our efforts and provide for our needs.

—Marianna

"I testify that while many circumstances in life may be beyond our control, none of us is beyond the reach of the Lord's infinite blessings."

Gérald Caussé

"Compensating Blessings," Apr. 2025

2 Kings 5:13

If the prophet had bid thee do some great thing, wouldest thou not have done it? how much rather then, when he saith to thee, Wash and be clean?

The Answer Is Simple

I love the story of Naaman. He was a powerful Syrian army commander who was also a leper. The young Israelite servant girl tells Naaman's wife that the prophet Elisha can heal him.

Excited about his potential freedom from his disease, Naaman goes to Israel with gifts. Elisha sends Naaman a message: wash in the River Jordan seven times and he'd be clean.

This is not what Naaman was expecting. I can relate in a sense. Years ago, on the eve of my hysterectomy, the Lord told me in a blessing I wasn't finished adding to my family. At the time, it didn't make sense. Ten years later, as we adopted our youngest, I saw God's wisdom and smiled.

For Naaman, the healing wasn't dramatic in process or effect. And so, rather than following the prophet's counsel, he walked away. Thankfully, with the encouragement of his servants, Naaman repented, washed, and was healed.

Many of us have this fantastic ability to overthink or overcomplicate things. But God doesn't do that. He keeps it simple. Have faith. Follow the commandments. Follow the prophet—even (or especially) in the simple things, and we will be blessed.

—Michelle

"The account of Naaman reminds us of the risk of picking and choosing the parts of prophetic counsel that fit our thinking, our expectations, or today's norms. . . . The most important words we can hear, ponder, and follow are those revealed through our living prophet."

Ronald A. Rasband

"The Things of My Soul," Oct. 2021

2 Kings 6:16

Fear not: for they that be with us are more than they that be with them.

Armies of Angels

My husband sent the hospital social worker to fetch me from the waiting room. Our daughter's heart had stopped three times during an attempted CT scan, and she was receiving active CPR. I needed to get to her immediately. The social worker and I sped down the hallway while she prepared me for the nightmare I was about to walk into. Suddenly, she grabbed me by the arm and pulled me to a stop. Tears ran down her cheeks as she asked, "How are you doing this? How are you standing? Why aren't you a puddle on the floor?"

I didn't know what to say, and I didn't have time to mull it over. But I opened my heart wide to see if God would send me an answer. Immediately, I knew that I was *not* standing in the hallway alone. Generations of family members on the other side of the veil had come rushing to my aid. They had their arms around me, carrying, supporting, and holding me together. It made perfect sense. Earthly family and friends from all over the country were flying, driving, and coming to help me in any way they could. Why wouldn't those in heaven do the same? The social worker smiled at my answer. Then together we stepped through a door into the terror of my daughter's medical crisis. And those angels went with me.

—Krista

> "When I speak of having confidence before God, I am referring to having confidence . . . that He sends angels to be with us and with those we love."
>
> Russell M. Nelson
>
> "Confidence in the Presence of God," Apr. 2025

2 Kings 8:2

And the woman arose, and did after the saying of the man of God.

A Great Woman

I have moved sixteen times in my married life. Most moves were for jobs, but I've never moved because a prophet told me to.

A Great Woman from Shunem often had the prophet Elisha to dinner in her home and made a spare room for him. Because of her hospitality, she was blessed with a son in her old age. When her boy died, the prophet raised him from the dead. Some time later, Elisha came and warned her there would be a famine and told her to go live somewhere else for seven years.

She didn't question or ask specifics. Instead, she "arose, and did after the saying of the man of God." She moved to Philistia for seven years. Upon her return, she discovered her land had been taken. Undeterred, this Great Woman took the prophet's servant and her son to the king. She explained that she was following the prophet which is why she left, and that her son had been raised from the dead by Elisha. The son and the servant both testified of her story. Even though the king did not follow the ways of God, he restored her lands.

Do we have the faith to follow the prophet no matter what, even if it means losing everything for a time? Are we that *Great*?

—Christine

> "As we focus on Christ and follow His prophet, we too will be led to Christ and the joy of His gospel."
>
> I. Raymond Egbo
>
> "Focus on Jesus Christ and His Gospel," Oct. 2024

2 Kings 9:36

This is the word of the Lord, which he spake by his servant Elijah the Tishbite, saying, In the portion of Jezreel shall dogs eat the flesh of Jezebel.

The Day of Judgment Always Comes

Years ago, we moved to a new city where we knew no one. We had bought a house, but it was too small for our growing family. So, with the money left over from the sale of our last home, we decided to add a couple of rooms onto the back of our new house. However, after the contractor had taken off the back wall of our home, he took our money and left the state, leaving us with a home completely open to the elements—and winter was coming. My husband and I considered suing him, but the lawyers said we would just lose more money. I was angry. This man had gotten away with it. But had he?

Even after Elijah proved that Israel's God was greater than her god, Jezebel continued to push her worship on the people of Israel. Though Elijah warned her she would die a terrible death if she did not change, Jezebel continued in her evil ways. It seemed she had gotten away with it until the Lord's judgment did come in the form of death foretold by Elijah. God not only sees us, but He is aware of those who try (and sometimes succeed) to do us harm. Though we may think they have "gotten away" with awful things, we can find peace knowing that God is a perfect judge, and all will be made right.

—Marianna

"We will be judged according to our actions, the desires of our hearts, and the kind of person we have become."

Dallin H. Oaks

"The Great Plan," Apr. 2020

2 Kings 10:16

*Come with me,
and see my zeal for the Lord.*

Come and See

I moved out of my home when I was seventeen into an apartment with a high school friend. I hit it off with my apartment manager, Denise, a single mom of a cute little two-year-old. One day, while talking with the missionaries in my singles ward, Denise popped into my head. The gospel had brought me so much joy, and I wanted her to feel it too. I invited her to "come and see." After learning about the beauty of the gospel and receiving her own answers, Denise was baptized. She was happy. She was changed.

Not every invitation leads to stories like this. But many stories like this start with an invitation to come and see. Come and see the gospel of Jesus Christ. Come and see the plan of happiness. Come and see hope and help and healing. Come and see a people who strives to love God and each other. Is there someone you can invite to "come and see" today?

—Michelle

> "As members of the Church, we are encouraged to immerse ourselves in the words of God. . . . Through sincere and humble prayer to our Heavenly Father, we learn to recognize the voice of the Holy Spirit. We accept calls to serve, teach, plan, minister, and administer. These opportunities allow us to grow in spirit, mind, and character. . . . We invite all of God's children throughout the world to join us in this great endeavor. Come and see!"
>
> Dieter F. Uchtdorf
>
> "Come and Belong," Apr. 2020

2 Kings 11:2–3

Jehosheba . . . took Joash the son of Ahaziah, and stole him from among the king's sons which were slain; . . . And he was with her hid in the house of the Lord six years.

Courage in Christ

Recently, my daughter came home from school visibly upset. During recess, a group of friends shared their opinions about a divisive topic. My daughter listened and felt confident enough to share what she believed to be true. But it didn't go well. Her friends turned on her in anger and then silence. She cried, "Mom, I wish I'd kept my opinion to myself."

I told her how proud I am that she politely and firmly stood her ground even in the face of opposition. And while there are times to keep our opinions to ourselves, there are also consequences for staying silent. The Lord needs people who are brave in defending truth and acting in righteousness.

I love the example of Jehosheba, who acted with tremendous bravery and trust in God. The Lord had covenanted with David that his house would endure forever, and that one day, the Messiah would come through his line (see 2 Samuel 7:12–16). When Jehosheba rescued her nephew, she preserved a nation's future and God's covenant. Sometimes protecting what is right requires bold, long-term courage.

–Krista

"As you proceed firmly in Christ and with courage not only to proclaim the truth but to live the truth, you will find comfort and peace during the turbulence that you shall encounter in these days."

Denelson Silva

"Courage to Proclaim the Truth," Oct. 2022

2 Kings 13:21

When the [dead] man was let down, and touched the bones of Elisha, he revived, and stood up on his feet.

Words of Life

While teaching seminary, I had a student approach me with a question. "Why didn't Christ write any of His own scriptures?"

I was surprised she'd ask that. "Didn't He write all of them? They are His words."

"Sort of," the student said. "But never directly. You'd expect it in the Old Testament, but in the New Testament when He was there, why didn't He write his own words? Instead, He used Matthew, Luke, or John."

I'd never thought of it that deeply, but the question made me pause. It was true. God uses His prophets to teach the words of Christ as much in times of old as today. If I had been wiser, I might have told the following story:

After Elisha died, the Moabites attacked. As soldiers were burying one of their dead, another band moved in. Quickly, they lowered the dead man's body into Elisha's sepulcher. As soon as it touched the prophet's bones, the soldier stood up. Alive. Healed. The prophet's words really do give us life by showing us the way to draw closer to Christ.

—Christine

"The words of prophets matter.
Prophets testify of the divinity of Jesus Christ.
They teach His gospel and show His love for all.

Ronald A. Rasband,
"Words Matter," Apr 2024

2 Kings 15:35

Howbeit the high places were not removed: the people sacrificed and burned incense still in the high places. He built the higher gate of the house of the Lord.

Hiding Sins in High Places

In the middle of the book of 2 Kings, many unrighteous kings reign in Israel. When Azariah became king, "he did that which was right in the sight of the Lord" (2 Kings 15:3), with one exception; he did not remove the altars in "high places" or on the hilltops away from the center of the city—the hidden places. Additionally, Azariah did not stop the people from sacrificing and burning incense in these places. Israel's hidden, worldly ways took them away from their Lord. Because of Israel's disobedience, Assyria conquered them and carried many of them away from their homeland.

Hezekiah, king of Judah, responded differently. He eliminated the high places and centralized all worship in Jerusalem. When the Assyrian army came to take over Jerusalem, the Lord protected Jerusalem from invasion (2 Kings 19:35).

To protect our family and home from worldly invasion, our family decided to establish certain restrictions on digital devices. Our rules to stop hidden sins included no phones and computers in the bedroom, parental controls on digital devices, and a regular review of the browsing history on computers. Israel tried to keep their worldly worship hidden, but God still saw it. God will see our hidden sins as well.

—Marianna

> "Overcoming the world is not an event that happens in a day or two. It happens over a lifetime as we repeatedly embrace the doctrine of Christ."
>
> Russell M. Nelson
>
> "Overcoming the World and Find Rest," Oct. 2022

2 Kings 17:13

Turn ye from your evil ways, and keep my commandments.

A Thousand Chances

Second Kings chapter 17 contains a pivotal moment in history, one that was prophesied thousands of years before and has been talked about for thousands of years since. It is the first major scattering of Israel. The scattering that we, today, have been working to regather. After they "sinned against the Lord" (2 Kings 17:7) and turned their backs on Him, in His patience and mercy, the Lord still warns them and pleads with them to come to Him. Why? Because "God is in relentless pursuit" of us, as Elder Patrick Kearon so beautifully said. He will give us as many chances as we will take.

If you feel you've had too many chances, that God is tired of hearing from you, that you've gone too far, or that you'll never be good enough, know that He doesn't feel that way. He is always in relentless pursuit of you. He loves you. He is patient and kind. You have all the chances you'll ever need—second, third, thousandths chances, and more.

As you go about your day today, I hope this brings you some peace and maybe even joy, and you can feel God's love for you.

—Michelle

> "Our Savior, Jesus Christ, knows everything about us we don't want anyone else to know, and He still loves us. His is a gospel of second and third chances, made possible by His atoning sacrifice."
>
> Gerrit W. Gong
>
> "Room in the Inn," Apr. 2021

2 Kings 18:5–7

He trusted in the Lord God of Israel. . . . For he clave to the Lord, and departed not from following him. . . . And the Lord was with him.

A Covenant Relationship with Christ

While I was teaching an institute class a few years ago, the topic of covenants came up. I invited two sets of young adults to come to the front of the room with me. I turned to the young man and woman to my left, neither of whom really knew each other. I asked the young woman, "If you needed five dollars, and he had five dollars, what could you do?" She shyly said, "Maybe ask him if I could borrow his five dollars?" Then I turned to the young man and woman on my right, who were married, and asked the young woman the same thing. She laughed. "I wouldn't. I make the money, but what I make is ours."

We talked about what made their responses so different. The ones on my left were living their own lives; the couple on my right were living one life together because they were in a covenant relationship.

We can have Jesus in our lives without making covenants. We can love Him and ask for His help. But when we enter into a covenant relationship with Him, we no longer invite Him into our lives. We create a new life *with* Him—a shared life with access and privileges only found in a covenant relationship.

—Michelle

"We must remember: it's not the course alone that will exalt us; it's the companion—our Savior. And this is the why of covenant relationship."

Emily Belle Freeman

"Walking in a Covenant Relationship with Christ," Oct. 2023

2 Kings 18:32–33

Hearken not unto Hezekiah, when he persuadeth you, saying, The Lord will deliver us. Hath any of the gods of the nations delivered at all his land out of the hand of the king of Assyria?

Let's Pause

Here we are in 2 Kings 18. The King of Assyria has laid siege to a vast portion of land in what we now call the Middle East. His armies have marched ruthlessly from city to city, slaughtering and pillaging. He has recently defeated the entire Northern Kingdom, scattered those ten tribes, and now he is literally standing with 185,000 soldiers at the gates of Jerusalem, mocking King Hezekiah's faith that the Lord will deliver them.

If we turn the page and read chapter 19, a miraculous turn of events will unfold. But can we pause here for a moment to appreciate the terror that King Hezekiah and his people must have felt? Looking at a map of all the land the King of Assyria conquered, we see that Judah is a tiny speck. There was no reason for the people of Judah to have hope, except that the prophet Isaiah promised that with faith, God would save them. They chose to believe, even though the enemy was right outside the door, even though logic told them it was hopeless. They did not have the foresight we do, that an angel was on his way, and that they would witness a miracle. They just believed. And God provided a way. Have faith in hopeless situations.

–Krista

> "When Helaman and his young warriors faced daunting challenges, Helaman was resolute. 'Behold, it mattereth not—we trust God will deliver us.'"
>
> Michael T. Nelson
>
> "In Support of the Rising Generation," Apr. 2024

2 Kings 19:34

For I will defend this city, to save it, for mine own sake.

A God of Miracles

When I was a BYU student, every day after lunch I would head to the back of the Wilkinson Center and watch *The Edge of Night* with my couch buddies. We were all addicted to the romance crime show. One semester I needed a course to graduate that was only offered then. I tried to go to class, but I hated missing the show. Soon I was skipping every other class and more. It was bad.

I prayed that I'd be strong enough, but I wasn't. One day after skipping class with extreme guilt and going to watch my show, I found it wasn't on. In tears, one of my couch buddies told me it had been cancelled. I was shocked and grateful! That was a battle I could not fight on my own, and the Lord took care of it for me.

I thought of the Jews in Jerusalem fighting the Assyrians with King Hezekiah and the prophet Isaiah. The ten northern tribes had already been taken hostage and were outnumbered. That night a miracle occurred. An angel smote the Assyrian camp, killing 145,000 of the enemies. In terror, the Assyrians left on their own, never to return.

Sometimes our personal battles may be an addiction or other personal weakness, or they may be struggles with personality clashes or obedience. Most of the time as we turn to the Lord, He will strengthen us or show us a way to escape. Still, every once in a while, He does fight our battles for us, and I'm still grateful.

—Christine

> "As you . . . let God prevail in your lives, you will experience for yourselves that our God is 'a God of miracles.'"
>
> Russell M. Nelson
>
> "Let God Prevail," Oct. 2020

2 Kings 22:16

Thus saith the Lord, Behold, I will bring evil upon this place, and upon the inhabitants thereof, even all the words of the book which the king of Judah hath read.

Reading the Scriptures Brings Safety

Huldah, the prophetess, becomes the mouthpiece for a very important prophecy about the kingdom of Judah and their righteous King Josiah. She warns Judah that they have brought evil to their land because they have not followed the words of the scriptures: "They have forsaken me [and therefore] my wrath shall be kindled against this place" (2 Kings 22:17). But King Josiah will be blessed because "thine heart was tender and thou hast humbled thyself before the Lord" (2 Kings 22:19). Huldah told the people to internalize the scriptures that had been read to them. Because King Josiah did what Huldah counseled, he was protected and so was his country.

Huldah reminds me of mothers who bring spiritual safety to their homes. As a mom, I make sure that my family daily reads the scriptures. As a family, we make studying the scriptures a centerpiece of our home life. If I can inspire my family to be faithful in their scripture study, like Huldah tried to inspire Israel and King Josiah, then they will be protected.

—Marianna

> "The answer is to transform our homes into a sanctuary of faith and a center of gospel learning. And how do we do that? By focusing on Heavenly Father and Jesus Christ, making Them the center of our family life, the most important influence in our home."
>
> Russell M. Nelson
>
> "Overcoming the World and Find Rest," Oct. 2022

2 Kings 23:25

And like unto him was there no king before him, that turned to the Lord with all his heart, and with all his soul, and with all his might . . . neither after him arose there any like him.

A Good Plot Twist

I recently read a story about a man who'd been in prison for ten years. After reading the Bible in solitary confinement, he longed for more. One day, he found a copy of the *Ensign* in a prison trash can. This plot twist led him on a path that not only changed him but those around him.

By chapter 23, King Josiah had already been ruling over the Kingdom of Judah for seventeen years. Judah had been in a deep state of spiritual corruption and idolatry. Then, in chapter 23, the Book of Law was found in the temple and given to Josiah. And then, plot twist! Everything changed. Josiah changed, and in turn, he changed the kingdom through his humility, repentance, and reformation of the laws of the land.

I heard someone say that God is less interested in where we've been and more interested in who we are now and where we are going. Regardless of our struggles or even past choices, we can experience the miraculous plot twist of the Atonement of Jesus Christ as we give our minds and hearts over to Him.

—Michelle

> "Whether we start in abundant or difficult circumstances, let us keep our sights and our slopes pointed heavenward. As we do, Christ will lift us to a higher place."
>
> Clark G. Gilbert
>
> "Becoming More in Christ: The Parable of the Slope," Oct. 2021

2 Kings 25:1, 8–9

Nebuchadnezzar king of Babylon came . . . against Jerusalem, and . . . a servant of the king . . . burnt the house of the Lord.

Old Testament Meets Book of Mormon

The Book of Mormon prophet Lehi and his family lived in Jerusalem during the reign of King Zedekiah (see 1 Nephi 1:4). The people had become wicked, so the Lord sent many prophets, including Lehi, to prophesy that if they didn't repent, the people of Jerusalem would be destroyed. Despite the prophets' warnings, the people, including Laman and Lemuel, did not believe that the Lord would destroy Jerusalem (see 1 Nephi 1:13). Why?

Only a few chapters back, in 2 Kings 19, we read of Jerusalem's miraculous deliverance when the Lord's destroying angel killed the entire Assyrian army. It became a cultural tradition that the temple was so sacred that God would protect it at all costs. But it wasn't the temple that saved Jerusalem; it was the people's righteousness. They forgot and grew complacent, drifting from righteousness. Lehi and his family were sent into the wilderness, and then the unthinkable happened. Babylon attacked. Jerusalem and the temple were destroyed, and the people were scattered.

Sacred temples can be rebuilt, but what God cares about is our hearts. I live near a temple. In the end, the Lord probably won't ask how close I lived to a temple. But He will look at my heart and see if I was worthy to enter the temple, and how I used the resources available to me to follow Him.

—Krista

> "In return for His priceless payment for each of us, the Lord asks us for a change of heart. The change He requests from us is not for His benefit but for ours."
>
> Rebecca L. Craven
>
> "Keep the Change," Oct. 2020

1 Chronicles 2:1–2

These are the sons of Israel; Reuben, Simeon, Levi, and Judah, Issachar, and Zebulun, Dan, Joseph, and Benjamin, Naphtali, Gad, and Asher.

Remembering Who You Are

The first book of Chronicles begins with Adam and lists twelve names before even including an "and." In fact, the first nine chapters record the names of the princes of Israel in every tribe. A friend of mine said she loves the "begats" because they provide a scaffolding for the scriptures and show the divine connection of family which is important and eternal. I like reading them because they review Old Testament stories and reawaken the lessons each one has taught me.

But, at the time these words were written, the list had a completely different purpose. Judah had only recently been freed from Babylon, and returned to a Jerusalem in ruins. The people were expected to rebuild the temple with limited resources and others fighting against them. As they struggled, some must have wondered if they were still God's chosen. By starting with Adam, the Jews affirmed their legitimacy as God's covenant people. Their children could see they owned the birthright. It must have worked, for the temple was rebuilt, and they grew again into a great nation.

By reviewing the faithful trailblazers in our own histories and their stories, our children might also learn of their divine heritage. That gift may lift them past moments of struggle and help them realize they are more. They, too, are God's chosen.

—Christine

> "Still very much alive, our ancestors deserve to be remembered."
>
> Gerrit W. Gong
>
> "We Each Have a Story," Apr. 2022

1 Chronicles 5:1

Now the sons of Reuben the firstborn of Israel, for he was the firstborn; but, forasmuch as he defiled his father's bed, his birthright was given unto the sons of Joseph the son of Israel.

Birthright

I am the oldest of twelve children. I love being the oldest, but it does come with certain responsibilities. I was the one who always did everything first. I was the first to date, I was the first to drive, I was the first to leave for college, and I was the first to have a baby. I had other family responsibilities, such as changing diapers, babysitting younger siblings, and supporting my siblings as they got older. I did not see these responsibilities as a burden, but as a blessing to serve my family.

In the Old Testament, the birthright was usually given to the oldest son of the first wife. There had been exceptions, such as when Esau sold his birthright to Jacob for a bowl of stew. But Reuben lost his birthright because of sin. The birthright then went to the firstborn son of Jacob and Rachel, who was Joseph. Even though Ephraim was the second son of Joseph, Jacob blessed Ephraim with the birthright before Manasseh, who was the elder son. Thus, Ephraim was given the birthright for the house of Israel and has the latter-day responsibility of taking the restored gospel message to the world. People who accept the gospel of Jesus Christ shall "fall down and be crowned with glory, even in Zion, by the hands of the servants of the Lord, even the children of Ephraim" (D&C 133:32).

—Marianna

"I have studied the gathering, prayed about it, feasted upon every related scripture, and asked the Lord to increase my understanding."

Russell M. Nelson

"Let God Prevail," Oct. 2020

1 Chronicles 9:1

So all Israel were reckoned by genealogies; and behold, they were written.

You Count

I have a confession. In my calling as Relief Society president, I'll often open my Tools app and scroll through the list of all the sisters in the ward. I want to know every sister, but I struggle. There are some I don't know. Sometimes I forget the names of those I'm getting to know. And at other times, my mind is so full of other things that certain sisters I know just aren't on my mind. But I love that they are always on God's mind. When I look through the names that are recorded, invariably I receive inspiration regarding these sisters.

I am so grateful He is a God of order and that He asks us to record the names of His children. It helps us to be seen and to see others, to remember God knows us, and to know others. Most of all, I love that it shows that we count. Literally.

Though you might feel momentarily unseen or forgotten, know you are not. Heavenly Father is aware of you right now. You matter. Your name is recorded in heaven and on earth. You are counted, and you count.

—Michelle

> "We are all 'children of the covenant' stretching across the earth in nations and cultures on every continent, numbering in the millions, as we await the glorious return of our Lord and Savior."
>
> Neil A. Andersen
>
> "Drawing Closer to the Savior," Oct. 2022

1 Chronicles 11:11

And this is the number of the mighty men whom David had.

Modern-day "Mighties"

The Lord anointed David as king, but this chapter reminds us of the loyal friends and allies who supported him and fought fiercely beside him. The best of these men even had a cool group nickname—the "mighties" (see 1 Chronicles 11:12). They could have been jealous of David's rank and power, but instead, they offered valiant service, even risking their lives for their friend and king. They served not for personal gain but out of deep loyalty and love.

My son Walker is a modern-day "mighty." Since he was a little boy, he has promised the Lord that he would serve a mission. Walker joined the Marines right after high school, and just as he was preparing to submit his mission papers, the Marines asked him to serve a deployment. Walker served his country faithfully, and when he returned, even though he is older than most missionaries, he kept his promise. By the time this book is published, Walker will be in South Africa serving out of deep loyalty and love for the Savior.

I want to be like my son and like David's friends. I want to be a "mighty" for Christ.

—Krista

> "Faith in Jesus Christ is a bond of trust forged in loyalty and love."
>
> Sandino Roman
>
> "Faith: A Bond of Trust and Loyalty," Apr. 2025

1 Chronicles 13:9–10

Uzza put forth his hand to hold the ark for the oxen stumbled. And the anger of the Lord was kindled against Uzza, and he smote him . . . and there he died before God.

No Parties

We moved into a new ward during COVID. It was hard to get to know people when you couldn't meet them face to face. At last, most restrictions were lifted, and I thought the parties would begin. Nope. Our ward went month after month without a single activity. No parties at all. A couple was called to oversee activities, but still nothing. Oddly, they were soon released. We had one Christmas dinner put on by the Relief Society that year, and that was it. My grown children lived nearby, and we invited a few neighbors over, but most of the ward weren't friends, and I worried about it.

Finally, I decided to put my hand up to steady the ark. I went to the bishop and volunteered to help with activities, if he felt inspired to take me on. The bishop kindly refused. He said he was very busy and was happy with having less to do. Luckily, I wasn't "smote" down like Uzza. About a month later, the stake called a new elders quorum president—someone who *loves* parties! He began organizing monthly activities, which increased the Relief Society's efforts as well. It has been wonderful to see the growth in both participation and fellowship. I should have had more faith in priesthood power.

—Christine

"Through callings and councils, men and women, young and old, can participate in priesthood work. It is a work of miracles, attended by angels.

Russell M. Nelson

"Preaching the Gospel of Peace," Apr. 2022

1 Chronicles 16:1, 8

So they brought the ark of God, and set it in the midst of the tent that David had pitched for it: and they offered burnt offerings and peace offerings before God. . . . Give thanks unto the Lord, call upon his name, make known his deeds among the people.

Praise God for a Temple

On a recent visit to Addis Ababa, Ethiopia, I attended a small ward in the city. That same weekend, the Saints were preparing for the dedication of the Nairobi Kenya Temple. This temple will change how often the Saints in Ethiopia can go to the temple. Previously, the closest temple was across the continent in Lagos, Nigeria, about 3,300 miles away. Now, the temple is in the neighboring country of Kenya and is only 932 miles away—so much more accessible!

That Sunday, all the sacrament meeting talks centered on the importance of the temple and the Saints' gratitude for having a temple so close. A young couple with a two-year-old son shared their testimony of the importance of the temple. They spoke of past efforts to be sealed in the temple—efforts that never quite came together. But now, with joyful tears, they look forward to being sealed together as an eternal family.

When the ark of God was brought to a place of rest, David sang and danced for joy. He wrote a psalm of thanksgiving for the Abrahamic covenant and God's law. We, too, should feel joy and gratitude when we think of the house of the Lord.

—Marianna

> "The only way to return to live with Them and with our family is through the ordinances of the holy temple."
>
> Henry B. Eyring
>
> "I Love to See the Temple," Apr. 2021

1 Chronicles 18:14

So David reigned over all Israel, and executed judgment and justice among his people.

Mad at Me Again

My kids were angry with me a lot when they were younger. I was too strict. I wanted the house too clean. I wanted them to brush their teeth and go to bed each night. It often felt like any effort I made to teach truth, enforce expectations, and allow them to experience consequences incited frustration in my children. I often felt like a failure. Then, one day, I read a quote by Merrilee Boyack. She said, essentially, "If your children are mad at you, you're doing it right." I *was* doing it right!

My sweet friends, successful parenting doesn't look like obedient, compliant, quiet children. It looks like you praying, learning, developing Christlike attributes, and loving. As you "execute judgment and justice" in the vein of Christlike love, you're doing it right, whether or not your kids think so.

Stay close to God. Keep trying. Teach truth. Be strong. Your children will be okay, and so will you.

—Michelle

"You are doing much better than you think. Just keep working at it. . . . One day your children will echo the testimony of Enos: I know my parents are just, 'for [they] taught me . . . in the nurture and admonition of the Lord—and blessed be the name of my God for it.'"

Jan E. Newman

"Preserving the Voice of the Covenant People in the Rising Generation," Oct. 2023

1 Chronicles 21:27

And the Lord commanded the angel; and he put up his sword again into the sheath thereof.

Letting Go

Day after day, I sat on my couch spinning in a dark, inescapable whirlpool of regret and agony. The doctor had reassured me that Elora's brain tumor and death were not my fault, but I couldn't believe him. Moms were supposed to know those things. If I'd paid better attention or been more worthy to receive revelation, I might have sought medical attention earlier and saved her life. It wasn't the truth, but it's what I believed.

But now she was gone, and all I could focus on were my failings as a mother—all the little things during my daughter's brief life I wished I could take back, do over, do better. It's one thing to have regrets about life, but quite another to regret actions that have affected someone else's life. I didn't feel worthy of absolving myself of these things, and even though Christ had atoned for this exact purpose, I felt even more guilty about heaping my problems on His innocent back. These were my regrets, and I was the only one who should have to bear them. After weeks of mental agony, I knew I needed help. I needed to let Christ teach me how to forgive myself. It was hard work. But the process taught me to know Him better and trust Him. He is a loving, forgiving, miraculous Savior. His mercy extends to us all. He is willing and strong enough to carry every burden. It's up to us to let Him.

—Krista

"I testify that He lives. He is our Savior and Redeemer. He loves us. He has compassion for us, He is filled with mercy, and he can heal you."

Peter F. Meurs

"He Could Heal Me!," Apr. 2023

1 Chronicles 23:3–5

Now the Levites were numbered . . . Of which, twenty and four thousand were to set forward the work of the house of the Lord . . . and four thousand praised the Lord with instruments . . . to praise therewith.

The Song of the Righteous

The other day, I was wasting time on social media, and I came across a YouTuber listening to "Come Thou Fount" for the first time. The Tabernacle Choir sang in the Conference Center in the video he was reviewing, and their voices sounded like angels. Tears streamed down this young man's face as the music touched his heart. There is such power in music, and the Lord knows that. Worship through music has been a priority from the beginning of His church.

One fun fact is that one in six of the Levites serving in the first temple were assigned to be musicians. Four thousand in all. They played the cymbals, harp, and psaltery. And, much of the book of Psalms was their hymnal. In our dispensation, the first choir in Christ's restored Church was formed only 29 days after arriving in Salt Lake Valley. This group evolved into the 360-member Tabernacle Choir we enjoy listening to today. Music matters to the Lord. Let's have good music fill our lives, homes, and hearts, especially as we praise the Lord every day.

—Christine

> "Scripture records that 'the song of the righteous is a prayer unto [God]' in which His soul delights. So let's sing! And praise Him!"
>
> Patrick Kearon
>
> "Welcome to the Church of Joy," Oct. 2024

1 Chronicles 26:12

Among these were the divisions of the porters, even among the chief men, having wards one against another, to minister in the house of the Lord.

Becoming a Gatekeeper

In 1 Chronicles 24 to 26, the temple duties of the Levites are carefully enumerated. Each Levite was called to a specific task, without being given a choice. They were assigned to be singers, musicians, and porters. The porters were the gatekeepers of the temple and had charge over the treasures in the temple.

As an ordinance worker, every time I serve in the temple, I am given a line of duties. When I first began serving, the standing positions were the hardest for me to enjoy. I sometimes felt unnecessary—simply standing in place for long stretches of time. But then, a quiet realization came to me: I was acting as a porter or gatekeeper, showing patrons the way to safety and sacredness. I came to see how meaningful it was to guide others where to go for sealings, initiatories, and endowments. Now, those standing positions bring me joy. I feel honored to point the way for Saints as they come to participate in holy ordinances.

I imagine the Levites felt a similar joy and peaceful fulfillment as they served in Solomon's temple. No matter their task, each role held purpose. This is part of the beauty of the temple.

—Marianna

> "Serving in the temple is a rich and powerful experience for people of all ages."
>
> Kent F. Richards
>
> "The Power of Godliness," Apr. 2016

1 Chronicles 29:20

And David said to all the congregation,
Now bless the Lord your God.
And all the congregation blessed the Lord God.

The End of an Era

David's character arc was complicated, yet beautiful. He was chosen by God to lead the people because he had a heart like the Lord's (see 1 Samuel 13:14). He was kind and faithful. Though he struggled with sin and weaknesses, he repented with humility and zeal. During his reign he united the tribes of Israel, established a capital in Jerusalem, led his people in military victories, and reigned with a righteous heart. Many refer to his forty-year reign as "The Golden Age of Israel." Despite his many accomplishments, David left his leadership and life the way he entered it—praising God and inviting others to do so. This is why David was "successful." God's cause was his cause.

David wasn't perfect, and yet God used him to do amazing things. I find so much peace in this! Some days, I am kind and faithful. On other days, I mess up. Then on other days, I repent with zeal. I am not perfect, but I am *so* grateful to know that if I keep my focus on God and make sure His cause is my cause, I know God can do amazing things in and through me.

—Michelle

"To David, the *cause of God was the most important cause.*"

Andrea Muñoz Spannaus

"Faithful to the End," Apr. 2024

2 Chronicles 2:9

For the house which I am about to build shall be wonderful great.

Caulking at Its Finest

I have a pretty amazing secret skill. I'm a really good caulker. My dad used to build and install custom cabinetry, and my mom did all the caulking. She taught me how to cut and shape the end of the nozzle to run a perfect bead of caulk. And I've spent hours learning to clean and shape flawless lines and corners.

When King Solomon built his temple for the Lord, he demanded the finest materials and quality of work. He hired master craftsmen, each an expert in their respective field, to ensure that every aspect of the construction was exquisite. If Solomon had known about caulk, he might have hired me. Not because I know how to build every part of a temple, but because I excel in this one area.

When we think about giving the Lord our finest, we may make the mistake of thinking we must *know* everything, *do* everything, and *be* everything. Perfectly. But I believe the Lord is just asking us to give the best of what we have. You offer the best of your time, energy, resources, and talents—whatever that is—and I'll offer mine. We can't build an entire temple on our own, but together, we can build something extraordinary for Him. My caulk gun is ready and waiting. What will you bring?

—Krista

"Jesus taught that our offering may be large or it may be small, but either way, it must be our *heartfelt all.*"

Dieter F. Uchtdorf

"Our Heartfelt All," Oct. 2022

2 Chronicles 3:17

And he reared up the pillars before the temple, one on the right hand, and the other on the left; and called the name of that on the right hand Jachin, and the name of that on the left Boaz.

What's in a Name?

When I first heard of the names of famous Native American Chiefs like Crazy Horse, Sitting Bull, and Black Hawk, I wanted a name like that. A name that really meant something and reflected my personality. Like Dancing Dreams or Laughing Friend. Hebrew names are much like those of Native Americans. Not only do they have meanings, but often those meanings are prophetic. For example, Daniel means "God is my judge." Esther means "Star." And Sarah means "Princess."

When Solomon built his temple, he named the two great pillars at the front of it *Jachin,* which means "He will establish," and *Boaz,* which means "In His strength." There are dozens of interpretations of what that means from different Jewish and Christian religious leaders. The best interpretation I heard came from a recently returned missionary who said to me: "When you go to the temple, *you* have to stand between the pillars, so together they will say, 'He will establish *you* in His strength.'" The pillars are prophetic, and that is the gift of attending the temple and doing His work.

—Christine

> "In this day of confusion and commotion, I testify that the temple . . . will help preserve us, protect us and prepare us for the glorious day when . . . our Savior returns."
>
> Neil L. Andersen
>
> "Temples, Houses of the Lord Dotting the Earth," Apr. 2024

2 Chronicles 6:2–3

But I have built an house of habitation for thee, and a place for thy dwelling for ever. And the king turned his face, and blessed the whole congregation of Israel: and all the congregation of Israel stood.

Thy Resting Place

Solomon built the temple as a final resting place for the ark of the covenant. He offered a dedicatory prayer for the temple and prayed for mercy and blessings for penitent Israel.

I compared Solomon's dedicatory prayer (2 Chronicles 6) with Joseph Smith's dedicatory prayer for the Kirtland Temple (D&C 109). I was surprised to discover many similarities between them. Both prayers ask for God's presence in His holy house (6:18; 109:4–5), warn the Saints that they must turn from sin (6:26; 109:20–21), acknowledge that only the righteous shall enter His holy house (6:31; 109:11–13), plead for the protection of the Saints from the world (6:34–35; 109:48–54) and bless those who attend the temple with peace and rest (6:39–41; 109:36–40; 79–80).

In the temple, we can experience God's instruction, guidance, peace, and eternal covenants. The temple can become our "resting place . . . and the ark of [God's] strength" (2 Chronicles 6:41).

—Marianna

"Whenever any kind of upheaval occurs in your life, the safest place to be spiritually is living inside your temple covenants!"

Russell M. Nelson

"The Temple and Your Spiritual Foundation," Oct. 2021

2 Chronicles 7:15

For now have I chosen and sanctified this house, that my name may be there for ever: and mine eyes and mine heart shall be there perpetually.

His House

Serving as a Relief Society president twice, I've visited with a lot of sisters over the years. I love the convenience of texting. I don't mind a phone call. And I adore the meet-up at our local frozen custard place. But, none of those compare to meeting a sister in her home. They are . . . different there. Not only can I see them, but I can *feel* more about them when I come to the place they have made their own.

To me, it's the same with the temple. I love the convenience of prayer and scripture study. I enjoy participating in my ward calling and Sunday gatherings. I love taking the sacrament. But there is something special about going to *His* house—the house of the Lord. The place He has literally made His own. Not only can I make and keep sacred covenants and focus on the Savior, but I can *feel* more of Him when I'm there. He has created an oasis in this crazy and complicated world and invited us to spend time with Him. He didn't make a house to live in alone. He made a spiritual home where we can be with Him.

—Michelle

> "Jesus Christ is the reason we build temples. Each is His holy house. Making covenants and receiving essential ordinances in the temple, as well as seeking to draw closer to Him there, will bless your life in ways no other kind of worship can."
>
> Russell M. Nelson
>
> "The Answer It Always Jesus Christ," Apr. 2023

2 Chronicles 9:1

When the queen of Sheba heard of the fame of Solomon, she came to prove Solomon with hard questions . . . with a very great company, and camels . . . and gold in abundance, and precious stones: and when she was come to Solomon, she communed with him of all that was in her heart.

Come and See

The Queen of Sheba heard of the wisdom of Solomon and came to see if the reports of his wisdom were true. After spending time with King Solomon, she was convinced of the truthfulness of the teachings she had heard and realized that the one true God loved Israel. She said: "Blessed be the Lord thy God, which delighted in thee to set thee on his throne, to be king for the Lord thy God" (2 Chronicles 9:8). After her conversion, she returned to her own country taking her testimony back with her.

People around the world hear reports about The Church of Jesus Christ of Latter-day Saints and wonder if they are true. Francisco had always wondered about what happened in an LDS temple. A temple open house was happening in his city, and a friend invited him to "come and see." When he sat in the celestial room of the temple, he felt the Spirit of God and a peace he had never experienced before. If the people we invite to a sacrament meeting service, a Church activity, a lesson with the missionaries, or a temple open house are unbiased seekers of truth, they will come to know that this is the restored gospel of Jesus Christ and that all the good reports about our Church are true.

—Marianna

"The invitations we extend to you to learn about . . . our message grow out of the positive effects the gospel of Jesus Christ has had in our lives."

Neil L. Andersen

"Temples, Houses of the Lord Dotting the Earth," Apr. 2024

2 Chronicles 12:14

And he did evil, because he prepared not his heart to seek the Lord.

German Spotlight

My family used to love to play lawn games. One of my favorites was German Spotlight. When my youngest siblings went to bed, the rest of us would run upstairs and put on black clothing. Some of my friends who were really committed would even cover their faces with charcoal from the grill. Once we were ready, the game began. The person that was "it" stood on the porch with a flashlight and swung it back and forth slowly. We all began at the edge of the yard behind a rock wall. Once the flashlight was on, we tried to make our way to the porch and tag it before being caught in the beam. Often the person that prepared the best became the winner. They didn't even have to be the fastest.

At the end of King Rehoboam's life, it was said that "he did evil, because he prepared not his heart to seek the Lord." Rehoboam, King Solomon's son, inherited Israel when it was at its largest. Due to his weakness, the kingdom was divided and the temple ransacked.

We also need to prepare our hearts to seek the Lord. Perhaps that is why the sacrifice He requires of us today is a broken heart and a contrite spirit, which means being willing to do whatever the Lord asks. And like in my game, those who are the most prepared will most certainly win the prize.

—Christine

> "He will not refuse you or those you love when you bring to Him your broken hearts and contrite spirits."
>
> Patrick Kearon
>
> "God's Intent Is to Bring You Home," Apr. 2024

2 Chronicles 14:11

Help us, O Lord our God; for we rest on thee.

Lean Into Jesus

You and I may not be at war in the traditional way, with swords and shields, but that doesn't mean our enemies and struggles are any less threatening. I love the righteous King Asa, who, when besieged by his enemies and outnumbered, taught his people to rest on the Lord.

My mother-in-law passed away two years ago after a battle with cancer. Her fight was tough, and we watched her learn to rest on the Lord. She commissioned my daughter to paint a picture of her wrapped in the Savior's embrace. My mother-in-law displayed the painting proudly and gave copies to everyone she knew, with an admonition to "lean into Jesus."

When I'm feeling stressed or worried, I follow my mother-in-law's advice. I envision my Savior sitting on a bench in the most beautiful park. He motions for me to sit beside Him. As He puts an arm around my shoulders, I lean into His embrace. Sometimes I talk out loud to Him. Sometimes I simply rest, knowing He loves me. His rest is real. We never have to face our burdens and battles alone. With Him on our side, we will conquer!

—Krista

"Jesus has overcome the abuses of this world to give you power to not only survive but one day, through Him, to overcome and even conquer—to completely rise above the pain, the misery, the anguish, and see them replaced by peace."

Patrick Kearon

"He Is Risen With Healing in His Wings: We Can Be More Than Conquerors," Apr. 2022

2 Chronicles 17:6

And his heart was lifted up in the ways of the Lord.

The Joy of Obedience

Grace was six years old when she walked through our door for the first time. She'd lived with her birth mother in various places and had been in three different foster homes. Her survival instinct was strong. At first, it seemed like a good thing. She was very polite and obedient. She followed the rules, attended church, and learned about the commandments. But after she became more secure in our home, things began to change. Rules made her angry, and commandments made her feel trapped, which triggered her fight to survive. She wanted to fight against everything and everyone who told her what to do.

Without realizing it, she was pushing against the very things that I knew would bring her the peace and joy she so desperately wanted and needed. It took many years of consistent teaching, love, nurturing, counseling, and more love for her to recognize the blessing of obedience to good and true principles. As she grew, she felt the peace of forgiveness, the joy of genuine relationships, the satisfaction of sacrifice and growth. In short, as she grew in our home and the gospel, Grace could experience a joyful life; one found through obedience to the laws that made it possible.

—Michelle

> "The Lord's commandments are given out of love and caring; they are intended for our joy in this life just as much as they are intended for our joy and exaltation in the next."
>
> Von G. Keetch
>
> "Blessed and Happy Are Those Who Keep the Commandments of God," Oct. 2015

2 Chronicles 20:15

And he said, Hearken ye, all Judah, and ye inhabitants of Jerusalem, and thou king Jehoshaphat, Thus saith the Lord unto you, Be not afraid nor dismayed by reason of this great multitude; for the battle is not yours, but God's.

The Battle Is Not Yours, But God's

When I lived in the Northwest, our school district was considering a new controversial curriculum. I knew it would not reflect the principles I believed in, but I also did not want to "rock the boat" or alienate neighbors who felt differently. I prayed about it and felt led to step into the arena. I became actively involved in trying to prevent the curriculum's adoption. My opinion was not the popular one. I often felt alone, overwhelmed, and discouraged, while pouring in so much time, effort, and heart. At my lowest point, the Lord lifted me up and supported me in this conflict. When the school board finally voted, the curriculum was not adopted.

The people of Judah and Jerusalem were surrounded by enemies determined to defeat them. In their desperation, they turned to the Lord for help. In the end, the Lord fought their battle for them, causing their enemies to turn on one another. Judah was left with the spoils of war, without ever lifting a sword.

The battle for righteousness is ours and God's. What a blessing it is to be on His side and receive his guidance, strength, and help.

—Marianna

> "But followers of Jesus Christ should set the example for all the world to follow."
>
> Russell M. Nelson
>
> "The Power of Spiritual Momentum," Apr. 2022

2 Chronicles 24:4, 10

Joash was minded to repair the house of the Lord. . . . And all the princes and all the people rejoiced.

Pardon Our Dust!

Reading sections of scripture like this about the rise and fall of righteous and wicked kings frustrates me. Isn't it obvious that nations thrived when leaders were righteous and failed when they turned from God? So, why did so many of them choose to fall away?

This is usually the point in my thought process when the Lord delivers a dose of humility. He reminds me that it's easy to see the patterns of righteousness and wickedness when you cover several kings' lifetimes in a single chapter. But how often do I take stock of my personal "kingdom" and discover, like Joash, that the house of the Lord has been sitting too long in disrepair? Joash followed the Lord for most of his life. He repaired the temple, but somewhere along the way, he stopped repairing himself. We don't have a record of the small, subtle, day-to-day decisions that led to the disrepair of his faith. But we can take stock of our own.

Are there repairs I need to make in my life that will keep me close to God? When asked in humility, the Lord will put to our minds where we can improve so we can continue to receive the blessings that come from following Him.

—Krista

"If . . . you or I believe we could be afflicted with and by pride, then we consistently will do the small and simple things that will protect and help us."

David A. Bednar

"In the Space of Not Many Years," Oct. 2024

2 Chronicles 25:18

And they withstood Uzziah the king, and said unto him, It appertaineth not unto thee, Uzziah, to burn incense unto the Lord, but to the priests the sons of Aaron.

The Recommend Desk

Everyone entering the temple must first pass the recommend desk. Temple workers supervise the desk to make sure that all who enter have a current recommend from their priesthood leaders showing that they are worthy to enter this holy place. If not, they are stopped at the desk and not allowed to enter. I was running late for my temple shift when I realized I forgot my recommend. Even though the people at the recommend desk knew me, they could not let me enter until I was cleared as having a current recommend.

King Uzziah did not have the right to enter the temple and burn incense, yet he was determined to do it. After King Uzziah entered the temple, the high priest and eighty other priests went after him to stop him because he did not have the priesthood authority to burn incense in this holy place. Only the priests, the sons of Aaron, were consecrated to burn incense in the sanctuary.

King Uzziah was angry. He was the king. How could they defy him? Immediately, the Lord cursed King Uzziah with leprosy—right there in the temple—to keep the temple holy and sacred. King Uzziah was a leper until the day he died and had to live alone, away from society, because he tried to desecrate the house of the Lord.

–Marianna

> "I am forever grateful that holders of the Aaronic Priesthood . . . do bless all of us."
>
> Steven J. Lund
>
> "Divine Authority, Sublime Young Men," Apr. 2025

2 Chronicles 29:36

And Hezekiah rejoiced, and all the people, that God had prepared the people: for the thing was done suddenly.

This Is All So Sudden . . .

Hezekiah replaced his father, Ahaz, as king and immediately was on a mission to reclaim reverence. Within the first month of his reign, he opened the temple and began restoring worship within. In a matter of days, the false idols were put away and the people could again worship their God. How did they respond? They rejoiced! *This is repentance!*

Complete repentance can be a long process. I know. I've walked that path. But it always begins with a sincere desire and a choice to change. This part of repentance can be sudden; it can happen *now.* I love how Amulek described it: "If ye will repent and not harden your hearts, immediately shall the great plan of redemption be brought about to you" (Alma 34:31).

Immediately! I love that! Repentance is simply the act of removing what's between us and the Savior. We don't have to wait to start changing our minds, hearts, and habits. We can begin to feel and be different today simply by choosing Him. Today, we can feel His love and rejoice too.

—Michelle

"Repentance opens our access to the power of the Atonement of Jesus Christ. . . . When we choose to repent, we choose to change! We allow the Savior to transform us into the best version of ourselves. We choose to grow spiritually and receive joy—the joy of redemption in Him."

Russell M. Nelson

"We Can Do Better and Be Better," Apr. 2019

2 Chronicles 30:5

So they established a decree to make proclamation throughout all Israel . . . that they should come to keep the passover unto the Lord God of Israel at Jerusalem: for they had not done it of a long time.

Don't Forget to Spray the Pan!

When my daughter was a teenager, she discovered a love for baking. But more often than she'd like me to reveal, her hard work resulted in cakes stuck in their pans and cookies glued to their trays. I would ask, "Did you remember to spray the pan?" She forgot so often that even now, years later, if she sets foot in my kitchen, someone will inevitably call out, "Don't forget to spray the pan!"

Humans are prone to forgetfulness. Our Father in Heaven knows this. It's why He established repetitive traditions and ordinances such as the Passover Feast and the sacrament to help our fallible minds remember the sacrifice and saving power of Jesus Christ. In a personal effort to more intentionally "always remember Him" (D&C 20:77), I began writing in a journal this year titled "How I Saw God's Hand Today." Every evening, I review my day, looking for evidence of His love, help, and influence. Recording these experiences has fine-tuned my ability to recognize His constant care and reminds me daily how much I need Him.

—Krista

"Partaking of the sacrament is not a passive religious ritual implying our mere consent. It is a powerful reminder of the reality of the Savior's infinite Atonement and the need to always remember Him and keep His commandments."

Kevin W. Pearson

"Are You Still Willing?," Oct. 2022

2 Chronicles 32:8

With him is an arm of flesh; but with us is the Lord our God to help us, and to fight our battles.

War Tactics

Our family used to love playing the game Splendor. For months we were evenly matched and enjoyed pitting our wits against each other. I say "used to" because one of my sons ruined it for us. You see, he figured out the perfect strategy. Now every time we play, he wins. A good strategy can trump even the best skills.

When Jerusalem was under siege by the Assyrian army, the Israelites laid out their strategy which proved successful. Here are a few of their tactics: They strengthened the wall around them, prepared many shields and darts, and spoke comfort to all, saying God is with us. Even when spies came in their midst they only listened to the prophet and were not deceived.

Today we are also in a battle. As with my son, using the best strategy by strengthening our faith, praying, and listening to the right voices will allow us to win every time.

—Christine

> "If we think celestial, we will receive the confirmation in our hearts that Jesus Christ is indeed our Rescuer."
>
> Juan Pablo Villar
>
> "His Hand Ready to Help Us," Oct. 2024

2 Chronicles 35:25–26

And Jeremiah lamented for Josiah: and all the singing men and the singing women spake of Josiah in their lamentations to this day.

Righteous Funerals

I recently attended the funeral of a friend of forty years. As young moms, we had raised our babies together in New York, far away from either of our families. She had lived such a righteous, giving life, and her death came too early. She and her husband had been serving as senior missionaries in England when she found out she had a brain tumor. Her death was sudden, but she had her entire family surrounding her as she passed away. Her funeral became a celebration of her righteous life. Her children sang hymns of praise to God that she had taught them. There were tables laden with memorabilia of all the service she had given others. All of the funeral speeches talked about Christ, the Atonement, and her testimony of the Savior.

King Josiah lived a righteous life. By following the Lord and His prophet's counsel, Josiah brought the tribe of Judah back to worshiping only the Lord. He destroyed the high, secret places and stopped the people from worshiping Baal. He led the people in observing a solemn Passover. King Josiah's leadership ended too early. He was killed by an Egyptian archer in a battle. The prophet Jeremiah and all of Judah mourned his swift end, but his acts of goodness and his example of righteousness are long remembered.

—Marianna

"I invite all who feel sorrow, all who wonder what happens after we die, to place your faith in Christ."

S. Mark Palmer

"Our Sorrow Shall Be Turned into Joy," Apr. 2021

2 Chronicles 36:15

And the Lord God of their fathers sent to them by his messengers . . . because he had compassion on his people.

The End Is Just the Beginning

I sat in my bishop's office in tears. My fiancé and I had just broken up, and I felt heartbroken and lost. My bishop listened to and consoled me. Then, he asked me if I would pray about serving a mission. It was the furthest thing from my mind. But, that small invitation—that small ray of light in that dark time—led me to a mission that changed me.

What, if anything good or inspiring, can come from such a dark chapter like 36? It is the ray of hope, the arm of mercy the Lord extended. Amidst all of this, the Lord sent them prophets.

In this account, it doesn't seem to make a difference. But, when you realize that these were the very prophets that caught Lehi's attention and set in motion everything that led to the Book of Mormon and the Restoration and temples that we love today—that ray of light in the darkness is bright and beautiful. It was God's love for them then *and* for us today.

Sometimes, when things seem darkest, that's when His light shines the brightest. Sometimes hard endings are part of the new beginnings that God has created for you and me.

–Michelle

> "Our Eternal Father and His Son, Jesus Christ, show Their love by making it possible for us to have eternal relationships with Them and our family members, by calling modern-day prophets to teach and minister to us."
>
> Taniela B. Wakolo
>
> "God Loves His Children," Apr. 2021

Ezra 1:2–3

Thus saith Cyrus king of Persia, . . . Who is there among you of all his people? his God be with him, and let him go up to Jerusalem, which is in Judah, and build the house of the Lord God of Israel.

There's No Place Like Home

Going on vacation is thrilling and relaxing, but it only takes a few days before I start craving my own bed, my own shower, and my own space! Coming back home—reuniting with familiar places and my most precious people—is one of the greatest feelings.

The children of Israel had been exiled in Babylon for decades when the new King of Persia, Cyrus the Great, was stirred by the Spirit to let them return home and rebuild the temple. The Israelites were so elated that they "wept with a loud voice; and many shouted aloud for joy" (Ezra 3:12).

This instinct to return home seems like a God-given heavenly compass embedded in our spirits, pointing back to Him. And I can't help thinking that the Israelites' reaction will match ours when we get there. We will reunite with loved ones we have long awaited to see, in a place that will be familiar and safe, and I believe we will weep and shout for joy to have come home.

—Krista

> "Deep inside each of us is a desire to return to our heavenly home, and Jesus Christ is our heavenly guidance system. He is the way."
>
> Sergio R. Vargas
>
> "Our Heavenly Guidance System," Apr. 2025

Ezra 5:9–10

Then asked we those elders, and said unto them thus, Who commanded you to build this house, and to make up these walls? We asked their names also . . . and thus they returned us answer saying, We are the servants of the God of heaven and earth.

Our Spiritual Identity

According to *Psychology Today*, a person's self-identity is formed in three ways: (1) discovering and developing one's potential, (2) choosing one's purpose in life, and (3) finding opportunities to exercise that potential and purpose.

When my husband and I first arrived at the nonprofit boarding school where we chose to serve as houseparents, we found many children who struggled with self-identity. Some had no clear concept of their potential or purpose, and floundered. Others had chosen self-identities that were harmful to themselves and others. Sadly, we saw that those with harmful identities exerted themselves on others. Finally, a few did understand they could do more and had a dream of what they wanted to be. These were the kids who flourished.

Our spiritual identity is just as essential and has the power to shift and expand our self-identity. Knowing that we are indeed the servants of God encompasses both our divine potential as children of our Heavenly Father and our purpose as His disciples in our daily walk through life. With that self-identity, we will flourish.

—Christine

> "We really are God's children. That truth is breathtaking! Stunning! And it is not figurative."
>
> Patrick Kearon
>
> "Receive His Gift," Apr. 2025

Ezra 6:7

Let the work of this house of God alone; let the governor of the Jews and the elders of the Jews build this house of God in his place.

Building Temples with the Help of God

Ezra was given the job of rebuilding the temple in Jerusalem. The work had started under the benevolent guidance of Cyrus, but Darius was now king of Persia and people were worried about the work continuing.

Darius renewed the decree made by Cyrus to build and protect the temple. He even went so far as to give Ezra money to finish and take care of the building. Darius also gave Ezra political power to protect the Jews working on and living near the temple, so that other people not of the Jewish faith would not destroy the believers and their house of worship.

Today, many of the temples that have been announced meet with the same concerns and worries about governmental and community leaders allowing a temple to be built. The Church often experiences persecution, lawsuits, and the lack of government permits.

Things can get complicated, but we need not fear. Temples are built with the help of God. Even in the face of adversity, temples will dot the earth in these latter days.

—Marianna

> "The temple will provide direction for you and your family in a world filled with chaos."
>
> Gary E. Stevenson
>
> "Sacred Homes, Sacred Temples," Apr. 2009

Ezra 9:5–6

And at the evening sacrifice I arose up . . . [and] fell upon my knees, and spread out my hands unto the Lord my God, And said, O my God.

He Prays for Us

There are so many ways to show love: hugs, serving, giving gifts, investing time, and more. Countless are the ways. I let my husband show his love for me by buying the things I tuck into my Amazon cart. It makes me feel all warm inside.

But there is another way we can show love. We can pray for others. Not the "I'll keep you in my prayers" sentiment we throw out like a "bless you" after a sneeze, but a sincere "I am going to talk to God on your behalf" prayer.

Pleading with God for someone else is beautiful and powerful. Taking the part of our hearts that we've given to those we love and placing it before Heavenly Father is, perhaps, one of the most Christlike ways we can use and express our love.

Ezra was frustrated by the choices of the people of Israel, but instead of leaving, he prayed for them with all the energy and emotion he had. He did it because he loved them.

Our prophet today loves us. He and the Brethren all do—and they show that love through praying for us *every day.* This brings me so much peace! No matter who or where we are, we are known, loved, and prayed for by a prophet of God.

—Michelle

> "I pray for you every day."
>
> Russell M. Nelson
>
> "Preaching the Gospel of Peace," Apr. 2022

Ezra 10:3–4

Let it be done according to the law. Arise; for this matter belongeth unto thee: we also will be with thee; be of good courage, and do it.

Clean and Sober

My friend Kelli grew up in an abusive home and later endured an abusive marriage. She began using alcohol at a young age to numb the pain and got caught in a twenty-seven-year cycle of severe alcoholism and drug abuse. One day, when she heard a knock at the door, she was too drunk to care who it was, so she opened the door wide and invited the missionaries into her home. Less than two months later, she had taken her last drink, been baptized, and begun the incredibly challenging work of staying sober, setting healthy boundaries, and learning to trust God. Kelli recently celebrated twenty years clean and sober! She tells everyone about the love and grace of Jesus Christ. She knows Him deeply and loves Him fiercely. Kelli is one of my biggest heroes.

Repentance involves hard work and sacrifice to avoid habits, systems, or environments that compromise our relationship with Christ. But when we put Him first, His blessings of help, healing, and strength more than compensate for what we've left behind. Choosing Him may require an arduous journey, but He is always the right decision.

—Krista

> "The invitation to repent is an expression of God's love. Saying yes to that invitation is an expression of ours."
>
> Tamara W. Runia
>
> "Your Repentance Doesn't Burden Jesus Christ; It Brightens His Joy," Apr. 2025

Nehemiah 2:12

And I arose in the night, I and some few men with me; neither told I any man what my God had put in my heart to do.

Hard Answers

When we moved to Nebraska, I was called as Relief Society president. My daughter and her husband were living with us and expecting their first baby. My youngest son had recently come home from a mission, and I had several personal projects. Then, I got a call from another son who was in his senior year of college, studying computer science. Once I heard the tension in his voice, I knew something was terribly wrong.

"My computer died and I've lost everything!" he said at last. I remember thinking, Why would the Lord let this happen? I tried to suggest solutions, but he was done and wanted to scrap the semester and come home. I lay in bed that night, awake and praying. Then the Lord gave me a terrible answer. "Just go to him."

"But, I've got an activity this week, and my daughter could have her baby, and Greg is stressed out at work and . . . "

Much like Nehemiah, I arose in the middle of the night and did what "God had put in my heart to do." For the next week, I sat beside my son in Idaho. Using my computer, he retrieved what he could, informed professors, worked long days, and finished the semester with passing grades. It was a sacrifice to go, but it was also the right thing to do. The Lord does answer our prayers. Some answers are just harder than others.

—Christine

> "God hears every prayer we offer and responds to each of them according to the path He has outlined for our perfection."
>
> Jeffrey R. Holland
>
> "Motions of a Hidden Fire," Apr. 2024

Nehemiah 4:14

And I looked, and rose up, and said unto the nobles, and to the rulers, and to the rest of the people, Be not ye afraid of them: remember the Lord, which is great and terrible, and fight for your brethren, your sons, and your daughters, your wives, and your houses.

Battling the Enemy Outside Our Walls

Nehemiah saw the need to rebuild a wall around the city of Jerusalem for protection from outside enemies. When neighboring peoples heard that the walls of Jerusalem were being rebuilt, they came together to fight against Jerusalem to stop their work. The fighting became so intense that Nehemiah set a watch day and night while the builders worked on the wall. The workmen also had one hand in their work and the other hand holding a weapon. Nehemiah told the people not to be afraid but to remember the Lord and they would be safe.

As I battle in my home against the adversary, I too must be vigilant and hard working. Elder Boyd K. Packer pointed out that the world is in our homes through our entertainment, our media, and our language. He offered counsel about how to spiritually survive: "The key word is discipline—self-discipline. . . . Be a disciple/follower of the Savior, and you will be safe. You can resist temptation" (Boyd K. Packer, "How to survive in enemy territory," The 100th Anniversary of Seminary). That is how I can build a wall to protect my family and keep the enemy outside of my home: become a disciple of Christ.

—Marianna

> "Let Him know through your prayers and your actions that you are serious about overcoming the world."
>
> Russell N. Nelson
>
> "Overcome the World and Find Rest," Oct. 2022

Nehemiah 6:3

I am doing a great work, so that I cannot come down: why should the work cease, whilst I leave it, and come down to you?

Squirrel!

The other morning I went into my office to study my scriptures when I noticed a few books out of place. Four hours later, I had rearranged my shelves, put away my laundry, and painted my toenails. All good things, but things that had distracted me from what was most important. Maybe you can relate. Sometimes we just . . . squirrel!

Other times we get distracted by things that aren't good. For example, entertainment that chases the Spirit away, or feeding negative thoughts, can keep us from focusing on what the Lord would have us do.

I really admire Nehemiah. He had a goal: rebuild the wall. There were a lot of things to distract him (not good things), like gossip, temptations, invitations by enemies, and fatigue, to name a few. How did he avoid these distractions? He focused on his cause (6:3), prayed (6:9), and kept working. No distractions. No squirrels. Just the best work—the Lord's work.

—Michelle

> "One of Satan's most powerful weapons is to distract us with good and better causes which, in times of need, may blind and bind us away from the best cause—the very work that called us into this world."
>
> Bonnie H. Cordon
>
> "Come Unto Christ and Don't Come Alone," Oct. 2021

Nehemiah 8:2

And Ezra the priest brought the law before the congregation both of men and women, and all that could hear with understanding, upon the first day of the seventh month.

Battling the Enemy from Within

After being under Babylonian captivity for about seventy years, many of the Jews had stopped living the law of Moses, did not remember it, and stopped worshiping their God. Nehemiah not only rebuilt Jerusalem's walls, but he also rebuilt the faith of the Jewish refugees who were resettling the promised land. He instituted moral and social reforms, rededicating his people to Yahweh. He reminded the Jews to keep the Sabbath day holy; he reminded those who were wealthy to help the poor. He even set an example by sharing his own wealth with others. He knew they needed to return to the Lord to be worthy to rebuild the city as a Jewish center of worship and faith.

Ezra, the priest and scribe, led a second group of Jews back to Jerusalem. He knew that the most important enemy the Jews needed to battle against was the enemy within themselves—their selfishness, their greed, their ingratitude, and their pride. Ezra read the law to all of the people to remind them of who to worship and how to worship.

Our prophets today have the same task—to help us remember and obey the Lord.

—Marianna

"Some might attempt to hide from God because they don't want to be discovered or exposed, and they feel shame or guilt. However, numerous scriptures teach us that hiding from God is impossible."

Scott D. Whiting

"Beware the Second Temptation," Apr. 2025

Nehemiah 9:3

And they stood up in their place and read in the book of the law of the Lord their God one fourth part of the day.

What Part of Our Day Do We Give?

Pew Research did a survey some years ago that found most mothers spend about 13.5 hours a week with their children. Fathers spend less than that—not even two hours a day! I was shocked and a little saddened, but then I thought about my Father in Heaven. He is always willing to spend time with me. How much time do I give to Him?

In the end of the book of Nehemiah, we read of the victory of this sweet servant of the Lord who organized the people to rebuild the wall around Jerusalem in fifty-two days. Then, with that protection in place, they dedicated the new temple. For the first time in seventy years there was a house of the Lord on the earth. The people in attendance spent one-fourth of that day reading the scriptures and another fourth in worship.

What part of our day do we give to the Lord? Too often my morning and evening prayers are short because I'm tired. Scripture reading lasts as long as breakfast with my husband. Any long prayers are car prayers while I'm driving somewhere. Setting aside specific time for the Lord needs to be a better priority. I don't think I've ever put it on my to-do list. The only thing I have to give Him that he doesn't have is my time and a willing heart. Am I giving Him the better part or the extras?

—Christine

> "Whatever is on your to-do list, give equal time, not spare time, to the Lord."
>
> Ronald A. Rasband
>
> "Right Before Our Eyes," Apr. 2025

Nehemiah 12:27,30

And at the dedication of the wall of Jerusalem they sought the Levites out of all their places, . . . to keep the dedication with gladness. . . . And the priests and the Levites purified themselves, and purified the people, and the gates, and the wall.

Invite Him In

When temples and meetinghouses are built or remodeled, they're dedicated—set apart—as sacred places for worship and other religious activities. But did you know you can dedicate your home? While not dedicated for the same purposes as a temple or meeting-house, our homes are sacred places where we can invite the Lord's presence to be with us.

In section 18.15.2 of the Church's *General Handbook,* we learn that a Melchizedek Priesthood holder "dedicates the home as a sacred place where the Holy Spirit can reside and gives other words as guided by the Spirit. For example, he might bless the home to be a place where family members can worship, find safety from the world, grow spiritually, and prepare for eternal family relationships." (For more information on how to dedicate a home, refer to *General Handbook* 18:15.)

No matter the size, location, or value, our homes can be places where the Savior is welcome if we intentionally invite Him in. Every time we've moved, my husband and I have set aside a special family day to dedicate our home. It's like a holiday. We've spent weeks unpacking and cleaning, and the celebration of reaching our day of dedication feels like the final step of turning a house into our home—a place dedicated to family, service, and worshipping the Lord.

—Krista

"The finest characteristic of any home is the image of Christ reflected in the home's residents. What matters is the interior design of the souls of the inhabitants, not the structure itself."

L. Whitney Clayton

"The Finest Homes," Apr. 2020

Nehemiah 13:31

Remember me, O my God, for good.

How She Saw Me

I will never forget the last conversation I had with my mom in the hospital before she died. As I laid my head on her chest, all the memories of my rebellious years came to mind. I had tried to be a good person, but mistakes were made, apologies given, and forgiveness received. Still, the guilt was there.

"Mom," I said into her hospital gown. "I'm so sorry."

"For what?" she asked.

I sat up and looked into the eyes of this woman who, time and time again, had told me throughout the years how proud she was of me. All I could see was love. She saw the good in me. No disappointment. No regret. Just love. "Never mind," I said through a smile. "We can talk about it later."

We are not perfect children of God. But I believe what matters to Him is that we try. We are *His* children. He loves effort. Through our Savior, we can set aside guilt and shame, and give Them our best effort. And we can trust that when They look at us, They don't see messed up people; They see the good.

—Michelle

> "We may ask of our offering, as Andrew the disciple did of the loaves and fishes, 'What are they among so many?' (John 6:9). I assure you: it is sufficient to give or to do what you are able and then to allow Christ to magnify your effort."
>
> Ian S. Ardern
>
> "Love Thy Neighbor," Oct. 2023

Esther 1:19

Let it be written among the laws . . . that Vashti come no more before king Ahasuerus; and let the king give her royal estate unto another that is better than she.

Golden Goblet Syndrome

King Ahasuerus threw a six-month party just to show off his riches and majesty. Can we say ego-trip? And when the fair Queen Vashti refused to parade herself for the king and his guests, he threw a fit. The princes of Persia easily convinced him that Vashti was no longer worthy of being queen and that he should find someone better.

It's easy to shake our heads at Ahasuerus's drama and ego—until we admit that maybe he's not the only one who struggles with "golden goblet" syndrome. Pride wears fancy robes and is highly attractive. Heaven knows I've had plenty of days when I hoped someone would notice my new jeans or comment on my haircut. I've felt jealous when someone else was winning or achieving. And I've boasted when I should have lifted those around me. We all want to be noticed, appreciated, even celebrated.

But our Father isn't impressed with showmanship. He's looking for humility—hearts that hold compassion and patience. He needs disciples who choose people over possessions and peacemaking over power. Our worth isn't shown in our highlight reel, wardrobe, or finances (thank goodness!). We are valued because we are His. And we show the best of ourselves in how we care for others and point them to Him.

—Krista

"We always must be on guard against a pride-induced and exaggerated sense of self-importance, a misguided evaluation of our own self-sufficiency, and seeking self instead of serving others. . . . We cannot look to and focus upon Jesus Christ as the 'mark' if we only see ourselves."

David A. Bednar

"In the Space of Not Many Years," Oct. 2024

Esther 3:6

Wherefore Haman sought to destroy all the Jews that were throughout the whole kingdom.

Unseen Biases

Five hundred years before Esther was born, King Saul fought the Amalekites, took the spoils of the city, and let King Agag live despite the command of God. This act lost Saul his position in the sight of the Lord. Haman was a descendant of Agag. My guess is that Haman was taught his hatred for the Jews by his father and his father before him, back over a thousand generations. That sort of bias is difficult to change, and we may not even notice it. We may think it is obvious or "common knowledge" and not even question beliefs that we have been raised with. But, as we grow close to the Lord, He has a way of opening our eyes and changing our hearts.

Today, we live in a world filled with biases. Some, like those of Haman, are many generations old. Others may have been gained in our own lifetimes. Any attitude that divides us from others before we even get to know them is not of God and breeds contention. Political affiliations, cultural differences, hair and clothing choices, homeschoolers, and working moms—each label can come with preconceived holes we drop people into and dismiss who they really are. May we open our hearts and learn to love all people by turning our hearts to the Lord and letting Him heal attitudes we may not fully admit we have.

—Christine

"Contention prevents the Holy Ghost from being our constant companion."

Russell M. Nelson

"Confidence in the Presence of God," Apr. 2025

Esther 4:14

For if thou altogether holdest thy peace at this time, then shall there enlargement and deliverance arise to the Jews from another place, but thou and thy father's house shall be destroyed: and who knoweth whether thou art come to the kingdom for such a time as this?

No Coincidences

I was working in the temple and felt a prompting to walk down a certain corridor. There, I found a young woman lost and confused. It was her second time attending the temple, and she did not know where to go. I believe it was not a coincidence that I was led to help her.

The beautiful Jewess Esther was a member of the Jewish community. Mordecai, her cousin, told her to hide her Jewish heritage. After Esther became queen, Haman plotted to exterminate all the Jews in the kingdom on a certain day. Whether the book of Esther is an allegorical story or historical fact, part of the purpose of the book of Esther is to teach us that there are no coincidences with the Lord. Esther was put into her position as queen so she could save her people from the vengeance of Haman.

When we follow the Lord and put our lives in His hands, He will make sure that we are in the right place at the right time.

—Marianna

"Many of you have witnessed miracles, more than you realize. They may seem small in comparison to Jesus raising the dead. But the magnitude does not distinguish a miracle, only that it came from God."

Ronald A. Rasband

"Behold, I Am a God of Miracles," Apr. 2021

Esther 8:3

And Esther spake yet again before the king, and fell down at his feet, and besought him with tears.

Courage Repeated Here

Esther inspires me to practice repeated courage. Twice before, she had risked her life to approach the king uninvited—an act in and of itself a cause for death—first to invite him to a feast (Esther 5:2) and then to admit her own heritage and expose Haman's plot against her people (Esther 7:4). And now, risking her life yet once again, she came before the king for a third time. The king extended his royal scepter (8:4), showing that Esther still needed royal approval to speak. This time she pleaded for the lives of her people and their safety. Her repeated acts of selfless courage saved her family and her people.

In today's world of contention, deception, and confusion, it takes repeated courage to choose love and truth. It takes repeated courage to live a covenant life so different from others, and to be peacemakers all the while. And sometimes, it just takes courage to brave the storms of life.

As we, like Esther, focus on the eternal things greater than ourselves and ask for divine help, we will be courageous time and time again because we know who and whose we are.

—Michelle

"As we remember who we are, knowing that there is a divine plan of mercy and drawing courage in the strength of the Lord, we can do all things. We will find calm."
Mark A. Bragg
"Christlike Poise," Apr 2023

Job 1:12

And the Lord said unto Satan,
Behold, all that he hath is in thy power.

When God Doesn't Explain

Have you ever asked God *why*? It's a complex concept for us to consider: that our loving Father allows temptation and suffering. He is all-powerful, all-knowing, perfectly in control, and infinitely caring. So why do bad things still happen? Why does God allow some tragedies but prevent others? It's the question I asked when my daughter died. It's the question I've asked countless times over my autistic son's challenges. It's the question I've asked when someone else's agency hurts me. We don't always get answers to these questions, but like Job, we can trust God and His plan for us, even when—especially when—we don't understand why.

The Lord is helping us become like Him in ways we can't fathom. Even though it's a painful and frustrating process, He knows which experiences, opportunities, and yes, even which trials, have the greatest chance of teaching us, refining us, changing our hearts, and turning us to Him. Though the "why" may never come in this life, we can anchor our hearts in the truth that He is still good, still near, and still leading us home. Trust isn't about having all the answers—it's about knowing who holds them. And someday, when we see Him again, He will help us understand.

—Krista

"Tribulation and challenges are the common experiences of mortality. Opposition is an essential part of the divine plan for helping us grow, and in the midst of that process, we have God's assurance that, in the long view of eternity, opposition will not be allowed to overcome us."

Dallin H. Oaks

"Be of Good Cheer," Oct. 2020

Job 2:6

And the Lord said unto Satan, Behold, he is in thine hand; but save his life.

The Best Kind of Workout

One of my personal pet peeves happened in Sunday School class when someone said, "God didn't really put Job in Satan's hand. He's too nice and wouldn't do that." Urgh! Have you read the story of Adam and Eve? Think of that sweet, innocent couple who didn't even know the difference between good and evil. God allowed Satan to tempt them. He put them in Satan's hand. But the result brought us all into the world and began the plan of redemption.

I'm too prideful to share the many times I feel I've been dropped into Satan's hand. Sometimes, like Job, I've completely resisted and come out worse for wear but stronger. Other times, like Eve, I've fallen a little but found the Savior to lift me back to a point I can keep going on the path.

The thing I do hang my hat on is that no matter the challenge or temptation, the Lord is watching over us and won't give us more than we can bear without providing an escape. Often that escape is the temple. Remember, during these times of challenge, we are doing spiritual weightlifting. It is an opportunity to become stronger. Maybe that's what the Lord meant when He said that we needed to "work out" our salvation before Him.

—Christine

> "One reason [for the temple] is that amid the turmoil and temptations of the world, He has promised to strengthen and bless His covenant Saints, and His promises are being fulfilled!"
>
> Neil L. Andersen
>
> "Temples, Houses of the Lord Dotting the Earth," Apr. 2025

Job 3:1, 11

After this opened Job his mouth, and cursed his day. . . . Why died I not from the womb? Why did I not give up the ghost when I came out of the belly?

I'm a Terrible Person

I went through a stage in my life when I used the phrase "I'm a terrible person" way too often. Any time I made the slightest mistake or something bad happened in my life, I would say it. I did not even realize how often I used the phrase until my loving husband brought it to my attention.

Job was going through a tough time. He cursed the day he was born and wanted to die. But Job only cursed himself, not God. He asked God why so many catastrophes happened to him even though he tried to live a righteous life. The book of Job takes us on his spiritual journey to gain understanding about why bad things happen to good people—because Job was a good guy. Through his suffering, Job learned that he wasn't a terrible person and that God loved him. His reward in heaven would make up for all the injustices he suffered on earth.

As I gained confidence in the Lord, my protestations that "I am a terrible person" were replaced with my praises to Him for His saving grace. Job, too, gained this same perspective.

—Marianna

> "We live in a time when 'peaceable followers of Christ' experience unique challenges. Those who believe in, humbly worship, and testify of Jesus Christ have always experienced trials, tribulation, and adversities."
>
> Quentin L. Cook
>
> "Be Peaceable Followers of Christ," Oct. 2023

Job 10:1

My soul is weary of my life.

It Will Get Better

Confession: There have been times in my life that were dark. And I've wondered if, when all the spirits were cheering for the chance to experience the challenges of mortality, maybe I thought we were cheering for all-you-can eat chocolate and naps. Because life is hard. And it's scary. And it hurts. A lot. Sometimes we just feel weary of life.

In those times, I do think chocolate and naps can definitely help. But there is something deeper that can offer true relief. Job knew. It was the Lord. Even in his darkest depths of grief, anger, confusion, despair, and pain, he never fully rejected or abandoned God.

If you are reading this on a day that seems darker, know that God is here, right now. He sees you. He hears you. He knows you. He loves you. And if you let Him, He can shine light even in your darkest days. Remember, God can do anything. He can help you. It will get better.

—Michelle

> "To any who may be struggling to see that light and find that hope, I say: Hold on. Keep trying. God loves you. Things will improve. Christ comes to you in His 'more excellent ministry' with a future of 'better promises.'"
>
> Jeffrey R Holland
>
> "An High Priest of Good Things to Come," Oct. 1999

Job 13:5

O that ye would altogether hold your peace!

Sitting in the Mud

Job's friends started strong. They sat in silence for seven days, grieving with him. But then . . . they opened their mouths. Instead of comfort and support, Job got lectures, spiritual clichés, and accusations of sin. Ouch!

We've all been there. Faced with someone's deep grief, we search for meaningful, helpful words to ease the pain but end up repeating platitudes like "At least she lived a long life" or "At least he's in a better place."

Grievers don't need speeches or quick fixes. They need someone willing to sit beside them in the mud, hold their hand, and say, "This is hard, and I'm here."

Jesus wept with Mary and Martha before raising Lazarus. He didn't start with "At least he's not suffering." He started with tears. Our presence, our tears, can be evidence to a griever that God hears their prayers for relief and keeps His promises of help and support.

So the next time someone's world falls apart, pull up a chair. Bring chocolate. Cry if you can. Just be there. Your quiet, loving presence will speak volumes.

—Krista

> "Our covenantal blessing is to partner with Jesus Christ in providing relief, both temporal and spiritual, to all of God's children. We are a conduit through which He provides relief."
>
> Camille N. Johnson
>
> "Jesus Christ Is Relief," Apr. 2023

Job 16:2–3

I have heard many such things: miserable comforters are ye all. Shall vain words have an end? Or what emboldeneth thee that thou answerest.

Miserable Comforters

Comforting people when they are going through terrible times of loss is often difficult for me. I just don't know what to say. I worry about saying the wrong thing or opening wounds they are trying to heal. Often, I keep quiet but give a hug or drop off a meal or baked goods so that they know I care about them and I'm thinking of them. It's how I show comfort and care.

Job's friends came to visit him after his tragedies. Their "comfort" ended up being judgments and false teachings about why bad things happen to people. These comforters speculated that Job had hidden sins or that his sudden lack of wealth meant that God did not love him anymore. Job's friends also would not leave him alone! The Lord kicked them out by saying that "ye have not spoken of me the thing that is right" (Job 42:7). These miserable comforters left Job and did what the Lord commanded them to do: offer up a burnt sacrifice and ask for forgiveness for their untrue words.

Now, before I give comfort, I seek the Lord's advice to know how best to comfort those in need.

—Marianna

> "If you are feeling lost, if you have questions or lack wisdom, if you are struggling with your circumstances or wrestling with spiritual dissonance, turn to Him. Pray to Him for comfort, love, answers, and direction."
>
> Alan T. Phillips
>
> "God Knows and Loves You," Oct. 2023

Job 19:25–26

I know that my Redeemer liveth, and that he shall stand at the latter day upon the earth: And though . . . worms destroy this body, yet in my flesh shall I see God.

Finally

Our stake in Dallas would perform *The Messiah* every year. I really wanted to sing "I Know That My Redeemer Liveth." I dreamed of bearing my testimony through song. So I auditioned, but they gave me "He Shall Feed His Flock." Well, imagine my joy twenty years later when I got Job 19 for this devotional! Finally! Although you can't hear the musical version which would have sounded much better back then, this is what would be going through my head as I sang:

I know that my Redeemer liveth. Just last night I was lying in bed berating myself for all I needed to do. I felt Him whisper that He loves me. It calmed me so I could sleep. He is there for us now. He lives and can be part of our lives today.

And that he shall stand at the latter day upon the earth. When I heard Elder Renlund talk about the Primary child afraid for this day, I shook my head. He is coming and I can't wait!

And though worms destroy this body, yet in my flesh shall I see God. The gift of Christ's resurrection is that I get to be in His presence again and hug my babies and have a completeness of joy. All because of my Savior. I know Him. I *love* Him!

—Christine

"But He'll return as scriptures say; it will be a joyful day when our beloved Savior comes again."

Dale G. Renlund,
quoting "When the Savior Comes Again"

"Personal Preparation to Meet the Savior," Apr. 2025

Job 19:26–27

Yet in my flesh shall I see God: Whom I shall see for myself, and mine eyes shall behold, and not another.

I Can't Wait to See Him

I discovered I loved the story of *Wicked* years before I saw the musical. I had read the book, but I thought it could be improved upon. Then I heard that the musical had come out. The songs were incredible, and it looked like the plot had been refined. Secretly, I read everything I could on the subject and wanted so badly to see it, but we lived in rural Minnesota. There was no way. A few years later we moved to Portland—right after it had left the area. Flying to Broadway in New York City was not an option, so I continued to memorize the words to the entire score, and pined for the day that would never come. Then it came! There was a showing over two hours away. I didn't care how far it was. I bought tickets which were more expensive than any tickets I'd bought before. I didn't care about the cost. I still remember my excitement, and the show was everything I dreamed it would be. Simply wonderful!

Take that experience and multiply it by a thousand. That's how I feel about seeing my Savior. I've felt His help, inspiration, and love. I've read all I could about Him and am still learning how to follow Him each day. But the thought of seeing Him with my own eyes—of being right there when He comes again and feeling Him near—is so thrilling that any distance or cost has no meaning. I can't wait to see Him!

—Christine

> "The best is yet to come, my dear brothers and sisters, because the Savior is coming again!"
>
> Russell M. Nelson
>
> "The Lord Jesus Christ Will Come Again," Oct. 2024

Job 27:6

*My righteousness I hold fast,
and will not let it go.*

Hold Fast

Years ago, I read a metaphor that has always stuck with me. It went something like this: Imagine you receive a gift wrapped in beautiful paper and tied with a piece of twine. Chances are, you'll quickly untie the twine and toss it aside to get to the present without giving it a second thought. Imagine, then, you are hanging over a cliff, a hundred feet above rocky ground, and the only thing keeping you alive is a long piece of twine you're holding onto. Not only are you paying attention to the twine, but you are holding onto it for your literal life.

The twine could have been the same piece of twine in both cases, but its meaning and value changed with its purpose. When it appeared to be a barrier to our personal desires, we tossed it aside. But when it becomes our literal lifeline, we hold fast to it.

When we come to see the gospel of Jesus Christ not as a barrier to keep us away from fun or freedom, but as a literal lifeline—one that can save us from grief, fear, heartache, confusion, and more—we will hold fast to it and not let go. Especially when we know who is holding onto the other end.

—Michelle

> "I promise you, as you hold on to the iron rod, you will walk hand in hand with Jesus Christ."
>
> Andrea Munoz Spannaus
>
> "Faithful to the End," Apr. 2024

Job 30:1

But now they that are younger than I have me in derision, whose fathers I would have disdained to have set with the dogs of my flock.

Don't Touch the Water!

The boat sat low in the water of the Chao Phraya River. Our guide had arranged for a scenic tour of some of Bangkok's most iconic buildings—beautiful temples, stately government highrises, and lavish homes. In the center of the river, choppy waves sent splashes over the edges of the boat, water heavy with the scent of questionable cleanliness. Someone near the front called out, "Stay away from the edge! Don't let the water touch you!" And we all scrambled to the inner edges of our seats, laughing nervously and screaming in panic with each splash.

The guide announced a detour down an offshoot of the river the locals had dubbed "The Venice of Bangkok." With "oohs" and "ahhs" of excitement, the boat changed course, and we all craned our necks to get a first glimpse. Then suddenly, we all fell silent. The Venice of Bangkok is a shanty town of terribly humble homes built on stilts over the water. A young mother washed dishes at the river's edge, an older man hauled water into his home with a bucket and rope, and a group of joyous boys waved and hollered to us as they leaped from a wooden platform to swim. The water I had just squirmed over was the water sustaining their life. How easily our perspectives and perceptions get misaligned. I'm forever thankful that for those few moments, God let me see through His eyes.

—Krista

> "I believe God was asking me, 'Can't you see that everyone around you is a sacred being?'"
>
> Robert C. Gay
>
> "Taking Upon Ourselves the Name of Jesus Christ," Oct. 2018

Job 34:28

He will deliver his soul from going into the pit, and his life shall see the light.

The Fourth Friend

After my last baby was stillborn, I lay in bed mourning. I asked my husband not to let anyone in. I just wanted to feel miserable for a long time. My friend Meghan wouldn't listen. She barged into my room, jumped in my bed, and put her arms around me. It began the healing process and encouraged me to turn to the Lord for answers rather than wallow.

In the book of Job, Elihu was that kind of friend. He didn't speak up until chapter 32, after Job's other three friends tried to convince the stricken man to "curse God and die." Even Job's words were more about denying their claims than about turning to God.

When Elihu, the fourth friend, entered, he bore a strong testimony of trusting in God. Soon after, Job heard the voice of the Lord and was made whole. It was that fourth friend that lifted Job so that he could hear Him. May we each listen, act, and have the blessing of becoming that fourth friend.

—Christine

"Wholeness is born of faith in and conversion to Jesus Christ."

Camille N. Johnson

"Spiritually Whole in Him," Apr. 2025

Job 37:14

Hearken unto this, O Job: stand still, and consider the wondrous works of God.

To Stand Still

I am constantly busy. Every day, I have a list of things I must get done before I go to bed. After accomplishing my list, I often take a break by watching a show, listening to a book, or scrolling through social media. My mind is always going to a variety of places in a variety of ways.

The counsel from God to Job is to "stand still." I don't think that means to physically stop moving (though it can mean that). I can stand still and still be looking at my phone or writing an email. I think the Lord's commandment to "stand still" refers to stopping our minds from being agitated by worldly concerns. Obviously, Job had a lot of worries on his mind—his children were dead, his wealth was destroyed, and his health was gone. He was not going anywhere, but the Lord wanted him to think about God rather than himself.

A standstill (noun) is very different from standing still (verb). A standstill is a stop in progress, such as an accident bringing cars to a standstill on the freeway. But the action—to stand still—is a conscious effort to find peacefulness in our lives. We begin to reflect on the wondrous works of God, rather than the frustrations of the world of man. There, we can find peace.

—Marianna

> "Thus, 'be still' may be a way of reminding us to focus upon the Savior unfailingly as the ultimate source of the spiritual stillness of the soul that strengthens us to do and overcome hard things."
>
> David A. Bednar
>
> "Be Still, and Know That I Am God," Apr. 2024

Job 40:8

Wilt thou condemn me, that thou mayest be righteous?

Finding Eyes

My family has a serious problem. They sometimes don't see things that are sitting in plain sight: the cereal in the pantry, the ketchup in the refrigerator, their socks. You name it. I can't tell you how many times I've told them where something is, and they *still* come back with "You're wrong. I don't see it." They're staring right at it, yet I'm wrong. Years ago I started replying, "Use your finding eyes." Nine times out of ten, they end up seeing what was always there.

This is kind of what was going on here between Job and God. God has knowledge, power, and righteousness, and yet, because it wasn't apparent to Job, he told God He was wrong. "Though I cry, 'I've been wronged!' I get no response; though I call for help, there is no justice" (NIV, Job 19:7). God's power is there and real, but because Job can't see it, God is wrong.

When we feel abandoned or angry or afraid, rather than condemning or accusing God, we can use our spiritual "finding eyes," with the help of the Holy Ghost. Chances are, we will see His love, His help, and His hand in our lives all along.

—Michelle

> "In the midst of this refiner's fire, rather than get angry with God, get close to God. Call upon the Father in the name of the Son. Walk with Them in the Spirit, day by day. Allow Them over time to manifest Their fidelity to you. Come truly to know Them and truly to know yourself. Let God prevail."
>
> D. Todd Christofferson
>
> "Our Relationship with God," Apr. 2022

Job 42:12

So the Lord blessed the latter end of Job more than his beginning.

In the End

My dad often says, "If I'd known grandkids were so much fun, I'd have had them first!" Now that I'm a grandma myself, I agree entirely! I love my kids fiercely, but being a grandparent means I get to relive the best parts of raising children but with fewer "no's" and much more sleep.

There are many ways that the Lord blesses us in the end more than at the beginning. Every day of life grants us wisdom, experience, and skills we didn't have before. And though there are many trials I would like to have avoided, who I am today, what I've learned, and my relationship with my Savior are precious gains that I would not exchange for anything.

When we leave this world and return to our heavenly home, I imagine we will find this principle infinitely true. We agreed to come to Earth to obtain a body and earthly experiences that help us become more like our heavenly parents. And when that day comes, with our eyes reopened to what we were like before we came to Earth, we will fully appreciate all we have gained by having lived! Compared to our pre-Earth beginning, our post-Earth end will be a glorious blessing.

–Krista

"In the end, it is the blessing of a close and abiding relationship with the Father and the Son that we seek. It makes all the difference and is everlastingly worth the cost."

D. Todd Christofferson

"Our Relationship with God," Apr. 2022

Psalm 1:3

And he shall be like a tree planted by the rivers of water, that bringeth forth his fruit in his season; his leaf also shall not wither; and whatsoever he doeth shall prosper.

Deep Roots

We bought an abandoned property that looked like a junkyard. The weeds were waist-high and every window of the house was broken, but as you drove in, there was a gorgeous willow tree. It was twenty feet high and as healthy and beautiful as it could be. It looked like it belonged in a garden instead of surrounded by trash and weeds. Even in an unruly yard, the tree thrived. Why? Because it grew near a riverbed. Regardless of what was happening around it, the tree was strong because it was fed by a stream of living water.

The very first Psalm teaches that if our "delight is in the law of the Lord," then we will be like that tree. The key is that we stay where we can be fed. It's a lot like Lehi's vision of the tree of life "whose fruit was desirable to make one happy" (1 Nephi 8:10). But in the psalm, instead of partaking from the tree, you become the tree.

Can you imagine being so rooted in the gospel and your love for the Savior that you lose the ability to stray from the truth? Being a tree that would offer the fruit of Christ's love to others? That's the goal. May we each become more rooted every day.

—Christine

"The healthy, fruitful tree of faith requires intentional effort. And a vital part of that effort is making sure we are firmly rooted in Christ."

Dieter F. Uchtdorf

"Nourish the Roots, and the Branches Will Grow," Oct. 2024

Psalm 8:3–4

When I consider thy heavens, the work of thy fingers, the moon and the stars, which thou hast ordained; What is man, that thou art mindful of him? And the son of man, that thou visitest him?

Consider the Heavens

My husband and I owned a summer home in New Harmony, Utah. Our large front windows looked out upon the majestic peaks and crimson walls of Kolob Canyon. It was a spectacular sight!

But the greatest view was at night. Because of the lack of light pollution, the night sky was a vibrant array of stars. I could go out at night and see in great detail the majesty of the heavens like I had never seen it before.

To get a closer view, I went with the astronomy club that met late at night to see planets rising amidst the stars and enjoy the Milky Way galaxy. I looked through the telescope, and I was amazed at the vastness of the heavens.

What is man in comparison to these works of God?

—Marianna

> "These wonderful creations were prepared entirely for our benefit and are living proof of the love the Creator has for His children."
>
> David A. Bednar
>
> "Our Earthly Stewardship," Oct. 2022

Psalm 14:2

The Lord looked down from heaven upon the children of men, to see if there were any that did understand, and seek God.

God's Love Language

Last year, we held a Relief Society activity about love languages (words of affirmation, acts of service, receiving gifts, physical touch, and quality time). We talked about our own love languages, then had a fantastic discussion about what Heavenly Father's love languages could be.

We agreed that He speaks all five languages (and then some). Many of the languages make sense. He offers words of affirmation through His prophets and the Holy Ghost; His entire work (service) and glory is for us; He gives us gifts of the Spirit, especially His Son; and He has given us bodies so we can have a physical experience and participate in physical ordinances. But, it's the quality time language that got me thinking the most. I've been taught since I was young that God wants us to spend time with Him in prayer, pondering, and worship. But as I considered time as a way He not only shows love, but *feels* love, it hit me deeply that *He* might want to spend time with *me.*

It still rings true and leaves me in awe. The God of the universe looks down and *wants* to be with me. If that's true for me, it must be true for you. I believe He longs to spend time with you because He loves you and loves to feel your love too.

—Michelle

"[God] yearns for us to commune with Him."

L. Todd Budge

"Seek Him with All Your Heart," Oct. 2024

Psalm 17:5

Hold up my goings in thy paths, that my footsteps slip not.

Slick Rock

My brother and I stood at the fork between two paths. Dad had taken us on a hike to a famous Yosemite waterfall, and we had a decision to make: walk the longer, safer, drier trail through the woods, or take the more adventurous route—a steep, rocky, wet path right next to the falls. I was nine, my brother was seven, and we were all in for an adventure.

As we neared the falls, the dirt trail morphed into deep-set stairs carved into the rock, slick with spray. Dad cautioned us to go slow and stay away from the edge. We climbed and were soon soaking wet, but the view of the falls, only feet away, was incredible. Halfway up, we came to a narrow turn in the path. My brother slipped and fell toward the edge. With lightning-fast reflexes, Dad caught him by the arm and pulled him to safety. He held us both for a minute to make sure we were all right. Then we pressed on and made it to the top.

Just as my dad watched over my brother and me on that hike, my Father in Heaven watches over every step I make. The path is often steep, rocky, and slick, but Christ's Atonement saves us from a terrible fall. Someday, I'll ask Him how many times He used His lightning-fast reflexes to pull me to safety. I'm guessing it's a lot. I can't wait to thank Him with a hug.

–Krista

> "Every book of scripture demonstrates how willing the Lord is to intervene in the lives of those who believe in Him."
>
> Russell M. Nelson
>
> "The Power of Spiritual Momentum," Apr. 2022

Psalm 20:7

Some trust in chariots, and some in horses: but we will remember the name of the Lord our God.

Hum Your Favorite Hymn

If you were asked what is the most quoted book in the Bible, your answer might be Isaiah, but you would be wrong. The book of Psalms which was the ancient hymnal of Old Testament times, is quoted by other biblical prophets almost twice as many times as Isaiah. In fact, Isaiah quotes Psalms at least ten times. For example, in Psalm 20:7, David talks about trusting in chariots and horses but encourages us by saying, "We will remember the name of the Lord." In contrast, Isaiah starts with that same scripture but turns it upside down. He warns, "Woe unto them that . . . stay on horses and trust in chariots, because they are many" (Isaiah 31:1).

Psalms are quoted in the New Testament 115 times, eleven by the Savior Himself. On the cross when Christ said, "My God, My God, why hast thou forsaken me," he was quoting Psalm 22:1. In good times and bad, using the words of the hymns of God can lift us. As we memorize the hymns chosen by our Church leaders, those words can stick with us. Especially the new hymns we've been given. They can allow us to lift our voices in joy and find solace in difficulty.

—Christine

"I love to sing the hymns of the Restoration. The combination of inspired lyrics and majestic melodies helps me to learn essential gospel principles and stirs my soul."

David A. Bednar

"But We Heeded Them Not," Apr. 2022

Psalm 22:1

My God, my God, why hast thou forsaken me? Why art thou so far from helping me, and from the words of my roaring?

Feeling Forsaken

Reading this psalm reminds me of the words of the Prophet Joseph Smith while he was unjustly imprisoned in Liberty Jail: "O God, where art thou? And where is the pavilion that covereth thy hiding place?" (D&C 121:1). Joseph had been in jail nearly four months when he asked these questions. The day before receiving this revelation, Joseph received a letter from Emma describing the suffering of the Saints. But more disheartening was Emma's description of her own troubles of being driven from their home in the middle of winter with their children and having only scant supplies. His family was destitute, and Joseph could do nothing to help them.

The answer from the Lord was one of comfort and hope: "If thou endure it well, God shall exalt thee on high" (D&C 121:7–8). This is the same conclusion the Psalmist describes: "The meek shall eat and be satisfied: they shall praise the Lord that seek him: your heart shall live for ever" (Psalm 22:26).

When I felt forsaken after the death of my parents, I thought of the cries of the Psalmist, the Savior on the cross, and the Prophet Joseph Smith in Liberty Jail. I took comfort and hope in the promises of the Atonement.

—Marianna

"It simply will not work 'to glide naively through life,' saying . . . 'Lord, give me all thy choicest virtues, but be certain not to give me grief, nor sorrow, nor pain, nor opposition.'"

Jeffrey R. Holland

"Waiting on the Lord," Oct. 2020

Psalm 23:1, 6

The Lord is my shepherd; I shall not want. . . . Surely goodness and mercy shall follow me all the days of my life: and I will dwell in the house of the Lord for ever.

The Good Shepherd and the Good Sheep

I was getting ready to teach a Gospel Doctrine lesson about sheep and shepherds and decided to talk to a farmer I knew who raised sheep. He said that sheep are dumb and are easily led astray. He had some sheep who fell off of a cliff because they followed another sheep who fell off the cliff. The purpose of a shepherd is to make sure the sheep go in the right direction. Without a shepherd, sheep do not know where to go and often make bad choices as to whom or what to follow. A good shepherd will not lead his sheep astray, and good sheep will follow their shepherd in faith and trust.

So, our responsibility is to become good sheep who follow the Good Shepherd. In Psalm 24, we are taught what we must do to become a good follower of Christ: "He that hath clean hands, and a pure heart; who hath not lifted up his soul unto vanity, nor sworn deceitfully" (24:4). We become wayward sheep when we are lifted up in pride and walk in our own paths. Good sheep have the pure heart of a disciple and follow the Shepherd wherever He leads. We give up our will to Him. In return, the Good Shepherd will make sure we safely return to our Eternal Home.

—Marianna

> "Jesus knows His sheep, calleth his own sheep by name, and, as the Lamb of God, gave His life for His sheep."
>
> Jonathan S. Schmitt
>
> "That They Might Know Thee," Oct. 2022

Psalm 27:1

The Lord is my light.

The Light in a Dark Place

Years ago, during a trip to Japan, I visited the Kiyomizu Dera Temple. Founded in the year 780, the temple sits on a lush green mountaintop near Kyoto, surrounded by cherry blossoms and sweeping views. It is magnificent. The highlight for me was the hidden lower room in Zuigudo Hall. You enter through a nondescript stairway, take off your shoes, and then descend a stairwell into utter darkness. The goal: to reach the sacred symbol at the bottom.

Prior to this, I had never been in total and complete darkness before, the kind of darkness where you literally cannot see your hand right in front of your face. The descent is relatively short. And even though I knew my family was near and I was safe, complete darkness has a way of stretching time and magnifying fear. It was uncomfortable, disconcerting. Even frightening.

Finally, as I neared the bottom, I saw soft light from a lamp shining onto the sacred symbol, and I let out my breath. At that moment, I wasn't focused on the symbol. It was the light I wanted to see, to soak in. The light was beautiful. It was hope.

Jesus Christ is the light that shines in a world that can feel dark. His light is beautiful. It is real. It is powerful. It is hope. Seek it. Find it. Love it. Soak it in.

—Michelle

> "[Jesus Christ] is our light, our life, and our way. His light will never dim."
>
> Timothy J. Dyches
>
> "Light Cleaveth to Light," Apr. 2021

Psalm 31:24

Be of good courage, and he shall strengthen your heart, all ye that hope in the Lord.

A Lightened Load

Halfway through my son's time at Marine boot camp, his courage was tested to its breaking point. While he was sick with pneumonia, his unit was scheduled for an eighteen-mile hike with fully loaded packs, gear, and weapons, and he didn't know how he would find the strength to finish. He started strong but soon found he was falling behind. He couldn't stop, couldn't quit, but in his sick and weakened condition, he was struggling like he never had before.

Suffering beneath the weight of his gear, barely putting one foot in front of another, he reached out in desperate, silent prayer to his Father. Suddenly, someone behind him took hold of his pack and lifted it, significantly lightening the weight. He turned to see who it was, but no one was there. Thinking he'd imagined it, he went back to his prayer. Again, someone lifted his pack. Again, he turned around, and again, no one was there. But his pack was definitely lighter than it had been. And it remained lighter. God had heard him and sent help. With buoyed courage, he kept walking and finished the hike.

Later, he sent me a letter detailing his experience. "Mom, it's real! Angels are real! And Heavenly Father really does help us!"

—Krista

> "It is in Him that we discover the strength to overcome, the courage to persevere, and the peace that surpasses all understanding."
>
> José L. Alonso
>
> "Jesus Christ at the Center of Our Lives," Apr. 2024

Psalm 34:13–14

Keep thy tongue from evil, and thy lips from speaking guile. Depart from evil and do good; seek peace, and pursue it.

Self-Talk and Guile

I recently had a job grading student papers at BYU–I. One of their finals entailed researching a communications technique and doing a PowerPoint presentation about it. About half of them were on negative self-talk. After going through over one hundred presentations, I felt like an expert on the subject.

According to these students, the way we talk to ourselves sets a standard for the way we treat others. Using cruel language when we talk or think about ourselves is one of the most destructive habits to our mental health. And I would add our spiritual health. The Lord doesn't think of us as evil or broken. He wants to love, lift, and heal us if we will let him.

Guile means dishonesty or deceit. When we speak ill of ourselves or others, we are not being honest. Either intentionally or unintentionally, we have distorted the truth. The answer is in Psalm 34:14: "Seek peace, and pursue it." We need to practice saying nice things, true things, about ourselves in our own head and about others out loud. As we pursue peace in the world and our own minds, we are letting virtue garnish our thoughts, rather than guile tarnish them.

—Christine

> "There's the key! In the Lord's own words, charity and virtue open the way to having confidence before God!"
>
> Russell M. Nelson
>
> "Confidence in the Presence of God," Apr. 2025

Psalm 40:1, 3

I waited patiently for the Lord; and he inclined unto me, and heard my cry. . . . And he hath put a new song in my mouth, even praise unto our God: many shall see it, and fear, and shall trust in the Lord.

Waiting Patiently

I have found that things often take longer than I want. Waiting for the birth of a baby, waiting to be able to buy a house, and waiting to be accepted into a graduate program—so many things simply take longer than I'd hoped. And it is hard to be patient when you want something to happen *right now.*

With all twelve of my children, I gave birth after the baby's due date. With one, I was more than three weeks overdue before the baby was born. I have found it *very* hard to be patient in those circumstances.

However, the Lord wants us to be patient in all things. I marvel at the example of others, especially those in sickness or pain, who wait patiently for the Lord to heal them. In the April 2025 general conference, Sister Camille N. Johnson said that the Lord may not provide healing from illness and disease: "That kind of healing is on the Lord's time. And in the meantime, we can choose to be made whole by exercising our faith in Him!" By being patient, we will be blessed with the faith and wholeness that brings everlasting healing.

—Marianna

"The Master Healer will heal all afflictions—physical and emotional—in His time."

Camille N. Johnson

"Spiritually Whole in Him," Apr. 2025

Psalm 46:10

Be still, and know that I am God.

Dessert

One of my most spiritual experiences happened while I was lying on the floor after a yoga class. At the end of each class, our teacher would have us lie on our mats while she talked us through some visualizations and meditations. I found it to be a lovely time to take a nap. Then, after a class, I wondered if there was something to this "stillness" she talked about. And so, when "dessert" came, I was all in.

She asked us to imagine we were in our favorite quiet place. Easy—a beach. Then, she invited us to imagine someone special there with us. I thought about all the people I could have there, then wondered what it would be like if God were sitting next to me. And so I did. This choice to think of God in my stillness led me to a string of experiences that not only strengthened my testimony of Him but also of the space that stillness creates for Him to dwell in. I love that no matter what's going on in my life, I can choose to find stillness on the floor, in prayer, in the temple, in the scriptures—anywhere. And in that stillness, I can find God.

—Michelle

> "I pray the Holy Ghost will enlighten each of us as we consider a higher and holier dimension of stillness in our lives—an inner spiritual stillness of the soul that enables us to know and remember that God is our Heavenly Father, we are His children, and Jesus Christ is our Savior."
>
> David A. Bednar
>
> "Be Still, and Know that I Am God," Apr. 2024

Psalm 47:6–7

Sing praises to God. . . . Sing praises unto our King, . . . For God is the King of all the earth: sing ye praises with understanding.

We'll Sing and We'll Shout!

The foundation of my testimony began with a song. I was eight years old, costumed in a pioneer dress and bonnet, standing onstage beside my mom for the ending scene of the Oakland Temple Pageant. The orchestra played the opening strains of "The Spirit of God," and I joined the ensemble, singing with all the energy of my young heart. The power of that chorus of people bearing testimony of Jesus Christ through song set my heart aflame. The last note rang through the auditorium, the audience cheered, and the red velvet curtain closed in front of me. I pulled on my mom's arm as tears spilled from my heart down my cheeks. Concerned, she knelt and asked what was wrong.

"I don't want to go home!" I cried, "I want to stay and do it again!"

My dear mother understood and explained, "Krista, that feeling is the Holy Ghost. It's telling you that the words you just sang are true!"

Few things bring the Spirit more quickly into the room and our hearts than music that praises our Lord.

—Krista

> "The music of the gospel is the joyful spiritual feeling that comes from the Holy Ghost. It brings a change of heart. "
>
> Wilford W. Andersen
>
> "The Music of the Gospel," Apr. 2015

Psalm 51:10

*Create in me a clean heart, O God;
and renew a right spirit within me.*

A Clean Heart

I remember this story as a young teenager. A group of boys snuck into the back of the school auditorium to look at an inappropriate magazine together. An old janitor found them. "I'd rather you boys were all rolling in the mud than looking at this filth," he said, snatching the magazine away. "Why?" asked one of the boys. The janitor shook his head. "If you roll in the mud you can have a bath, and it's over. But this dirt will stay in your head and heart, and come back again and again over the years. You may never be totally clean of it."

In those days, you had to seek out pornographic images. Today, it comes electronically into our homes. The statistics are harrowing. One poll claims 93 percent of boys and 62 percent of girls are exposed to porn online by age eighteen. As young adults, 26 percent reported seeking porn out. And 98 percent of all porn is viewed on smartphones. (See ballardbrief. byu.edu.)

Through repentance, we can become clean, but that process can take years of fighting at a cost to self-esteem, relationships, and mental health. The Lord will help you, but it's not easy. How much better to not turn down that road in the first place.

—Christine

"We need to avoid pornography, evaluate the appropriateness of what we are streaming in our homes, and avoid every form of sinful conduct."

Quentin L. Cook

"Be True to God and His Work," Oct. 2022

Psalm 55:22

Cast thy burden upon the Lord, and he shall sustain thee: he shall never suffer the righteous to be moved.

From Burdens to Blessings

The music and words of this psalm are in our hymnbook. Originally, this hymn was a part of Felix Mendelssohn's oratorio, *Elijah*, which was performed in Birmingham, England, in 1846. During a dramatic scene, Elijah is engaged in battle with the evil priests of Baal. As Elijah builds an altar, he cries out in mighty prayer. A choir of angels appears and sings to him, "Cast your burden upon the Lord." These words have brought comfort and peace to many believers of Christ.

As a young mother, I was called to the stake Relief Society presidency. I had six children, the oldest being eight years old. In 1985, the Yorktown New York Stake took in the area between Scarsdale, New York; New Canaan, Connecticut; and the Bronx, New York. This calling was a burden for me and my family. I traveled a lot on Sundays visiting wards, often bringing a nursing baby with me. I participated in stake meetings and spoke at ward conferences and stake Relief Society meetings. I cast this burden on the Lord and had faith and confidence that I could accomplish the service He had asked me to do. The calling became a great blessing in my life. I gained dear friends, learned about Christlike service, and became a better leader in the Church. My family was blessed with an increased portion of the Spirit. This burden became a blessing to my young family.

—Marianna

"As we are filled with the Savior's love, His yoke truly can be easy, and His burden can feel light."

J. Anette Dennis

"His Yoke Is Easy and His Burden Is Light," Oct. 2022

Psalm 61:1

Hear my cry, O God;
attend unto my prayer.

Our Floors Are Clean

When I was a teenager, I struggled with prayer. Not *saying* prayers—I prayed a lot. I needed to. My self-doubts, fears, and need for love kept me on my knees. My problem wasn't in saying them. It was believing that God heard them. Not because of Him, but because of me. I often felt like my prayers would hit the ceiling in my room and fall to the floor. Even though I pleaded with God to hear me, during a few hard times, it seemed my floor was a carpet of unheard prayers.

But I know now that He did hear my prayers. Every single one of them. Turns out my floor is clean. And so is yours.

He hears every prayer—your prayers too. He hears the prayers said on our knees, yelled in anger, delivered through tears, and whispered in grief. He hears the prayers in our cars, at the side of hospital beds, as we read our scriptures, or when we kneel as a family. He even hears the prayers we can't bring ourselves to pray.

God hears us. No prayer is left on the floor.

And He answers every prayer in His wisdom, His timing, and His love. So, keep praying, my friend. Because it works. I promise.

—Michelle

"I testify that the Lord hears and answers our prayers."

Ciro Schmeil

"Faith to Act and Become," Oct. 2021

Psalm 69:1–3

Save me, O God; for the waters are come in unto my soul. I sink in deep mire, where there is no standing: I am come into deep waters, where the floods overflow me. I am weary of crying.

Through the Deep Waters

Though Elora had survived emergency surgery, her little body was so broken and traumatized that there was little chance she would survive. My little girl wasn't coming back to me. I'd been clinging to the miracle of her recovery like a life preserver, but now, it had been ripped from my grasp and plunged me into a dark, churning, torrential river of pain and fear. I sobbed from a depth of sorrow I'd never known, unable to stop, barely able to breathe. Panic set in as the waters of terror rose higher and higher, and for several terrifying moments, I believed I would succumb to my grief—lie down on the floor and never get up. I was drowning and desperately needed saving.

I thought of the Apostle Peter drowning beneath waves he had momentarily walked upon, and I choked out the same three-word prayer: "Lord, save me" (Matthew 14:30). I envisioned Christ's arm stretched out to me, and I literally thrust my hand into the air above my head, symbolically taking hold of His, a gesture of choosing to believe in His help. As long as I held onto Him, He *would not* let me drown.

–Krista

"As we reach out to Him in faith, He will always be there, and in His time, He will be ready and willing to grasp our hands and pull us up to a safe place."

Juan Pablo Villar

"His Hand Ready to Help Us," Oct. 2024

Psalm 71:3

Be thou my strong habitation, whereunto I may continually resort: . . . for thou art my rock and my fortress.

My Fortress

There is only one time in my adult life when I felt like I wanted to run away. I was dealing with grief and couldn't get over it. The daily grind of taking care of my large family was all-consuming. I felt like I didn't have the time or space to heal. At last, my husband said, "You need to spend some time with your parents." I was shocked. This is a man that never cooks for himself or helps with the dishes, and I had seven children at home. I'd never spent a weekend off by myself since we married, but I left.

Surprisingly, my parents' home was not the resort I needed. Friends were always dropping by, and I wanted to be alone to process where to put all that I was feeling. Luckily, my folks' home was a short walk from the temple. That became my fortress. The place I could run to for support and love.

Within those sacred walls, I found balm for my broken heart. I literally felt my grief lifted from my shoulders and taken on by the Atonement. After a few days, I was ready to return home.

A fortress isn't a long-term living facility. It is a place of refuge during the most dangerous times of battle. Are we using that great gift to its full potential?

—Christine

> "The temple lies at the center of strengthening our faith and spiritual fortitude.'"
>
> Ulisses S. Soares, quoting Russell M. Nelson
>
> "Covenant Confidence Through Jesus Christ," Apr. 2024

Psalm 75:8

For in the hand of the Lord there is a cup, and the wine is red; it is full of mixture; and he poureth out of the same: but the dregs thereof, all the wicked of the earth shall wring them out, and drink them.

Drinking the Dregs

If you have ever drunk out of the same cup as young children, the backwash at the bottom of the cup can be pretty disgusting. These are the dregs: the sediment contained in a liquid that settles at the bottom. In wine, the dregs are the unwanted portion of the drink at the bottom of the barrel; they are filtered or wrung out from the good wine and are thrown away so that their taste does not affect the rest of the wine.

During the Final Judgment, the unrepentant sinner will need to drink the bitter cup of the dregs because they have not come unto Christ and partaken of His atoning sacrifice (or the good wine) to cleanse themselves. The Savior used wine during the first sacrament as a symbol of His blood that He spilt for us. He said: "And he took the cup, and gave thanks, and gave it to them, saying all of you drink from it; For this is in remembrance of my blood of the new testament which is shed for as many as shall believe on my name, for the remission of their sins" (JST, Matthew 26:23–24).

Christ has drunk the bitter cup for us. If we come unto Him, the bitter, evil parts of our lives will be separated from us.

—Marianna

"Partaking of the bread and water is a weekly reminder of His power working in you to help you overcome."

Emily Belle Freeman

"Live Up to Your Privileges," Oct. 2024

Psalm 82:6

I have said, Ye are gods; and all of you are children of the most High.

Who She Really Was

Years ago, I met a woman who lived in an apartment near mine. We hit it off despite our extreme differences. I was married with two toddlers, active in church with a loving family. She was a single mom of two slightly older kids from different dads who didn't believe in God and had a dysfunctional family. Not too long before, I'd been a full-time missionary. Not too long before, she'd been a full-time stripper. Still, we both felt a connection that was real.

As we got to know each other, we both opened up more about our lives and beliefs. She had a complicated relationship with men; therefore, the idea of God being a loving Father was really hard to accept. But the more we talked about it, the more the Spirit spoke to her soul. Finally, she allowed herself to believe He was her Father. This meant *she* was a daughter of God who was loved. For the first time, she began to see her worth and her value. For the first time, she saw herself, and she started to love who she saw. Who she really was. And she smiled.

—Michelle

> "I invite you to receive, either for the first time or to a greater extent than ever before, the magnificent realisation that you truly are God's beloved child. You must undo the bow, tear off the wrapping paper, open the box, and actively receive with grateful humility a true, pure understanding of this foundational truth. The Holy Spirit can bear witness to your heart that you are indeed a child of the Most High."
>
> Patrick Kearon
>
> "Receive His Gift," Apr. 2025

Psalm 85:8

I will hear what God the Lord will speak: for he will speak peace unto his people.

A Befuddled Bride

After Travis proposed, we took a trip to meet my family. I loved introducing him as my fiancé, and we spent the weekend giddy about being engaged. Sunday evening, Travis drove home so he could get back to work, and I stayed behind to begin planning my wedding. But Mom and I didn't get much done because once Travis was gone, I cried for three days straight.

I know. It sounds bad. But deciding who to marry is massively important, and I didn't think I'd received confirmation from God that Travis was the right husband for me. I was looking for lightning, fireworks, and a burning in my heart so hot there was no denying it! But when I prayed, the heavens seemed silent.

For three days, I woke up in an absolute stressed-out panic. Then I would worry and cry until I was exhausted. The only relief I found was a few minutes of stillness each time I prayed. Yep. Stillness. Peace. You see what I didn't, right? I'd been so focused on getting a loud answer that I'd completely missed God's soft reply: Marrying Travis would bring me peace.

Travis and I have been married for thirty years, and over all that time, Travis truly has been the peace in my storms. I'm thankful that God helped me recognize the value in that gift.

—Krista

"The peace you seek may not come as quickly as you desire, but I promise you that as you trust in the Lord, His peace will come."

Neil L. Andersen

"The Triumph of Hope," Oct. 2024

Psalm 92:10

But my horn shalt thou exalt like the horn of an unicorn: I shall be anointed with fresh oil.

Unicorns and Rainbows

Several young mothers were talking about not having their children wear symbols of unicorns and rainbows because they reflect beliefs they don't share. I laughed and said, "They are biblical symbols of Jesus Christ's power and promises."

Most people know that the rainbow was first given as a sign after the Flood that the earth wouldn't be flooded again, but in the Joseph Smith Translation of Genesis 9:21–25, it expands that promise to include the return of the city of Enoch at the start of the Millennium. Rainbows are so cool!

As for unicorns, the horn spoken of represents the power of God or the priesthood. It always made me laugh when I heard that persecutors of the early Church began a rumor that members of the Church had horns. They were right! We are the only church on the earth that has the authentic priesthood of God. And with that priesthood, we are anointed with oil and given incredible blessings in the temple. We are real unicorns!

So have your children wear the symbols of unicorns and rainbows, but teach them they are symbols of Christ and have them share what they really mean with their friends.

—Christine

> "We want our children to believe in Jesus Christ, belong to Jesus Christ and His Church through covenant, and strive to become like Jesus Christ."
>
> Amy A. Wright
>
> "Thou Art the Christ," Apr. 2025

Psalm 94:11

The Lord knoweth the thoughts of man, that they are vanity. Blessed is the man whom thou chastenest, O Lord, and teachest him out of thy law.

He Knows the Way

The Lord knows our thoughts and what we think we know. Often, we must be humbled by the Lord in order for our thinking to change. We must be humble enough to acknowledge "for my thoughts are not your thoughts, neither are your ways my ways, saith the Lord" (Isaiah 55:8). We must humbly learn to do His work His way, not ours.

When the Church changed from three-hour Sunday meetings to two-hour meetings, I questioned why. I missed not being with the Saints for that extra hour and especially not having Relief Society and Sunday School every week. Just six months before the COVID crisis, the Church instituted the home-centered gospel study program, Come Follow Me, preparing the Saints for the time when all Church meetings would be suspended. The Lord and His prophets knew what was going to happen. I must be humble enough to change my mind when the Lord and His prophets speak, so that His ways become my ways.

—Marianna

> "The Lord knows the way because He is the way and is our only chance for successfully negotiating mortality."
>
> Sheri L. Dew
>
> "Our Only Chance," Apr. 1999

Psalm 100:1–2

Make a joyful noise unto the Lord, all ye lands. Serve the Lord with gladness: come before his presence with singing.

Dance—I Mean Sing—Party

My grandkids were having a dance party the other day in their room. They had no idea anyone was watching. Their mom recorded the entire performance on the video baby monitor. The littles are five and two, and like most that age, they don't have the best dance moves. In fact, much of the two-minute video is them trying to dance and falling, laughing the entire time. They never worried if they were good dancers or not. They weren't trying to perform for anyone or look good. They were simply dancing from joy and feeling joy from dancing.

I mentioned at the beginning of this book that I am not a great singer. We are halfway through the Old Testament, and it's still true. But, I still love to sing. I even rejoined the ward choir. Why? I'm not a strong addition, but I'm not singing for the choir. I am not worried if I'm a good singer or hoping to perform well for my ward. I sing because I know that music makes the Lord happy. And the Lord makes me happy. So, I sing loudly and sometimes off-key with gladness.

—Michelle

> "As we sing, are we joining together to praise our God and King no matter the quality of our voices, or are we just mumbling or not singing at all? Scripture records that 'the song of the righteous is a prayer unto [God]' in which His soul delights. So let's sing! And praise Him!"
>
> Patrick Kearon
>
> "Welcome to the Church of Joy," Oct. 2024

Psalm 111:7–8

The works of his hands are verity and judgment; all his commandments are sure. They stand fast for ever and ever, and are done in truth and uprightness.

Perfect Like Him

Can you imagine what would happen if God lost His temper? Or got distracted and forgot to check in on our prayers? What would life look like if God got bored, tired, or frustrated? It's comical to imagine the chaos (and potential lightning strikes) that would emanate from an imperfect God. But honestly, aren't we grateful to have an unchanging, infinite, ever-present Father?

Being perfect and exalted like Him is our eternal goal, but I'm learning that it isn't about being perfect for our own sake. His work is all about His kids. Us. He is perfect so that we can always trust Him and rely on Him. And because He wants to give us all that He has, He's teaching us to be patient, attentive, gracious, forgiving, and every other good quality so that one day, if we choose to follow Him and take on the work that He does, we too will be perfect, unchanging, infinite, ever-present heavenly parents for our children. He sees our potential and knows how to help us reach it. So, let's keep trying and trusting in His perfect process. I'm excited to see what He has in store.

—Krista

"Our Heavenly Father wants you to become His heir and receive all that He has. He cannot offer you more. He cannot promise you more. He loves you more than you know and wants you to be happy in this life and in the life to come."

Dale G. Renlund

"Your Divine Nature and Eternal Destiny," Apr. 2022

Psalm 113:5, 9

Who is like unto the Lord our God. . . . He maketh the barren woman to keep house, and to be a joyful mother of children. Praise ye the Lord.

A Joyful Mother of Children

My daughter was very excited to go to a new book club. She met with a half-dozen women, most full-time moms like her, and hoped to build some new close friendships. Instead, they spent the entire time complaining about their husbands and children. She left feeling lonely and disappointed.

Being a mother at all is a gift from God. Not everyone gets that in this life. But being a *joyful* mother is a miracle that takes significant work. Might I suggest four ideas that made me more joyful even when I was drowning in dirty dishes and laundry:

1. Remember how short your time with your babies is. It is only a season, and you will never get it back. Believe that your time and choices are precious and important.
2. Find your covenant community. Life is more full when you can find another mom or two you trust. Then you can carry each other's burdens and lift each other up.
3. Keep an eternal perspective. Your goal is to teach your little ones to find Christ and become their best selves. Partner with your spouse and the Lord to find answers.
4. See the *joy,* because it's there. Count your blessings aloud, in front of your children and other moms. Please!

–Christine

"As sisters . . . we need to prepare the world for the Second Coming of the Savior Jesus Christ. . . . We will do that by creating a covenant community."

Camille N. Johnson

Worldwide Relief Society Devotional, Apr. 2025

Psalm 119:34

Teach me, O Lord, the way of thy statutes; and I shall keep it unto the end. Give me understanding, and I shall keep thy law; yea, I shall observe it with my whole heart. Make me to go in the path of thy commandments; for therein do I delight.

Knowledge Versus Understanding

Knowledge is knowing facts. Understanding is putting those facts into context—hopefully, the right context. I can memorize a lot of information without the background knowledge or experience to apply that knowledge in my life.

I recently went to the beautiful country of Ethiopia for the first time. Before leaving, I read up on the food, the history, and the culture of the country. I had the book knowledge. But when I arrived in Ethiopia, that knowledge was put into context. My understanding of the people and their lives was changed from facts and figures to personal appreciation for their situation.

Our immediate worldview can make it difficult for us to understand the eternal nature of God's law. We can study published works and worldly scholarship about the scriptures. But until we keep the law and observe it with our whole hearts, we will not have an eternal grasp of it. After we have learned and done His word, then the Lord will grant us His understanding of His word.

—Marianna

"Adam's obedience *preceded* his understanding and *prepared* him to receive the *sacred knowledge* that he was participating in a *sacred symbol* of the Atonement of Jesus Christ."

Tracy Y. Browning

"Seeking Answers to Spiritual Questions," Oct. 2024

Psalm 120:1

In my distress, I cried unto the Lord, and he heard me.

Running to the Rescue

I had known something was wrong for a few days, but I wasn't expecting this. What started out as a warm ache in my stomach had come and gone for three days. By Saturday morning, the ache had moved to my back as well. I thought I'd be okay, but suddenly, the pain intensified, piercing its way from my back through my stomach, as if someone was stabbing me from behind. It was searing and relentless. My husband was upstairs, unaware. I moved from the kitchen to the couch, determined to endure the pain alone, but it soon became unbearable.

Through sobs, I fixed my eyes on the stairs and managed to get out one word: "Jerey." Within seconds, my husband ran to my side. He didn't holler from above, asking what I needed. He didn't walk. He *ran* down the stairs to my side. "I need a blessing," I said, trying not to hyperventilate. Less than a minute later, his hands were on my head, and though I was still suffering, I believed in the promise I would be healed. And my husband stayed by my side until I was. (Turns out, kidney stones are no joke.)

I believe the Savior is completely attuned to us. He loves us. He knows our voice. He hears our cries, and He rushes to our rescue and stays by our side until healing comes.

—Michelle

> "The Atonement of Jesus Christ provides the ultimate rescue from the trials we face in this life."
>
> Quentin L. Cook
>
> "The Atonement of Jesus Christ Provides the Ultimate Rescue," Apr. 2025

Psalm 139:14

For I am fearfully and wonderfully made.

Don't Skip This One!

If you're like me, you woke up today with your head already spinning about all the things you need to get done and all the ways you wish you could do them better. We spend so much of our lives overwhelmed, stressed out, exhausted, anxious, afraid, lonely . . . you know the list. So today, let's pause. Come with me and stand in front of a mirror. Yes, even if your hair isn't done. Mine isn't either. Look yourself in the eyes, and then quote the verse at the top of the page. Out loud. Maybe say it three or four times until it sticks. Because it's true. We are His children, and we *are* fearfully and wonderfully made.

"Fearfully," not because we were made to be afraid, but because our creation is so miraculous that it inspires wonder and even awe-filled trembling.

"Wonderfully," because we are extraordinary, distinct, talented, and capable, created with intentional, unfathomable design.

The Mighty Creator of worlds without end took the time to ponder over and create *you*. So get out there and conquer the day like you believe it!

—Krista

"Thank you for being the kind of people you are and doing the things you do. May the blessings of heaven rest upon you. May your prayers be answered and your hopes and dreams become realities."

Gordon B. Hinckley

"To the Women of the Church," Oct. 2003

Proverbs 1:5

A wise man [or woman] will hear, and will increase learning.

Truly Hearing

In a marriage, you often meet unexpected challenges that require new skills. Your fifth baby has colic and cries 24/7 so no one can sleep, a new puppy decides your husband is the enemy, or you really don't agree on which house to buy—and I mean *really!* Each takes compromise, prayer and commitment. All those experiences paled in comparison to our most recent challenge—my husband's minor hearing loss. Even with hearing aids, when I make a random comment from the other room, expecting him to respond, he often can't hear me. If I talk louder, he can't understand me. It felt like I had lost my best friend. After talking to him, I realized that I was the one who couldn't hear what he needed. So I listened and learned.

Apparently, it takes time to distinguish background noise from someone's voice, especially if they speak without warning. I have to get up and get his attention before I say something. In the car I have to turn off the radio. When I do that, all is well.

I need to start using those skills when I pray. I can pause and draw closer to the Lord before I begin, then listen and learn.

—Christine

"President Russell M. Nelson has invited you to 'pour out your heart to your Heavenly Father. . . . And then listen!' Listen to what you feel in your heart and to thoughts that come to your mind."

Susan H. Porter

"Pray, He Is There," Apr. 2024

Proverbs 3:5–6

Trust in the Lord with all thine heart; and lean not unto thine own understanding In all thy ways acknowledge him, and he shall direct thy paths.

The Old Country Road

One day, I was driving uphill on a straight part of a two-lane country road. Beyond the crest, I could see the road stretching straight ahead. You can imagine my surprise, then, when I reached the top of the hill and realized I had been wrong. Though it had appeared to be one long road, they were, in fact, two different roads. Driving downhill, the road I was on veered to the left and continued in a completely different direction than the rest of the road I had seen from above.

This is so representative of life. We can be moving in one direction, believing we can see the outcome ahead, only to realize the path that God has us on is leading us in a completely different direction. As we trust Him, I know He can take us to where we need to be—even if we can't see it from where we are right now.

–Michelle

"The ultimate test of our discipleship is found in our willingness to give up and lose our old self and submit our heart and our whole soul to God so that His will becomes ours. . . . I testify to you that following the Lord's will in our life will enable us to find the most precious pearl in the world—the kingdom of heaven."

Ulisses S. Soares

"Aligning Our Will with His," Oct. 2024

Proverbs 6:20–22

My son, keep thy father's commandment, and forsake not the law of thy mother. Bind them continually upon thine heart, and tie them about thy neck. When thou goest, it shall lead thee; when thou sleepest, it shall keep thee, and when thou awakes, it shall talk with thee.

The Heritage of Righteous Parents

I was blessed with righteous parents who brought me up in the ways of the Lord. Both of my parents have been gone for many years now, but I still hear them in my thoughts. Their teachings guide my actions.

When I am discussing plans for a family reunion, I remember how my parents always had a spiritual theme with branded T-shirts. When I am reading scriptures with my grandchildren, I remember my mother doing scripture chases with my children. When I make a quilt for a new member of the family, I remember how my mother kissed the corner of a baby blanket with her red lipstick so that the baby would know she was always loved.

I know that not everyone has this kind of heritage, but each of us can be the start of a righteous family heritage for the next generation. We can become the ones who teach the law to our children and grandchildren so that they will have the word of the Lord continually in their hearts.

—Marianna

> "Help your children build faith in Jesus Christ, love His gospel and His Church, and prepare for a lifetime of righteous choices."
>
> Dieter F. Uchtdorf
>
> "Jesus Christ is the Strength of Parents," Apr. 2023

Proverbs 13:20

He that walketh with wise men shall be wise.

Wise Friends

During a particularly difficult time in my life, I allowed my thoughts to lean toward the negative. I was pretty hard on myself, to the point where I wasn't sure if I was doing anyone any good by being here. It was a brief moment, but a strong one. Thankfully, I had a good friend who saw what was happening and pulled me out of it. She was wise, and in a very non-dramatic way, she helped me redirect my thinking and my self-love. I will forever be grateful for her.

We are here to choose. Choose good, righteousness, opportunities, and joy. We also have the gift to choose (most of) the people in our lives. It's true, some people are given to us in our family, and others we must learn to work with out of necessity. But, we have a fantastic opportunity to surround ourselves with people who are wise—who see God's truth, light, and love, friends who can help us be wise ourselves.

Find people who will see you as God does, who love Him and will love you. People who will help you be wise. Then, be that friend to others.

–Michelle

"Find your strength in numbers. Find good friends. Be good friends. Support one another wherever you are. Stand with holy people."

Gary E. Stevenson

"Promptings of the Spirit," Oct. 2023

Proverbs 15:1

A soft answer turneth away wrath: but grievous words stir up anger.

Mothering Autism

By the time Noah was eighteen months old, my entire parenting playbook had been thrown out the window. Sticker charts, time-outs, and "the mom look" had worked well enough for my older children, but Noah's autism played by different rules. Every attempt to assert authority was met with opposition. If I raised my voice, Noah raised his louder. If I reacted in anger, Noah responded with wrath. And threats of punishment were met with threats of his own. Raising Noah required humbly abandoning old, failing methods and opening my heart to mothering in new, better ways.

Through the help of therapists, family and friends, countless prayers, and promptings from God, I learned to diffuse arguments, ease tension, calmly enforce rules, and help Noah express his feelings. It's taken years of tedious uphill work, but the effort of turning away wrath from our home has been a blessing. If you could meet eighteen-year-old Noah today, you'd agree he is a walking miracle: gentle, service-centered, and generous. In learning to soften my answers, I helped Noah soften his heart—and together, we found peace.

—Krista

"Anger never persuades. Hostility builds no one. Contention never leads to inspired solutions. . . In situations that are highly charged and filled with contention, I invite you to remember Jesus Christ. Pray to have the courage and wisdom to say or do what He would."

Russell M. Nelson

"Peacemakers Needed," Oct. 2023

Proverbs 23:7

As [a man] thinketh in his heart, so is he.

Why?

I had a clever two-year-old who discovered the word *why*. Every time I'd ask him to do something, he would ask, "Why?"

"It's time for bed."

"Why?"

"We've got to go to church."

"Why?"

"Red is my favorite color."

"Why?"

At first, I answered truthfully, wanting it to be a learning experience. But when the color question came up, I turned to him and asked, "Why do you want to know?"

He paused and said, "Because I like hearing you talk."

As adults, too often, we run around doing what we are asked to do. We build our daily routine, go to church, maybe even choose our favorites. Do we ask ourselves why? Do we even know what we are thinking in our hearts?

As we ponder on our motivations and let the Lord guide our choices, we can more intentionally act and become like Him.

—Christine

"I promise that as you ponder . . . the windows of heaven will open, and you will receive answers to your own questions and direction for your own life."

Mark L. Pace

"It Is Wisdom in the Lord That We Should Have the Book of Mormon," Apr. 2024

Proverbs 31:10–12, 30

Who can find a virtuous woman? For her price is far above rubies. The heart of her husband doth safely trust in her, so that he shall have no need of spoil. She will do him good and not evil all the days of her life. Favour is deceitful, and beauty is vain.

The Price of Rubies

The rare Burma rubies are the most expensive gemstones in the world. They are valued at over a million dollars per carat—much more than a diamond. These precious gems come in smaller stones and are flawless in color and clarity. There are other rubies that are not as perfect but are still beautiful and sought after. Some rubies may have a tiny speck in the middle of the stone or are cloudy in color, rather than a clear red. But these stones are still worth a lot—between $1,400 and $12,000 per carat.

The bottom line is that rubies have great worth, but not as much worth as good women have in the eyes of God. The twenty-verse description of this perfect woman can be a daunting standard to live up to! I do not make all my own clothes. I do overspend on household items sometimes. I do lose my temper occasionally.

I am not the flawless million-dollar woman described in Proverbs 31. I have flaws and am a little cloudy sometimes, but I am still worth a lot. Through the blood of the Atonement, I can become the perfect ruby I want to become.

—Marianna

> "No greater recognition can come to you in this world than to be known as a woman of God."
>
> Spencer W. Kimball
>
> "The Role of Righteous Women," Oct. 1979

Ecclesiastes 1:14 (ESV)

I have seen everything that is done under the sun, and behold, all is vanity and a striving after wind.

Can't Catch Me

When I was young, I loved playing tag. I was fast and agile. I could dodge the best of them. Except when my older brother played. I could never catch him. Not only was he fast, but he was smart and elusive. But I was determined. I wouldn't be happy until I tagged him. I let the pursuit of him rob me from having fun with others and invited anger, frustration, and a feeling of failure.

Solomon, one of the wisest men to live, called life's pleasures and pursuits "vanity"—like chasing the wind. How often do we chase success, comfort, and recognition, thinking once we get them, we will be happy?

True meaning isn't found in the things we build or buy. We won't get it if we paint our house the perfect color, get that promotion, or reach a certain number of followers on social media. We won't find it in the things that can evade us.

But we will find it in our relationship with God, when we focus on eternal things. Ask yourself today: Am I chasing wind, or walking with the One who gives life meaning?

—Michelle

"Worldly happiness, by contrast, does not last. It cannot. It is the nature of all earthly things to grow old, decay, wear out, or become stale. But godly joy is eternal, because God is eternal."

Dieter F. Uchtdorf

"A Higher Joy," Apr. 2024

Ecclesiastes 3:1–2

To every thing there is a season, and a time to every purpose under the heaven: A time to be born, and a time to die.

My Season to Live

I love pumpkins. And roller coasters and vintage children's books. Sushi is my favorite food, and being a grandma is even better than I expected. I make really good pie crust, and my dream is to go mudlarking on the foreshore of the Thames.

Eighteen years have passed since my daughter's death. I used to wish time would go faster, or that Jesus would come so I wouldn't have to live so long without my girl. But the Lord recently reminded me we only get one turn on this earth. Elora's turn was so short, she never got to ride on a roller coaster, or eat sushi, or learn how to bake a pie. And I know the Lord has promised that all we have lost will be made up to us, but how can I wish away days she never got to have?

This is the season the Lord has given me to live! To ride the rides, read the books, eat the foods, dance, sing, and wander. To dream, love, work, serve, and grow as old as God has designed. When I see Elora face to face, I will tell her about all the things, and she will know that I lived for both of us.

—Krista

> "Do you take time to discover each day how beautiful your life can be? You are one of the noblest of God's creations. His intent is that your life be gloriously beautiful regardless of your circumstances."
>
> Richard G. Scott
>
> "Finding Joy in Life," Apr. 1996

Ecclesiastes 4:5–6

The fool foldeth [her] hands together, and eateth [her] own flesh. Better is an handful of quietness, than both the hands full with travail and vexation of spirit.

Open Your Hands

I had a friend who planned her days so tightly that if you called her to do something, she would go to her calendar and say, "I'm doing laundry that afternoon." The idea of rescheduling something that wasn't time sensitive was more than she could handle. (Or maybe she was trying to avoid us.) Often, and I know because I've done it, when our life feels out of control, we seize onto the things we can control so tightly that we isolate ourselves and make matters worse, feeding our anxiety.

Some may have mental disorders that need professional help, but everyone feels the stress of the world we live in. At times, we may not deal with it in healthy ways. That's what we are being warned about in Ecclesiastes. If we fold our hands and worry, we aren't available to accept what may be the solution.

The gift of the gospel is peace. And the first principle of the gospel is faith in Jesus Christ. Before we feel too worried to accept an invitation from a friend, a calling, or even having another baby, we need to unfold our hands and open them to Him. If we feel so inspired, then even if it seems impossible, we say yes and expect miracles to follow. Say yes!

—Christine

"You can come to Christ with confidence in His loving-kindness and receive all his gifts . . . with your head held high, your arms outstretched, and your hands open."

Patrick Kearon

"Receive His Gift," Apr. 2025

Ecclesiastes 9:11

I returned, and saw under the sun, that the race is not to the swift, nor the battle to the strong, neither yet bread to the wise, nor yet riches to men of understanding, nor yet favour to men of skill; but time and chance happeneth to them all.

Time and Chance Happen to Us All

The race isn't always won by the swiftest runner. Extenuating circumstances may affect their performance. The battle is not always won by the strongest army. History teaches us that battles can be won because of weird weather or false information given to a commander. Smart and wise men are not always rich. In fact, the smartest and wisest people may be the poorest.

Time and chance happen to us all during this mortal life, whether we are righteous or evil. Life just happens, and it is not always fair. But life is not meant to be fair. Even the righteous get hit by a drunk driver, even the righteous lose money in the stock market, even the righteous can't make their mortgage payments, and even the righteous get old and die. The unfairness of life should not change our faith in the Lord, Jesus Christ. Instead, we have hope in the mercy and justice of the final judgment, rather than the happenstance of this mortal life.

Life may not always be fair, but God is always good, and He will help us in all our times of trouble and struggle.

—Marianna

> "Faith is a choice. Strengthen your faith and live to be deserving of the Savior's approving words: 'Great is thy faith.'"
>
> Neil L. Andersen
>
> "Faith Is Not by Chance, but by Choice," Oct. 2015

Ecclesiastes 12:7

Then shall the dust return to the earth as it was: and the spirit shall return unto God who gave it.

Three Small Goodbyes, One Big Hello

My mom died in July 2020. She'd been sick for a while, so it wasn't a complete surprise. When we thought it was the end, I hopped on a plane in the morning from Seattle and was by her side in Sacramento that night saying goodbye.

However, she seemed to rally some strength during the night and woke up the next day. By that night, she was failing again. And so, I stood by her bedside in the hospital and said goodbye once more. No one prepares you for one, let alone two, goodbyes. Then, in her Patti-style, she made another comeback. I found myself at the hospital again the next day. It was 2 a.m. We were both tired. This time, I could tell there was no coming back. She really was leaving. And I said goodbye for the third and last time.

A week later, I had finished dressing Mom in her temple clothes for her burial. As I walked out of the room, I turned one last time to see her. To say the fourth goodbye. But before I could, I heard her voice, sparkling with joy, say, "I'm not in there." I knew, in that moment, that Mom was alive and happy. I'd said goodbye to her three times, but she was experiencing a joyful hello in heaven. And I smiled.

—Michelle

"To return to God through the gateway we call death is a joy for those who love Him and are prepared to meet Him."

Russell M. Nelson

"Thanks be to God," Apr. 2012

Song of Solomon 1:1

The song of songs, which is Solomon's.

The Elephant in the Room

The Song of Solomon is a perplexing little book; a collection of passionate poetry without direct references to God, covenant, or salvation. It feels . . . out of place. During his translation of the Bible, Joseph Smith made only one note about this book: "The Songs of Solomon are not inspired writings" (see Song of Solomon footnotes). This raises honest and possibly uncomfortable questions: What do we do with scripture that may not be inspired? When Church history disappoints us? When a beloved leader says something that doesn't sit right? When policies change? When mistakes are made?

Here is a profound truth: God works with imperfect people. The ongoing Restoration includes both divine revelation and human limitation. Our church experience may include things that aren't equally inspired—traditions that linger past their usefulness, cultural blind spots, human errors. But if there's room in God's plan for a book of poetry mistakenly included in sacred canon, then there's room in His plan for our questions, wrestling, doubts, learning, and even our missteps. The gospel of Jesus Christ is big enough for imperfection. Let's be patient with our scriptures, our history, our leaders, and ourselves. Because the Lord is.

—Krista

> "Be kind regarding human frailty. . . . Except in the case of His only perfect Begotten Son, imperfect people are all God has ever had to work with. That must be terribly frustrating to Him, but He deals with it. So should we."
>
> Jeffrey R. Holland
>
> "Lord, I Believe," Apr. 2013

Isaiah 1:17

Learn to do well; seek judgment, relieve the oppressed, judge the fatherless, plead for the widow.

Becoming Mud in His Hands

Clay is fun to play with. There is something satisfying in taking a shapeless mound and molding it into a beautiful object. Even little children can roll clay into thin strings to make a snake or into balls to make a snowman.

The Savior wants to mold us into exalted, perfect people—like He is. If the Lord is our Potter and we are His clay, then we can become the workmanship of His hands: "But now, O Lord, thou art our father; we are the clay, and thou our potter; and we all are the work of thy hand" (Isaiah 64:8).

Elder Heber C. Kimball, a potter by trade, often used the analogy of the potter and the clay to teach the Saints the importance of obedience and allowing the Master Potter to shape and form us: "Now suppose I subject myself enough, in the hands of the potter, to be shaped according as he was dictated by the Great Master potter, that rules over all things in heaven and on earth, He would make me into a vessel of honor" (Heber C. Kimball, "The Potter and the Clay," *Ensign*, January 2011). As His vessel, we are molded in His image and accomplish His purposes by relieving the oppressed, supporting the fatherless, and pleading for the widow—that is what the Potter would do!

—Marianna

> "Like the clay on the potter's wheel, we must be centered as well. Our core, the center of our lives, must be Jesus Christ and His gospel."
>
> Richard J. Maynes
>
> "The Joy of Living a Christ-Centered Life," Oct. 2015

Isaiah 2:2

And it shall come to pass in the last days, that the mountain of the Lord's house shall be established in the top of the mountains. . . . And all nations shall flow unto it.

Code Words

The scriptures have certain code words that carry consistent meanings. For instance, lambs usually refer to Jesus Christ. Lions are the tribe of Judah. So when we sing "How Blessed the Day when the Lamb and the Lion shall lie down together," many people think it means lions eat lambs but in the Millennium they won't, which is true. But understanding those code words, it also means the lion or the Jews will accept the Lamb or Christ, and that's awesome!

When I was showing my son the scripture about the house of the Lord being established in the mountains, he nodded and said, "Yeah, it's just saying the Church is in Utah." Mountains are where the early prophets talked to God. Abraham, Moses, Elijah, and Ezekiel all communed with God in the mountains. Even Christ had some of His most sacred experiences on the Mount of Transfiguration and the Mount of Olives. Mountains are about revelation and are code for the temple.

And if you look, the above scripture says the temples will be established in the mountain*s*. As in more than one. Since the time of Moses, there has only been one temple on the earth. Now they are in all nations on many mountains so all nations can flow unto them. It is the last days!

—Christine

> "Increased time in the temple will help us prepare for the Second Coming of our Saviour, Jesus Christ."
>
> Russell M. Nelson
>
> "Confidence in the Presence of God," Apr. 2025

Isaiah 4:6

And there shall be a tabernacle for a shadow in the daytime from the heat, and for a place of refuge, and for a covert from storm and from rain.

Repetition

I love the words of Isaiah. I have to admit that wasn't always the case. In reading the Book of Mormon, I realized that the Lord's command about Isaiah was not only for the Nephites, but for me as well: "Yea a commandment I give unto you that ye search these things diligently; for great are the words of Isaiah" (3 Nephi 23:3). So, I began to study Isaiah. My favorite book about Isaiah is one where the author took the words of Isaiah and wrote them as poetry. Most of the book of Isaiah is poetry, except for the middle story of King Hezekiah and the salvation of the Kingdom of Judah. Isaiah often wrote in couplets, where two phrases say the same thing but in different ways. Isaiah used repetition to strengthen his points. By looking for the repetition of ideas and parallel structures, you will find the balance of meaning within a verse, a chapter, or the whole book.

In Isaiah chapter 4, Isaiah gives the righteous a glorious vision of the Millennial Day. The temple or tabernacle will become a protective place—a covering from the heat of the day and a refuge from the storm. The repeated symbol of the temple as a refuge, a covert, and a shadow from the world emphasizes the power of the temple to protect us in these latter days.

–Marianna

> "Repetition ingrains gospel principles in our minds and hearts.'"
>
> Susan W. Tanner
>
> "Glad Tidings from Cumorah," Apr. 2005

Isaiah 6:8

Also I heard the voice of the Lord, saying, Whom shall I send and who will go for us? Then said I, Here am I; send me.

I Accept

It was July 2022. I was sitting in my bishop's office, tears streaming down my face, as I confessed to being overwhelmed by life and my calling. My good bishop listened to me, then said something I wasn't expecting: "I'm going to be calling a new Relief Society president in September. Your name is the only one that's been given to me. But I want you to have time to counsel with your husband, to pray about it, and see if this is something you feel you want to do."

I was shocked. I had just served as Relief Society president in that ward eight years ago. And did he not hear that I was a failure and overwhelmed? I took a beat and a breath. This sweet bishop was giving me six weeks to decide if it would work for me. But, sitting in his office that day, I knew that call was coming from the Lord. I didn't need more time. "I accept," I said, my way of saying to the Lord, "Here am I. Send me."

There is a great work to be done, my friends. Despite our doubts or worries, if we are willing, He will do amazing things in and through us. Let Him send you today.

—Michelle

> "As baptized members of the Church, we are under covenant to care for those in need. Our individual efforts don't necessarily require money or faraway locations; they do require the guidance of the Holy Spirit and a willing heart to say to the Lord, 'Here am I; send me.'"
>
> Sharon Eubank
>
> "I'll Pray He Sees Us," Oct. 2021

Isaiah 9:6

For unto us a child is born, . . . and his name shall be called Wonderful, Counsellor, The mighty God, The everlasting Father, The Prince of Peace.

A Name for Every Need

At an event with a large group of women, we played a brilliant icebreaker that helped us connect quickly and meaningfully. Each of us took a turn explaining our name—what it means, or why our parents chose it. The stories were filled with history, culture, and tradition. Some were moving, others hilarious or unexpected, but all were unforgettable. By the end, we weren't just a room full of strangers—we were friends whose names carried stories. So, it was easy to remember each other.

Names matter. They're part of our identity, reminding us who we are and where we come from. The scriptures use hundreds of names for Christ. Each has a story, purpose, and meaning that teaches us about who He is and the very personal role He plays in our salvation. Do you have a favorite? One of mine is *High Priest of Good Things to Come.* This name reminds me that when I face trials or struggles, Jesus can always see bright days on my horizon. If I keep my hand in His, He will lead me there. Say His name. Call out to Him in pleading and thanksgiving. He will hear and answer.

—Krista

"Concerning Jesus's many names, President Nelson said, 'Study everything Jesus Christ is by prayerfully and vigorously seeking to understand what each of His various titles and names means *personally* for you.'"

Jonathan S. Schmitt

"That They Might Know Thee," Oct. 2022

Isaiah 11:8–9

And the weaned child shall put his hand on the cockatrice' den. They shall not hurt nor destroy in all my holy mountain.

Beware the Cockatrice for Now

It irks me when people try to flatten the brilliance of scripture. Take, for example, the cockatrice, a mythical creature that is half rooster and half serpent who can turn you to stone with one glance. Some say the cockatrice is a mistranslation of the "flying serpent" from the day of Moses, maybe a cobra. Although in the Book of Mormon a number of changes were made to Isaiah, the cockatrice is still there. Also, in Isaiah 59:5–7, he speaks of the cockatrice in our day: "They hatch cockatrice eggs, and weave the spider's web. . . . Their webs shall not become garments. . . . Their feet run to evil."

To me the cockatrice is mythical content, fantasy in all its digital and written forms. In our day, it especially captures boys from eight to teens (and older). It turns them to stone at their glance. Although much of it is inane, some is deadly poison. I read *Game of Thrones*, and it was fun and brilliant. When I watched it on HBO, it was a great story mixed with porn. A true cockatrice.

It makes me smile that in the Millennium there will still be art and creativity, but it won't be a gateway to smut and addiction. For now I can admire brilliant, colorful roosters but run (or put on parental filters) if I see they have a scaled tail.

—Christine

"He will respond to our sincere prayers through the Holy Ghost as we seek to understand truths we do not yet fully appreciate."

David P. Homer

"Trusting Our Father," Oct. 2024

Isaiah 13:1, 5

The burden of Babylon, which Isaiah the son of Amoz did see. They come from a far country, from the end of heaven, even the Lord, and the weapons of his indignation, to destroy the whole land.

A Time Warp

Science fiction novels and movies explain time travel as a product of manipulating the space-time continuum. Characters like Marty McFly in *Back to the Future* or Spock in *Star Trek* experience the interconnectedness of the past and future events. The Lord's prophets experience time differently.

Isaiah obviously saw different times in the future history of the world and often referenced both of them in the same verse or phrase, contrasting their similarities and differences. In Isaiah 13, Isaiah describes "the burden of Babylon" or the Babylonian captivity which is shortly to come upon errant Israel. The description of this event is also a warning about the destruction that Isaiah saw before the Second Coming. Both are times of wrath and vengeance against those who forget the Lord and fight against Him. Isaiah told Israel: "Behold, the day of the Lord cometh, cruel both with wrath and fierce anger, to lay the land desolate: and he shall destroy the sinners thereof out of it" (Isaiah 13:9). Is this verse referencing the Babylonian destruction or the Day of Judgment? Isaiah views the history of man through spiritual principles and helps us see the similarities between two events. One of these events has already occurred. We look forward to the other one and understand it better through the words of Isaiah.

—Marianna

"More than ever before, we are required to confront the reality that we are getting ever closer to the Second Coming of Jesus Christ."

Christoffel Golden

"Preparing for the Second Coming," Oct. 2021

Isaiah 18:3

All ye inhabitants of the world, and dwellers on the earth, see ye, when he lifteth up an ensign on the mountains; and when he bloweth a trumpet, hear ye.

Listen to Me

Recently, my husband and I took our children, spouses, and grandchildren out to dinner. We enjoyed the low chatter with those who were sitting near us. Then, suddenly, my granddaughter, Claire, who was three years old yelled, "Hey, everybody. Listen to me. Listen to my favorite song." Without hesitation, she proceeded to sing the entire primary song "Gethsemane" at the top of her lungs. *Gethsemane. Jesus loves me!* In that moment, this sweet little girl with no fear was commanding the attention of not only us, but everyone sitting near us.

I *love* living in these latter days when we have the fulness of the gospel on Earth! And I love that the Lord is using so many different means—technology, social media, members, missionaries, education, welfare programs, charity, and more—to get the attention of the world so they can hear Him say, "Hey, everybody. Listen to Me. Listen to my Son." The entire world is getting the chance to learn of and become connected to Jesus Christ, and we get to be a part of it. It is extraordinary, indeed!

—Michelle

"Our days are so extraordinary that they were even shown in a vision to the prophet Isaiah; he too saw and prophesied of this day of the Restoration of the Church of Jesus Christ and of its purpose."

Benjamín De Hoyos

"That Our Light May Be a Standard for the Nations," Apr. 2017

Isaiah 19:22

And the Lord shall smite Egypt: he shall smite and heal it.

Speeding Ticket

"Didn't you see my lights? I've been following you for two miles." The police officer was kind but obviously frustrated.

"I'm so sorry," I said, embarrassed. "My kids were crying, and I had the rearview mirror tipped down so I could sing to them." He shook his head and took my license back to his patrol car.

It was my first solo road trip with three young kids, and after multiple bathroom emergencies and throw-up in a car seat, we were hours behind schedule. The kids were cranky, and I was exhausted. For the last hour of driving, I'd been running a continuous prayer through my mind: "Heavenly Father, please keep us safe, please protect us, please help us get there . . . "

The officer returned with a speeding ticket. As he drove away, I cried, "Heavenly Father, where are you?! You were supposed to protect us!"

There was no mistaking His immediate, direct reply: "How can I protect you if you don't obey the law?" In my desperation to arrive at my destination, I had failed to obey the speed limit. That was on me, not God. Being "smitten" with a ticket had brought me low, but I was healed as I worked to repent of my misplaced frustration toward Him, and lifted as He taught me valuable eternal principles.

—Krista

> "Then what is humility? According to *Preach My Gospel*, it is a 'willingness to submit to the will of the Lord. . . . It is being teachable. . . . [It] is a vital catalyst for spiritual growth.'"
>
> Joni L. Koch
>
> "Humble to Accept and Follow," Oct. 2023

Isaiah 22:23

And I will fasten him as a nail in a sure place; and he shall be for a glorious throne to his father's house.

The Nail in the Sure Place

When I hear the phrase "the nail in the sure place," I cringe a little, thinking of the Savior on the cross and His pain. Nails were driven in the palms of the hands but also in the wrists to hold the weight of His body. It was horrible.

In Isaiah 22, that nail is given a different meaning. Isaiah tells of a new servant in the king's house that is given the key to David's house. His name is Eliakim, meaning "God shall cause to arise" (see Isaiah 22:20). He is like a nail with a lot of responsibilities hanging on Him. That nail will be cut down "and the burden that was upon it shall be cut off." This means that through the Atonement, our burdens will be taken away. They will simply be gone.

Jesus really does take on our burdens. When we have lifted the heavy burden of sin, guilt, or grief off our shoulders through faith and repentance, we can place them on the Sure Nail of His Atonement. In time, we will feel the effects of those burdens lifted. The echo of our trials is healed. So, the Nail in the Sure Place is not a sign of pain, but of consistency. It will always be there, able to take on any burden no matter how big. See, the Nail in the Sure place is JOY!

—Christine

> "Christ is the Nail in a Sure Place—never failing, never faltering, ever the most certain and reliable force in eternity."
>
> Jeffrey R. Holland
>
> *Witness for His Names*, Deseret Book, 2020

Isaiah 25:9

And it shall be said in that day, Lo, this is our God; we have waited for him, and he will save us: this is the Lord; we have waited for him, we will be glad and rejoice in his salvation.

Waiting for Good Things to Come

Sometimes, I have to wait a long time before good things come into my life. It took me and Steve ten years to finally have the money to buy a new car. We had been driving a twenty-year-old Oldsmobile Belvedere. It drove more like a tank than a car. Finally, we were able to afford a maroon Honda Civic with a manual transmission. We thought it was the swankiest car we'd ever driven.

We felt so blessed that we gave a prayer of gratitude. We told the Lord that we would use this car to serve Him. Immediately, Steve was called as bishop.

The Lord wants His people to enter into His rest—His fulness of glory. To do that, we must patiently wait for Him to let us in. While we wait, we can wisely use our time to prepare to be worthy of His glory. Serving others is the best thing we can do while we wait and prepare for His coming.

—Marianna

"For every infirm man healed instantly as he waits to enter the Pool of Bethesda, someone else will spend 40 years in the desert waiting to enter the promised land. . . . The path to holiness and happiness here and hereafter is a long and sometimes rocky one. It takes time and tenacity to walk it."

Jeffrey R. Holland

"Waiting on the Lord," Oct. 2020

Isaiah 28:10

For precept must be upon precept, precept upon precept; line upon line, line upon line; here a little, and there a little.

Trust the Crease

I love the paper art of origami. Through a series of creases and folds, you can create amazing things. More times than not, you fold your paper over just so, then move on to the next step. But occasionally, you're instructed to fold the paper, sharpen the crease, then unfold it again. At first, it seems like a useless crease, a wasted effort. But sometime later in the creation, you're instructed to tent or fold the paper in a way that could only be done because of the existing crease. In origami, some creases are for now, and others are for later. But all are needed to create the finished design.

So often, things happen in our lives that don't seem to make sense. We receive and follow an impression that appears to make no difference. It seems like wasted effort. But, when we follow God, there is no wasted effort. Every time we follow Him, we are creating creases that help make us who He knows we can be. Line up line, crease upon crease, He is creating something wonderful in us. Trust the crease. Trust God. It will all make sense someday.

—Michelle

"Even as we trust God's prior answers, we need to be open to further personal revelation. After all, few of life's destinations are reached via a nonstop flight. We should recognize that personal revelation may be received 'line upon line' and 'precept upon precept,' that revealed direction can be and frequently is incremental."

Dale G. Renlund

"A Framework for Personal Revelation," Oct. 2022

Isaiah 29:14

I will proceed to do a marvellous work among this people, even a marvellous work and a wonder.

Grandpa's Two Baptisms

When my Grandpa LaMar was almost eight, his mother asked him to ride into town to mail a letter. LaMar rode Bess across the river and down a road on the opposite bank. He soon met a vagabond man who stopped the horse and asked, "Young man, have you been baptized?" LaMar's baptism was scheduled for after his birthday, so he answered, "Not yet!" The man picked up an old tin can, scooped water from the river, and poured it over LaMar's bare foot. "There," the man said proudly, "now you have been."

LaMar was spooked. Had he just been baptized into the wrong church? Would God be mad? He forgot about the letter, turned Bess around, and rode hard all the way home. He told his mother what had happened. She reassured him that all was well because the restored gospel includes proper priesthood authority to baptize, and that man didn't have it. LaMar's first baptism didn't count. Only weeks later, LaMar had his second baptism, performed by his priesthood-bearing father, in the river only feet away from the spot of his first, tin can baptism. But this time, LaMar knew in his heart that this one was right.

—Krista

> "We also testify that the restored Church of Jesus Christ has been established to teach the fulness of His doctrine and to officiate with His priesthood authority to perform the ordinances necessary to enter the kingdom of God."
>
> Dallin H. Oaks
>
> "The Need for a Church," Oct. 2021

Isaiah 32:9

Rise up, ye women that are at ease; hear my voice, ye careless daughters; give ear unto my speech.

The Women's Movement

For me, the Women's Movement began in 1979. I was shocked when Camilla Kimball stood up in general conference. Her prophet husband was in the hospital and asked her to read his talk. Had this ever happened before? I was on the edge of my seat. As a freshman at BYU, I was thrilled by each word. She said that women would be the ones to bring "major growth" to the church to the degree they "are seen as distinct and different—in happy ways—from the women of the world" (Spencer W. Kimball, The Role of Righteous Women, Oct. 1979).

Describing our day, Isaiah is much less flattering. He warns the women of the Church to not be "at ease" or "careless daughters." He even tells us to "tremble" and "be troubled." Like Isaiah, I have been bothered by the *Secret Lives of Mormon Wives* type of women who try to push every boundary and don't have their hearts centered on Christ. Yet, I also stand in awe of the righteous mothers struggling to make ends meet, the women in the workforce who stand up for what is right even when it may harm their careers, the young women who hold strong against the attitudes of their peers in defending truth. Let's be the different and distinct ones!

—Christine

"You are the women he foresaw! Your virtue, light, love, knowledge, courage, character, faith, and righteous lives will draw good women of the world, along with their families, to the Church in unprecedented numbers!"

Russell M. Nelson

"You Are the Women He Foresaw," Apr. 2022

Isaiah 33:16

He shall dwell on high: his place of defense shall be the munitions of rocks: bread shall be given him; his waters shall be sure.

Rock, Bread, and Water

During my grandson's visit, I decided to take him on an easy hike in the foothills near my home. I had a destination in mind, but Weston wanted to look at the rocks. He inspected every stone and pebble along the way. After an hour of rock hunting, I brought out our treat—some water and homemade bread.

Rocks, bread, and water are symbols that all point us to Christ. These symbols are a part of everyone's life. Rocks are foundational for building and are also used as defensive weapons in a battle. Bread and water are the basics for nourishment that sustains us physically.

The Savior is our rock, our foundation. He will also be our defense when we battle against Satan. The bread and the water of the sacrament symbolize the Savior's flesh and blood. This bread and water spiritually sustain and nourish us. These are symbols we can teach to our children when we see rocks and eat bread and water.

—Marianna

"The gift of His Atonement is symbolically offered to us each week when a priesthood holder, representing the Savior Himself, offers us the bread and water. As we perform the action of eating and drinking the emblems of His flesh and blood, Christ symbolically becomes a part of us."

J. Anette Dennis

"Put Ye On the Lord Jesus Christ," Apr. 2024

Isaiah 36:4

What confidence is this wherein thou trustest?

Trust Him

When I was newly married, I worked as a receptionist at a computer software company. One of the software engineers was very analytical and very atheist. We genuinely liked each other and respected each other's beliefs. For nearly a year, we would chat about life and things. I'd often ask him through a smile, "Do you believe in God yet?" He'd always smile as he said no. On my last day of work, I asked him that same question: "So, do you believe in God yet?" He smiled, then said something I wasn't expecting and have never forgotten. "I don't know if I do, but I know you, and if you believe in God, then He must be real."

In all the times I talked about God, my coworker never once received a confirmation He was real. But, it was my confidence and belief in God that changed his mind. He knew me. And he knew who I trusted. And that, to him, was enough.

Do you believe in God? Do you love Him? Do you have confidence in Him? If not, ask Him to help you. And if you do, share your belief, love, and confidence with someone today. Who knows, it might be exactly what they need to believe.

—Michelle

> "We can always trust God."
>
> Gerrit W. Gong
>
> "Trust Again," Oct. 2021

Isaiah 38:5, 7

I have heard thy prayer, I have seen thy tears: behold, I will add unto thy days fifteen years. . . . And this shall be a sign unto thee from the Lord.

Alternate Miracles

Sometimes the Lord provides the healing or blessings we plead for; sometimes He doesn't. But I can look back and see evidence—signs—that He *always* hears me.

The most difficult "no" I've received from Him was the death of my daughter. I prayed for a miracle of healing with every portion of my soul and faith, but it did not come . . . at least not in the way I'd hoped. It's easy to think that because my daughter died, I didn't receive a miracle that day, but I've discovered that He never leaves us without a miracle. The healing may not have come for my daughter, but it *has* come for me. He has given me the miracles of friends and family who carried me through my darkest days, and deepened compassion for those who mourn. My relationship with Him has deepened, and I trust Him in ways I never did before.

I can see countless alternate miracles the Lord has given me, signs that He is there and loves me. I would never have chosen to lose my daughter, but the things I've learned and the person I've become along this journey are precious beyond measure. What signs has the Lord given you of His care and miracles?

—Krista

"As we follow Jesus Christ, God bears witness to us 'with signs and wonders, and with divers miracles, and gifts of the Holy Ghost, according to his own will.'"

Gérald Caussé

"Is It Still Wonderful to You?" Oct. 2015

Isaiah 40:9

[Lift] up thy voice with strength. . . . Be not afraid; say unto the cities of Judah, Behold your God!

Behold Your God!

My father had a scowl on his face whenever he was in deep thought. As a result, at church he'd often sit on the stand, scowling. When he was called as bishop, a number of young women were afraid of him. I told them they didn't know him. My father (I called him Daddy) was so kind and generous. He thought the best of people and would give them anything. He also was a fount of answers, not only to gospel questions but also to coping techniques and fresh ideas. He loved everyone.

Sometimes I worry that many people don't really know the Lord. They think He is mean and scary, like my friends did of my father. Or worse, they think He is overly permissive and is pleased by any choice you make. Because He loves us, it pains Him when we walk in crooked paths.

Just as I did years ago, we need to tell others about who Christ really is. We need to lift up our voices "with strength" and say, "Behold your God!" Then, we need to share about His kindness to us, His wisdom, His light in our lives, and even His correction when we've strayed, so others understand and better recognize His hand in their lives.

May we open our mouths.

—Christine

> "Our opportunity is to love, share, and invite in such a way that those we love can feel the love of God."
>
> Benjamin M. Z Tai
>
> "The Love of God," Apr. 2025

Isaiah 40:11

He shall feed his flock like a shepherd; he shall gather his lambs with his arm, and carry them in his bosom.

Bummer Lambs

Every once in a while, a mother sheep will reject her baby. There can be many reasons, but once the ewe has made up her mind, she will not change it. These lambs are known as "bummer lambs" and are said to often die of heartbreak, even before they pass from lack of food or warmth.

This is when the shepherd has to intervene. He will take the rejected lamb into his own home. He will hand-feed the little one, warm it by the fire, and hold it close to his own heart so that it can feel his heartbeat. Once the lamb is strong enough, it can be returned to the flock, but it will never forget.

As these sheep grow to maturity, they are the first to come when the shepherd calls. Perhaps it is because they feel most deeply loved of all the sheep. In truth, the shepherd loves all his sheep equally, but the bummer lambs were given the gift of seeing that love more clearly.

For those who have felt rejected, broken, or forgotten, Christ will gather His lambs in His arms—if you will let Him. I know that, and I will love Him forever for it.

—Christine

"You might know something secret about yourself that makes you feel unlovable. However right you might be about what you know about yourself, you are wrong to think that you have put yourself beyond the reach of God's love."

Karl D. Hirst

"God's Favourite," Oct. 2024

Isaiah 43:1

But now thus saith the Lord that created thee, O Jacob, and he that formed thee, O Israel, Fear not: for I have redeemed thee, I have called thee by thy name; thou art mine.

He Calls Me by My Name

When I teach a class, I memorize the students' names. They feel valued and respected when I call them by their name. If I don't know a student's name, I need to resort to saying, "Hey, you," or pointing at a student, which can seem rude and cause students to feel forgotten. In contrast, the Lord knows my name, without looking me up or finding my picture. He knows me as a parent knows His child. That fact makes me feel loved.

In Isaiah 43 and 44, the Lord calls us by name: "Yet now hear, O Jacob my servant; and Israel whom I have chosen" (Isaiah 44:1). We were chosen even before we were born. "Thus saith the Lord that made thee, and formed thee from the womb. . . . Fear not, O Jacob, my servant and thou, Jesurun, whom I have chosen" (Isaiah 44:2). The name Jesurun is a poetic or diminutive name for Israel found in the Hebrew Bible. God is calling us by name, as one of Jacob's descendants because we have been chosen by Him to bear witness to the world that He is the God of this world and there is no other God beside Him. The Lord said to us: "Ye are my witnesses. Is there a God beside me? Yea, there is no God; I know not any" (Isaiah 44:8). As we follow His call to us to acknowledge Him as our Father, we will feel His love.

—Marianna

"Did you know that Heavenly Father knows you personally—by name? The scriptures teach us that this is true."

Elaine S. Dalton

"He Knows You by Name," Apr. 2005

Isaiah 46:1

Bel boweth down, Nebo stoopeth, their idols were upon the beasts, and upon the cattle: your carriages were heavy loaden; they are a burden to the weary beast.

He Carries Me

In chapter 46, Isaiah mentions the gods Bel and Nebo, who were major gods of the Babylonian empire. Bel was the chief sky-god, and Nebo was the god of scribes and wisdom. The gods were man-made, likely crafted from heavy metals, such as gold or iron. These idols were so heavy that they had to be carried by beasts of burden. Instead of the loving care and bearing up of the God of Israel, the Babylonian gods did not save their people—they had to be saved by them. These gods became a hindrance and a burden, causing people to groan under the extra weight they had to carry.

In sharp contrast, our God has made us; He cares for us as a heavenly parent from birth to gray hairs and beyond this life. That is how I feel about my children and grandchildren. As babies, I carried them in my arms and cared for them when they were colicky or crying. Now that they are adults, I pray for them and support them in their triumphs and tragedies. I love them no matter what they do or what happens to them. Our heavenly parents feel the same way about each one of us.

—Marianna

"But we also need to appreciate that the Lord desires, through His Atonement and by the power of the Holy Ghost, to *enliven* us—not only to guide but also to strengthen and heal us."

David A. Bednar

"Bear Up Their Burdens with Ease," Apr. 2014

Isaiah 46:4

I am he; . . . I have made, and I will bear; even I will carry, and will deliver you.

That's Good Pie!

I fed my dad pie today. This might not seem significant. But it was. As I write this, my dad is in hospice care. By the time you read this, chances are he'll be in heaven with my mom. (And what a sweet reunion that will be!) Today I flew down to be with him. The nurses said he's lost interest in eating much. When I arrived, his dinner and dessert were untouched. After the initial confusion, then excitement of my unexpected visit, my dad perked up. After some coaxing, Dad ate a few bites of his sandwich. Then, he nodded to the pie. His hands were too shaky and weak to cut the pie and eat it. So, I cut it for him and gave him a bite. He lit up. "That's good pie!" We both smiled, him because the pie was delicious; I, because I got to help him experience some joy at this stage of his life.

Life can be hard, and often we feel too sad, too tired, or too weak to give ourselves what we need. But the Lord knows us and loves us. He wants to help us, to bless us, to heal us, to strengthen us. In our times of need, He can and will give us the things that are delicious to our souls if we let Him.

—Michelle

> "In mortality, we can 'come boldly' to the Savior and receive compassion, healing, and help. Even while we suffer inexplicably, God can bless us in simple, ordinary, and significant ways."
>
> Dale G. Renlund
>
> "Infuriating Unfairness," Apr. 2021

Isaiah 49:15–16

Can a woman forget her sucking child, that she should not have compassion on the son of her womb? Yea, they may forget, yet will I not forget thee. Behold, I have graven thee upon the palms of my hands; the walls are continually before me.

A Nursing Mom

I was a nursing mom to nine children. My nursing babies would not let me forget them. They cried to remind me when they needed to be fed. Conversely, I would never forget a nursing child. Physically, my body would not let me forget them because it was painful for me to miss a feeding or two.

But the most important reason why I would never forget them is my love for them. Through the pain, suffering, and joy of birth, they are each engraved upon my heart and upon my mind forever.

The Lord feels the same way about each of us. He allowed Himself to be crucified for us. Through His Resurrection, we are reborn after death. Through our covenant with Him at baptism, we are divinely reborn and become His spirit sons and daughters. The nail prints upon his hands and wrists are eternal reminders of His love for us.

—Marianna

"The reason for Mother's loving smile became clear years later when I read of Heavenly Father and His Beloved Son speaking of Their purpose in creating this world and giving spirit children the opportunity of mortal life."

Henry B. Eyring

"Tested, Proved, and Polished," Oct. 2020

Isaiah 52:1

Awake, awake; put on thy strength, O Zion; put on thy beautiful garments, O Jerusalem.

Fully Clothed

When I was asked to substitute the adult Sunday School class in our ward, I was thrilled. The lesson which was on Isaiah. I had a nursing baby at the time who became fussy right at the end of Sacrament Meeting. Rushing to the mother's lounge, I tried to top him off, but he had other ideas and wanted to nurse longer. At last, I ran down the hall minutes after the class started, handed the baby off to my husband, and began teaching. I was well prepared and had great activities to show how other prophets have quoted Isaiah and the rich meaning of so many layered phrases. As the class came to an end, everyone filed out without much interaction. Then I looked down. In my haste to get class, I had forgotten to do up my buttons and taught the entire lesson half dressed. I wondered how much people actually heard of what I said, or were they completed distracted by my attire?

Too often, we face our lives like I did that Sunday School class, more exposed than I should have been. Have we put on the whole armor of God today? Have we said our morning prayers, turned to the scriptures, reviewed our covenants and included the Spirit in our hearts as we start the day? Or are we running around half-dressed?

—Christine

"We need to get up off the couch, put down the remote, and wake up from our spiritual slumber. It is time to put on the full armor of God."

Russell M. Nelson

"We Can Do Better and Be Better," Apr. 2019

Isaiah 53:5

He was wounded for our transgressions, he was bruised for our iniquities: the chastisement of our peace was upon him; and with his stripes we are healed.

One for Thee

Rob Gardner's masterful oratorio, *The Lamb of God*, is one of my favorite musical pieces. One song is written from the perspective of the Apostle Peter after he realizes he has denied Jesus three times, as prophesied. He is overwrought with anguish and weeps as he sings his apology to his Savior and Friend: "As Thou hast taken stripes for me, could I not take but one for Thee?"

I cannot listen to these words without weeping. Through the trials of my life, I have come to know my Jesus personally, and I love Him. He has carried me through darkness and lifted burdens that are impossible for me to bear alone. He walks beside me as my Friend and Guide, and I am overcome when I consider my life without Him. With His stripes, *I am healed.*

For all He has done, all He saves me from, all He is leading me to, and all He has suffered, *can I not take but one stripe for Him?* Humble myself, forgive someone, break an addiction, sacrifice my time and talents, refocus my priorities, take one step closer to Him? It might be a small offering compared to His, but it's all He asks.

—Krista

> "If we are among the penitent,
> with His Atonement our sins are nailed to His cross,
> and 'with his stripes we are healed.'"
>
> D. Todd Christofferson
>
> "The Love of God," Oct. 2021

Isaiah 54:2

Enlarge the place of thy tent, and let them stretch forth the curtain of thine habitations: spare not, lengthen thy cords, and strengthen thy stakes.

Putting Up a Tent

While living in New York, we wanted to attend a family reunion in Utah. We did not have enough money to fly or stay in hotels as we traveled in a car across the country. So, we decided to buy a tent and camp. I bought a tent large enough for the family to sleep in, but did not have time before we left to practice putting it up or reading the instruction manual.

For the first night of our journey, we stopped in Tennessee. When we arrived at the campsite, it started to rain—not just a sprinkle but a downpour. We put up the tent as best we could, but the stakes were not strongly put into the ground and we did not lay a tarp down underneath the tent floor. Unsecured, the tent began sliding down the hill, and the downward slope caused water to pool in the back of the tent. My children felt as though they were sleeping in a lake!

The tent of the Church will cover the entire earth. We must be careful to stretch forth the tarp and strengthen the stakes so the tent is secure and the people inside are safe.

—Marianna

"In our families and in our stakes and districts, let us seek to build up Zion through unity, godliness, and charity."

D. Todd Christofferson

"Come to Zion," Oct. 2008

Isaiah 58:6,9

Is not this the fast that I have chosen? Then shalt thou call, and the Lord shall answer . . . Here I am.

God, Where Are You?

You know those stories where someone fasts and then suddenly a miracle comes as a direct result of their fasting? For me, the miracles from fasting come differently and are not as obvious.

Fasting helps me feel close to God. On my mission, that was the miracle I needed during the particularly hard times. I needed to really *feel* God near, and fasting helped me do that. I loved (and still do) that God had given me a way to show Him just how much I wanted Him to be with me. And I loved that He always showed up. He always replied with "Here I am."

If you are struggling to connect with God and you feel like asking Him, "God, where are you?," consider fasting. The miracles may not seem huge or immediate, but they will come. God will come. He always does. And, when you think about it, isn't that the greatest miracle of all? That we have the invitation to call upon the Lord and He will come?

—Michelle

"I bear witness of the miracles, both spiritual and temporal, that come to those who live the law of the fast. I bear witness of the miracles that have come to me. Truly, as Isaiah recorded, I have cried out in the fast more than once, and truly God has responded, 'Here I am.' Cherish that sacred privilege."

Jeffrey R. Holland

"Are We Not All Beggars?," Oct. 2014

Isaiah 60:1–3

Arise, shine; for thy light is come. . . . The Lord shall arise upon thee, and his glory shall be seen upon thee. And the Gentiles shall come to thy light, and kings to the brightness of thy rising.

Shine!

During my teenage years, my family lived in the California Bay Area. One day, I got a phone call from a neighbor I'd never met who was looking for a babysitter for her two daughters. "I see you outside playing with your little sisters. You're different from the other teenagers. You have a light."

There's a beautiful song by Julie de Azevedo called "Window to His Love" that describes my hopes for shining Christ's light. "I want to be a window to His love, so when you look at me, you will see Him."

We follow Christ, speak of Him, glory in Him, and shine His light because we never know who might be looking for it. His light in our eyes, our countenance, our speech, and our actions is a beacon to show others the way to Him. So be bold and shine!

–Krista

"My invitation today is simple: share the gospel. Be you and hold up the light. Pray for heaven's help and follow spiritual promptings. Share your life normally and naturally; invite another person to come and see, to come and help, and to come and belong. And then rejoice as you and those you love receive the promised blessings."

Marcus B. Nash

"Hold Up Your Light," Oct. 2021

Isaiah 61:10

I will greatly rejoice in the Lord, my soul shall be joyful in my God; for he hath clothed me with the garments of salvation.

I Will Greatly Rejoice

The other day, I was sitting in the temple complaining. Everyone says that when you serve a senior mission, your family will be blessed. We are preparing to leave in a week, and all I've seen is the opposite. Two of my boys were unemployed despite a good education and their best efforts. Others had issues of their own. "Why aren't you blessing our family?" I said in my heart, a little angry that my prayers went unanswered.

Now, I will acknowledge that even if I left with nothing changed, the Lord might be changing their hearts in important ways I cannot see. But yesterday so many miracles happened. Both of my sons were offered jobs! And both in Texas! The one that has struggled the longest has been asked to start right away. Our missionary farewell is this weekend, which will be his last activity in Idaho before he leaves. The Lord's timing is perfect.

Most precious of all, a child who hadn't been to the temple in a while asked when we want to go to the temple together before we leave. This is *huge*! I am filled with joy. Miracles happen, and I am *greatly* rejoicing in the Lord!

—Christine

> "I promise that as you serve, you will feel the love of the Lord in your life, you will know Him, He will know you, and 'how great shall be your joy.'"
>
> Ronald A. Rasband
>
> "How Great Shall Be Your Joy," Apr. 2025

Isaiah 66:18

For I know their works and their thoughts: it shall come, that I will gather all nations and tongues; and they shall come, and see my glory.

The Beginning and the End

The beginning and the end of Isaiah have many similarities. As you read Isaiah 66, compare the content with Isaiah 1. Find common themes and specific counsel that is most important for you to follow. Isaiah teaches us to practically prepare for the Second Coming of the Lord by learning to do well, relieving the oppressed, and pleading for the widow (Isaiah 1:17). The end and beginning of the book of Isaiah tells us to "Hear, O heavens, and give ear, O earth," and "Hear the word of the Lord" (Isaiah 1:2; 66:5).

Isaiah teaches us that at His Coming, the righteous will enjoy a glorious future: "For as the new heavens and the new earth, which I will make, shall remain before me, saith the Lord, so shall your seed and your name remain" (Isaiah 66:22). "Thou shalt be called, The city of righteousness, the faithful city" (Isaiah 1:26).

I look forward to His Coming and all the events leading up to it. As I hear His voice and do His will, I have no need to fear or to be anxious for the times ahead. Instead, I will become a citizen of His faithful city.

—Marianna

> "His instructions are neither mysterious nor complex. When we follow them, we do not need to fear or be anxious."
>
> Dale G. Renlund
>
> "Personal Preparation to Meet the Savior," Apr. 2025

Jeremiah 1:5

Before I formed thee in the belly I knew thee; and before thou camest forth out of the womb I sanctified thee, and I ordained thee a prophet unto the nations.

I Know You

Jeremiah was called as a prophet around 627 BC when the Kingdom of Judah was in a really fragile state. His mission would last forty years as he cried truth and hope, yet felt deep grief as the nation he loved would crumble. It would be so hard that Jeremiah would receive the nickname the Weeping Prophet.

I've had times in my life when I've felt like the Weeping Disciple—times when life was just hard and the doubts and fear seemed heavy. Times when I wanted to give up. In those times I turned to the Lord, wondering what He could or would tell me to help me.

What could the Lord tell Jeremiah that could help prepare him for such a difficult task ahead? What would give him strength and hope and faith to endure such challenges? God told him the same thing He has told me: *I know you. I've* ***always*** *known you. You have a purpose. And I am by your side.*

—Michelle

"*We really are God's children. . . .* Imagine you are hearing this for the first time! You really are His cherished daughter. You really are His precious son. . . . He knows exactly who you were before you were sent to earth and what you have experienced so far in your mortal life, and He has mercifully planned for your every tomorrow."

Patrick Kearon

"Receive His Gift," Apr. 2025

Jeremiah 1:19

And they shall fight against thee;
but they shall not prevail against thee;
for I am with thee, saith the Lord, to deliver you.

As Long as I Hear You, I Will Be Okay

When my son was in fifth grade, he fell over a railing onto the concrete, hitting his head and arm. The ER staff was more concerned about his head injury, ordering a CT scan first. I held Spencer's hand as they instructed him to not move when the cold table slid into the large white tube. He was nervous and in pain. I was so glad I was with him, but then I was told I couldn't be with Spencer during the test. I could watch from behind the one-way mirror shield.

Hesitantly, I left him, my heart hurting. From behind the shield, out of sight, I hollered, "Spencer, how are you?"

From the table, he called back, "Mom, as long as I hear you, I will be okay." Oh, the faith and love of that boy!

So often, we might not see God, and wonder if He is near. But, He is. He needs to stand behind the heavens, metaphorically speaking, while we take our "test," but He is near, just a breath away, watching, loving, and helping as much as He can. As long as we strive to hear Him, we will be okay.

—Michelle

"I have felt His presence when needing reassurance, comfort, or greater spiritual insight or strength, and I have been deeply humbled and am grateful for His divine companionship."

Ronald A. Rasband

"Standing by Our Promises and Covenants," Oct. 2019

Jeremiah 6:16

Stand ye in the ways, and see, and ask for the old paths, where is the good way, and walk therein, and ye shall find rest for your souls. But they said, We will not walk therein.

At Least Try

My son began struggling with mental health challenges at a very young age. I sought the best help from mental health specialists, holistic doctors, pediatricians, books, articles, dieticians, and more. But one day, as I was studying for a Relief Society lesson, I came across several quotes from Church leaders about the promised blessings of studying the scriptures as a family. That list of blessings was precisely what I'd been looking to give my son, but I instantly thought, "It can't be that easy." We were trying every method under the sun, except this "old path," this "good way" to "find rest" for our souls. I was hesitant to place my hopes in such an obvious "Sunday School" answer to our problems, but I thought, if it really is that easy, shouldn't we at least try?

So we did. Not perfectly, but with intent and hope. And over the years, as we've worked to make gospel study a priority in our home, we've seen the long-lasting effects and blessings that come from feasting on the word of God at the same table. That old path was exactly what we needed.

—Krista

"We can choose to harden our hearts, or we can choose to soften our hearts. In our daily lives, we can choose to do the things that invite the Lord's Spirit to come into and dwell in our hearts. I know that in these choices, there is peace and joy."

Christopher H. Kim

"Harden Not Your Heart," Apr. 2025

Jeremiah 10:2

Learn not the way of the heathen, and be not dismayed at the signs of heaven.

The Way of the Heathen

I used to love aerobics class. There was a nursery for my preschoolers, and for a time I'd go every morning. Our instructor stood at the front, the music would start, and we would play an adult version of Simon Says. Whatever she did, we would imitate. At first, some of her moves were impossible, but the more I went, the better I got until I could shimmy with the best of them.

When Jeremiah tells us that in the last days we should not "learn the way of the heathens," I think he was warning us against the kind of learning I did in aerobics class. When we admire someone and watch them closely, we naturally take on their movements and sometimes their attitudes. We may not even notice it's happening. When we do, we are not watching and preparing for the signs of heaven.

I have a daughter-in-law who takes Jeremiah's warning seriously. I was sharing with her how nervous I was about the national debt, the weakness of the dollar, and how young families couldn't even make it in this economy. She smiled and said, "Mom, the Lord is in charge. It'll be okay." I was dancing in the way of the heathens, not trusting in the Lord. Some of these difficulties have been prophesied, but He will support His covenant people. I need to "buckle up, buttercup," and watch for His holy signs without dismay.

—Christine

"Confidence in God's answers implies accepting that His ways are not our ways and that 'all things must come to pass in their time.'"

Taylor G. Godoy

"Call, Don't Fall," Apr. 2024

Jeremiah 13:10

This evil people, which refuse to hear my words, which walk in the imagination of their heart, and walk after other gods, to serve them, and to worship them, shall even be as this girdle, which is good for nothing.

Birthday Questions

At our family birthday parties, while we are eating the birthday person's favorite meal, we ask questions to find out more about what is in this person's heart. We try to see how well we know him or her.

Each person around the table has the chance to ask a question to the birthday person. Before the person gives the answer, everyone else says how they think that person will answer. The people who guess it right win a point. The person with the most points at the end of the dinner wins the game.

Some of the questions are silly: Who is the movie star you think you look like the most? Others are more profound and show a person's character and heart: If you had a million dollars, what would you do with it?

The Lord knows the imaginations of our heart. He would know how we would answer every question and would win every birthday question game.

Ask yourself how you would answer this question: What God do you worship? God knows the answer.

—Marianna

> "Asking seems simple, and yet it is powerful because it reveals our desires and our faith."
>
> Milton Camargo
>
> "Ask, Seek, and Knock," Oct. 2020

Jeremiah 15:16

Thy word was unto me the joy and rejoicing of mine heart.

His Words Have Power

One night, during perhaps the most challenging part of my full-time mission, I knelt by my bed and prayed. This was back when we could only call our parents twice a year. Without access to my mom, and with a companion I was struggling with, I didn't have anywhere to turn. It was the first time in my life that I truly had only Heavenly Father to rely on. I was so very discouraged. And so, I prayed with a fervor I never had before. Then I remembered the words He told me in a blessing before I left, and I knew I would be okay.

This is where we find Jeremiah in chapter 15. He is well into his four-decade-long mission. The people have refused to follow, let alone listen, to him. He was feeling discouraged, abandoned, and even angry. Jeremiah longs to hear and see the Lord, and in this raw and reflective moment, He remembers how God's word once brought him joy and identity. His faith and trust in God shines, even when he questions his own ability and mission. God's words have power. Hear them, read them, remember them. And you will be okay.

—Michelle

"[The scriptures] teach us about Jesus Christ and His gospel, the magnitude of His Atonement, and our Father's great plan of happiness and redemption. Daily immersion in the word of God is crucial for spiritual survival, especially in these days of increasing upheaval."

Russell M. Nelson

"Hear Him," Apr. 2020

Jeremiah 18:6

Behold, as the clay is in the potter's hand, so are ye in mine hand.

Shimmery Scars

I have a cherished necklace—a silver heart interlaced with cracks filled with gold. Kintsugi is the Japanese art of mending broken pottery by joining the pieces with golden lacquer. My necklace symbolizes how the Lord has repaired my broken heart.

We are created in His image, clay in His hands, but there are so many bumps, blunders, or battles in this life that might knock us off the shelf. Thankfully, the hands that created us are no less adept at repairs. He can gather our shattered pieces and slowly, lovingly put us back together.

His healing may take time and patience, but just as a Kintsugi vessel is considered even more beautiful and valuable than before its repair, so too are we more precious after His grace has restored us. The gold in our cracks tells a story—not just of brokenness, but of redemption. Each fracture mended by His hands becomes a testimony of His mercy and power.

If you find yourself in pieces, don't despair. You're still in the Potter's hands. And He's not finished with you yet.

—Krista

> "Jesus specializes in the seemingly impossible. He came here to make the impossible possible, the irredeemable redeemable, to heal the unhealable, to right the unrightable, to promise the unpromisable."
>
> Patrick Kearon
>
> "He Is Risen with Healing in His Wings: We Can Be More than Conquerors," Apr. 2022

Jeremiah 23:7, 8

Therefore, behold, the days come . . . that they shall no more say, The Lord liveth, which brought up the children of Israel out of the land of Egypt; But, The Lord liveth, which brought up and which led the seed of the house of Israel out of the north country.

The Sandbox or the Fruit Bowl

In most families there is some great miracle everyone remembers because it was so amazing. Like the crossing of the Red Sea, it may have happened years ago. In our family it was the lost keys. My keys ended up missing while my husband was away. We looked everywhere and prayed like crazy. Feeling inspired, I walked out to the sandbox. There was a pan lid and I lifted it. Nothing. Then came the inspiration to dig. Six inches below the surface, I found where my nonverbal toddler had buried them. This happened thirty years ago.

While focusing on whether I had an equally impressive but more current miracle, my husband lost his glasses. They were his only pair and had been gone for two days. It was also the morning of our departure for an eighteen-month mission. We prayed, and I looked up at the kitchen counter. There was a stack of mail for my son on the fruit bowl. I lifted it up, moved a few apples to the side, and there were the glasses. My husband said it was a miracle! The heavens are open, and the Lord blesses us today . . . but maybe we just have to stop losing things.

—Christine

> "I testify that miracles have not ceased, angels are among us, and the heavens are truly open."
>
> Shayne M. Bowen
>
> "Miracles, Angels, and Priesthood Power," Apr. 2024

Jeremiah 25:5

They said, Turn ye again now every one from his evil way, and from the evil of your doings, and dwell in the land that the Lord hath given unto you and to your fathers for ever and ever.

Playing Statue

When I was a little girl, my favorite outdoor game was Statue. The sculptor or statue maker would twirl you around and around and then let you go so that you tumbled onto the grass. When you stopped moving, you were in an awkward position, but you needed to stay in that position and become like a statue.

The sculptor would then figure out what statue you looked like. He would tell you what you were and then you had to act it out. If you fell on all fours, the sculptor might tell you to act like a cat. Then, you had to "meow" or "purr" and walk on all fours, while the "buyers" (or other children playing the game) guessed the name of your statue.

Turning and swirling makes us dizzy and often puts us in awkward positions. When we turn to evil doings, we are not thinking straight. We are like statues in a childish game forced to do what another person tells us to do. To become free, we must turn from these evil ways, stand up straight, and follow our Savior.

—Marianna

"The commandments of God provide the guiding and steadying force in our lives."

Dallin H. Oaks

"Following Christ," Oct. 2024

Jeremiah 29:11

For I know the thoughts that I think toward you, saith the Lord, thoughts of peace, and not of evil, to give you an expected end.

A God of Good Endings

Years ago, I met an atheist at a pizza place. I can't remember how the conversation started, but it landed on God. This man was a Vietnam vet and couldn't accept that a loving God would let bad things happen to innocent people. I didn't have the answers he wanted, but I gave him the only answer I had: *God loves all of His children. He's with them. And in the end, it will all make sense. He is a God of good endings.*

In 597 BC, Lehi and his family were gone from Jerusalem, and many of the Jews were in exile. The family was far from home and probably discouraged, confused, hurting, and angry—but God wanted them to know that He still had a plan. Even though it would take seventy years, restoration was coming. And He would be with them until then.

Life is a complicated blend of agency, opportunity, purpose, beauty, pain, and growth. Regardless of whether our challenges come from God, ourselves, or others, one thing remains the same: God wants what is best for us. He loves us. He wants us to have joy. He's doing all He can to give us strength and relief.

—Michelle

> "I know that our Father in Heaven desires goodness and hope for each of His children."
>
> Kristin M. Yee
>
> "Beauty for Ashes: The Healing Path of Forgiveness," Oct. 2022

Jeremiah 31:13

I will turn their mourning into joy, and will comfort them, and make them rejoice from their sorrow.

Like a Rubber Band

Imagine holding a rubber band with both hands. Now, try to stretch one end of it in one direction while leaving the other end untouched. You can't, right? I know—it's impossible. Sorry for asking you to do something that defies the laws of physics. We all understand that when you pull a rubber band, both ends move. It stretches as a whole.

In Alma 36, the prophet Alma describes to his son Helaman what it was like to be called to repentance by an angel. In verse 20, after recounting his torment and guilt, he describes what happened when he finally cried out to Jesus: "And oh, what joy, and what marvelous light I did behold; yea, my soul was filled with joy as exceeding as was my pain!"

Alma had felt the most profound sorrow of his life. Are you thinking about the most profound sorrow of yours? I am. Just like Alma, those hard experiences stretched the rubber band of our hearts painfully far in one direction, but can you recognize that when relief came, it stretched just as far the other way? Alma explained that the depth of his sorrow expanded his capacity for joy. And it's the same for us. The sorrow we feel now doesn't stay one-sided forever. God knows how far we've been stretched—and He will compensate with joy to match.

—Krista

"The nights may seem long, but the morning does come, and oh, how exquisite is the peace and resplendent joy we feel as the Savior's Atonement frees us from sin and suffering."

Craig C. Christensen

"There Can Be Nothing So Exquisite and Sweet as Was My Joy," Apr. 2023

Jeremiah 32:39

And I will give them one heart, and one way, that they may fear me for the good of them.

Be Afraid, Be Very Afraid

My son Camron was a clever child. When he was still in grade school, he would make lovely things in our woodworking shop and come up with really creative projects. Almost everything he did worked out, which left him with the sense he could do anything. That is dangerous.

We lived in Minnesota. Normally, the area was lovely and safe, but when the snow melted off the bluffs, the runoff created a fast-moving river of freezing water that fed into an underground culver. Well, this clever boy decided he was going to make his own raft and ride the raging river. The freezing temperatures were dangerous enough, but if he had gotten sucked into the culver, he would have drowned and might even have been irretrievable. It's terrifying to think about.

Luckily, a neighbor called me as he was marching over to the river's edge with his makeshift raft. I raced outside and scooped that boy up, trying to convince him of the danger around him. The power of that water was nothing to play with. It should be respected, and we need to treat it with an element of fear.

God is far more powerful than that frigid water. Although we love Him, we also need to respect and even fear what He says so that we don't find ourselves drowning, trapped, or even worse.

—Christine

"The word *reverence* can be traced to the Latin verb *revereri* which means to 'stand in awe of.'"

Ulisses S. Soares

"Reverence for Sacred Things," Apr. 2025

Jeremiah 36:2

Take thee a roll of a book, and write therein all the words that I have spoken unto thee against Israel, and against Judah, and against all the nations, from the day I spake unto thee, from the days of Josiah, even unto this day.

Burnt Writings

In Louisa May Alcott's book *Little Women*, Amy March is so upset with her sister Jo that she throws her writing into the fire. Jo is devastated because she has painstakingly worked for a long time on this manuscript. But that does not stop her from writing. She continues to write until she finally gets her first book published.

Jeremiah is told by the Lord to write on a scroll the Lord's words against Israel and Judah so that they will repent from their evil ways. Jeremiah is to read these words in the Lord's house on the day of fasting. When King Jehoiakim reads the book, he takes his penknife and cuts it into shreds and throws the scroll into the fire.

I'm sure Jeremiah was disheartened to have his work destroyed. But the Lord told Jeremiah to take another scroll and write His words again. Jeremiah was obedient, and the Lord blessed his writings by giving additional words for Israel to hear (36:32).

—Marianna

"I wrote down a few lines every day for years. . . . Before I would write, I would ponder this question: 'Have I seen the hand of God reaching out to touch us or our children or our family today?'"

Henry B. Eyring

"O Remember, Remember," Oct. 2007

Jeremiah 39:18

For I will surely deliver thee . . .
because thou hast put thy trust in me, saith the Lord.

Straight into the Pit

Sometimes faith lands us in unexpected places. Thousands of years ago, faith led to a prophet getting thrown into a pit to die and a servant of a disobedient king being sent to save him. In both cases, faith led them to very unexpected situations. However, as they both turned to the Lord in faith, they were given unexpected solutions.

My faith has led me to serve a mission, write books, adopt a daughter—none of which I'd planned on, but all of which have been lovely. Other times, my faith has led me into more undesirable situations—unemployment, a hysterectomy, loss of friends.

If your faith has led you to an unexpected place, it doesn't mean it didn't work. Faith, I've learned, is more about *who* we follow, not *where* He takes us. Whether you are in a pit or called to rescue, choose to keep your eyes on the Savior. Trust Him, for He will always deliver you in His time and way.

—Michelle

"Whatever change in life's circumstance may come our way, and whatever unexpected path we may have to travel, how we respond is a choice. Turning to the Savior and grasping His outstretched arm is always our best option."

W. Christopher Waddell

"Turn to the Lord," Oct. 2017

Jeremiah 44:4–5

Howbeit I sent unto you all my servants the prophets. . . . But they hearkened not.

A Living Prophet

I once heard a story about a woman who was trying to explain the beliefs of our church to a friend. When she mentioned that we have a living prophet, her friend was stunned. "There's a prophet alive right now? What does he teach?" To her embarrassment, the woman couldn't remember. From that day on, she made a commitment to stay current with prophetic teachings.

We are so blessed to live in a time when the heavens are not silent—when God speaks through a living prophet to guide, warn, and comfort us. But this gift comes with a responsibility.

Let's follow the example of the woman in the story and make a personal commitment to know what the prophet is teaching, to treasure his words, and to live by them. You never know when someone might ask what he teaches, and we'll be ready—not just with a summary but with a heart that lives those teachings.

–Krista

> "I promise as you follow the inspired counsel of our dear prophet, President Russell M. Nelson, his counselors, the Apostles, and other Church leaders, . . . you will be filled, deep in your heart and soul, with the spirit and the work of the Restoration. I promise you will see the hand of God in your lives, hear His promptings, and feel His love."
>
> Ronald A. Rasband
>
> "Fulfillment of Prophecy," Apr. 2020

Jeremiah 48:11

Moab hath been at ease from his youth and he hath settled on his lees.

Settle on Your Lees

In England, I recently bought some spray starch and was ironing shirts. It was a brand I'd never tried before, and I was surprised how weak the solution seemed. Then my husband shook the bottle. Suddenly, it worked great for one shirt and was weak again. The key to success was consistently shaking the bottle every few passes.

Anciently, making wine was a little like that spray starch. If you didn't turn the bottle as it fermented, the top became water, and the bottom grew into a thick substance called lees. So, if you are too lazy or distracted to consistently keep turning your wine as it aged, then you "settled on your lees."

Today, as we attempt to live covenant lives, it is easy to forget to keep things up. In our hectic world, we can fall into a routine of going to church, saying meaningless prayers, and living a life of obligation rather than building a relationship with Christ. When we do that, we are settling on our lees. Turning the bottle requires daily repentance driven by a heartfelt desire to stay close to the Lord. The difference will make our life turn out sweet and lovely, instead of goopy at the bottom.

—Christine

"Discover the joy of daily repentance. . . . Please do not fear or delay repenting. Satan delights in your misery. Cut it short."

Russell M. Nelson

"The Power of Spiritual Momentum," Apr. 2022

Jeremiah 50:6

My people hath been lost sheep: their shepherds have caused them to go astray, they have turned them away on the mountains: they have gone from mountain to hill, they have forgotten their resting place.

Finding a Comfy Mattress

A comfortable bed is necessary to enjoy a good night's sleep. The story of "The Princess and the Pea" is a perfect illustration of my point. Even a small, annoying problem at bedtime, such as the pillow is too high or the mattress is too hard, can ruin your sleep.

When Steve and I needed a new mattress, we took this purchase very seriously. We went to a variety of stores and tried many mattresses in search of the perfect one. The mattress we finally found has served us well for many years. But it has also made it difficult to sleep away from home. When I travel and sleep in a hotel bed, my back and neck often miss their normal resting place. It is hard for me to forget the peace, the quiet, and the comfort of my own bed.

Our Heavenly Father has the comfiest beds waiting for us in His mansion above. All we must do is remember our way home.

—Marianna

"When the tour group entered an endowment room, the boy pointed to the altar, where people kneel to make covenants with God, and said, 'Oh, that's nice. Here is a place for people to rest on their temple journey.'"

Russell M. Nelson

"Overcome the World and Find Rest," Oct. 2022

Jeremiah 51:10 (NIV)

The Lord has vindicated us; come, let us tell in Zion what the Lord our God has done.

I Told You So

Four words that most people don't like hearing are "I told you so." Maybe it's a pride thing, but we don't like to be wrong.

And yet, how many of us relish the chance to say it? At the end of the book of Jeremiah, Jeremiah gets to lay out the ultimate two-fold "I told you so." First, to Babylon, the mighty empire that once crushed nations and mocked the Lord and then fell, just as it had been prophesied.

But there is a deeper, more beautiful "I told you so" here. The fulfillment of prophecy reminds us that God sees, remembers, and acts—in His time. And even as Jerusalem fell, grace flickered in the release of Jehoiachin, showing us that God's story never ends in despair. He weaves mercy into judgment and hope into ruins. His "I told you so" is soft, hopeful, and loving. "I told you l love you." "I told you I'd help you." "I told you I'd save you." "I told you, you'd be okay."

—Michelle

> "As home and Church are gathered together in one in Christ, we may be troubled on every side, but we will not be distressed in our minds and hearts. We may be perplexed by our circumstances and challenges, but we will not be in despair. We may be persecuted, but we will also recognize that we are never alone. We can receive spiritual strength to become and remain firm, steadfast, and true."
>
> David A. Bednar
>
> "Be Still and Know That I Am God," Apr. 2024

Lamentations 1:12

Behold, and see if there be any sorrow like unto my sorrow.

Structured Sorrow

Unless you've memorized the Hebrew alphabet and happen to be reading the Bible in Hebrew, you might not recognize that Jeremiah wrote his book of Lamentations in the form of alphabet acrostic poetry. Let me explain.

The Hebrew alphabet has twenty-two letters. Chapters 1, 2, and 4 of Lamentations each have twenty-two verses. The first verse in these chapters begins with the letter *Aleph,* and each subsequent verse begins with a successive letter of the alphabet—*Bet, Gimel, Dalet,* and so on. Chapter 3 is a double acrostic poem with sixty-six verses. Every set of three verses follows the same alphabet pattern.

Why does it matter? Jeremiah is employing an intentional literary device to help him articulate his despair over the loss of Jerusalem and the suffering of his people. Using the entire alphabet, from *Aleph* to *Tav,* suggests a fulness to his expression of grief. Nothing is left out. Jeremiah is showing us that God can handle every kind of sorrow, from A to Z. There is nothing beyond His strength and knowledge to heal, nothing we can't tell Him. Even in the chaos and turmoil of our grief, we can count on the order and faithfulness of our God and His love.

—Krista

"I testify of Jesus Christ, He who has all power."

Kelly R. Johnson

"Enduring Power," Oct. 2020

Ezekiel 3:1–3

He said unto me, Son of man . . . eat this roll and go speak unto the house of Israel. . . . Then did I eat it; and it was in my mouth as honey for sweetness.

Scriptures for Breakfast

Have you ever had a moment when something is a perfect set-up and you totally miss it? That happened to me with the following scripture. A shy girl was asked to give our morning seminary scripture. That day she showed up with a brown bag and pulled out a dinner roll, then read Ezekiel 3:1: "Eat this roll." She took a big bite and read, "And it was in my mouth as honey." She patted her belly and sat down. I was shocked.

"Wait," I said. "Is that a real scripture?" She showed me, and I sat there silently while the class president took attendance and reviewed the scripture mastery. What a missed opportunity!

In the previous chapter, the angel tells Ezekiel to take the "roll of a book." The scriptures, duh. He was simply saying the same thing that Nephi said in his last words: "Feast upon the words of Christ" (2 Nephi 32:3) Or like Alma said, speaking of faith "that it beginneth to be delicious unto me" (Alma 32:27). Or as Christ Himself said during His time of temptation, "Man shall not live by bread alone, but by every word that proceedeth out of the mouth of God" (Matthew 4:4). Although I can't relive the moment in seminary and come back with "we are doing that right now, ha-ha," I can partake of my scriptures for breakfast every morning from now on. And they are delicious!

—Christine

"I promise that if we 'feast upon the words of Christ' that lead to salvation . . . the powers of heaven will pour down upon us."

Ronald A. Rasband

"Words Matter," Apr. 2024

Ezekiel 12:27

Son of man, behold, they of the house of Israel say, The vision that he seeth is for many days to come and he prophesieth of the times that are far off.

It's Going to Happen

Israel had been told by prophets for many years that if they did not repent, they would be conquered and carried away by the Babylonians. The people thought this meant some time in the future. They were hoping that another generation would experience these consequences, but not them. Now, the prophet Ezekiel was told: "Thus said the Lord God; There shall none of my words be prolonged any more, but the word which I have spoken shall be done" (Ezekiel 12:28). The Babylonians did take the Israelites captive, did destroy their city, and did force them to the land of the Chaldeans.

Our prophets today have been talking a great deal about preparing for the Second Coming of the Lord. We may feel like they are prophesying about a time that is far off in the future. We may think that other latter-day prophets said the same thing and the Savior didn't come in their lifetimes, so why should we prepare? Everyone will stand in the presence of the Lord sometime, and we must be prepared for that day!

—Marianna

"For centuries, prophets have foretold this gathering, and it is happening right now! As an essential prelude to the Second Coming of the Lord, it is the most important work in the world!"

Russell M. Nelson

"Let God Prevail," Oct. 2020

Ezekiel 18:31

Cast away from you all your transgressions . . . and make you a new heart and a new spirit.

In a Moment, It Was Gone

For the longest time, I carried a hurt in my heart. It was deep. I didn't want to hurt, but I also didn't want the anger and resentment that came with it. I'd prayed and counseled with others. I really *wanted* the pain to go away. But no matter what I did, it remained.

I decided to attend an event where I knew the Spirit would be strong. I went with one goal: to feel at peace about the pain. I prayed and asked God to do what He would with my heart.

Then, in the most unexpected moment, while listening to a song, I felt it. I felt His love. And then, I felt the hurt leave. In a moment, it was gone. It was as if He held my heart in His hands and gently extracted the pain I'd been feeling. All that was left was Him. I haven't had an experience like that before or since, but I'll always remember that one time when I gave Him my heart, and He gave me a new one in return.

–Michelle

"What is the key to this breakthrough in contented, happy living? It is embedded there in the text in one sentence: "The love of God . . . did dwell in the hearts of the people." When the love of God sets the tone for our own lives, for our relationships to each other and ultimately our feeling for all humankind, then old distinctions, limiting labels, and artificial divisions begin to pass away, and peace increases."

Jeffrey R. Holland

"The Greatest Possession," Oct. 2021

Ezekiel 24:3–5

Set on a pot, . . . and also pour water into it: . . . Fill it with the choice bones . . . and make it boil well.

A Boiling Pot

God told Ezekiel to put a pot on the fire, fill it with choice bones and meat, then let it boil. After some time, the pot became corroded, and even boiling couldn't save the ruined meat. This metaphor was a warning from God to a prophet about the spiritual and moral decay of the people of Jerusalem and the coming destruction of the city.

While the current political tensions, personal hardships, and moral compromises of today's world may differ significantly from those of ancient Israel, the pot is still boiling. I'm sure, like me, you feel the tension and unrest around us. It floods my social media and news feeds. I see truth twisted and evil promoted as freedom. It's hard enough to navigate on my own, but I feel desperate to help my children and grandchildren travel safely through the mists of darkness that have crept in around us.

Our prophet is aware of the struggle to maintain our spiritual health and fortitude in the heat of a boiling pot, and has given us direct counsel from God about how to keep ourselves protected: "In coming days, it will not be possible to survive spiritually without the guiding, directing, comforting, and constant influence of the Holy Ghost" (Russell M. Nelson, April 2018). Let us learn from the history recorded in scripture and be diligent in following our prophet's counsel. He is a watchman on a tower; he can see what's coming, and will help guide us through.

—Krista

> "Brothers and sisters, now is the time for you and for me to prepare for the Second Coming of our Lord and Savior, Jesus the Christ. Now is the time for us to make our discipleship our highest priority."
>
> Russell M. Nelson
>
> "The Lord Jesus Christ Will Come Again," Oct. 2024

325

Ezekiel 37:12

Thus saith the Lord God; Behold, O my people, I will open your graves, and cause you to come up out of your graves, and bring you into the land of Israel.

A Scriptural Parfait

Most Church members have seen a missionary or teacher hold their Bible and Book of Mormon together and recite, "Join them one to another into one stick; and they shall become one in thine hand" (Ezekiel 37:17). But I don't believe that the "stick of Joseph and the stick of Judah" scripture is the coolest in this chapter. Ezekiel 37 begins with the prophet being carried by the Spirit into a valley of dry bones. He hears "a noise" and feels "a shaking." Then the bones reassemble themselves "bone to his bone." Soon they are covered with sinew and flesh, and breath is put in them. They go from being dead to completely alive!

I love the layered meaning of this prophecy. First, it is a clear representation of the physical resurrection, a point of debate in the ancient church. Second, Ezekiel taught the people during the exile in Babylon, and it was a prophecy about their return to Israel. That their dead country of Israel would live again. Finally, this prophecy feeds into verse 17 because both the Bible and the Book of Mormon are as *voices from the dust.* (See Isaiah 29:4; 2 Nephi 26:15; Moroni 10:27.) As we read the words of ancient prophets which touch our hearts, they come alive, too. Some may ask which one of the three is the real meaning. The answer is all of them; it's a scriptural parfait. And a delicious one!

—Christine

> "Ancient voices from the dust plead with us today."
>
> David A. Bednar
>
> "In the Space of Not Many Years," Oct. 2024

Ezekiel 47:22

They shall have inheritance with you among the tribes of Israel.

Our Abundant Inheritance

In Ezekiel's vision of future Israel, he was brought to the door of the temple and saw waters rushing out of its threshold. These waters healed the Dead Sea and all the land surrounding it. The trees were full of fruit and the fish were abundant. The healing temple waters caused the land to expand in beauty and usefulness, even land that used to be uninhabitable.

This new land of growth and abundance shall be divided into lots for an inheritance for Israel and the strangers who live in Israel. "They shall have inheritance with you among the tribes of Israel. And it shall come to pass, that in what tribe the stranger sojourneth, there shall ye give him his inheritance, saith the Lord God" (Ezekiel 47:22).

Isn't that what is happening in our temples today? Whether you were born into a family that has been a part of the Church for generations or are the first in your family to join the Church, you are not a stranger to the Lord. You are brought into the family of Israel and given an inheritance as a member of His household. Temples heal families and bring family members together as co-inheritors of God's grace and salvation. All people who have accepted the covenants outlined by the Lord in His holy temple, starting with the waters of baptism, receive the same inheritance and eternal abundance of blessings.

—Marianna

"No matter the outcome, all will be well because of temple covenants."

Henry B. Eyring

"All Will Be Well Because of Temple Covenants," Apr. 2024

Daniel 2:44

And in the days of these kings shall the God of heaven set up a kingdom, which shall never be destroyed: and the kingdom shall not be left to other people, but it shall break in pieces and consume all these kingdoms, and it shall stand for ever.

His Kingdom Now and Forever

Daniel was a faithful young man taken captive to Babylon, and yet, he stayed true to God in a foreign land. He was gifted with wisdom and the ability to interpret dreams and boldly testified of God's power. This came in handy when Nebuchadnezzer, the very king responsible for Daniel's captivity, had a dream that no one—except Daniel—could interpret. More important than what he saw in the dream was what it *meant.* Through Daniel, the Lord wanted the king to know that a true kingdom is not made by man but by *His* authority. His plan was unfolding and *His* kingdom would never fail.

This gives me so much peace: God's kingdom is here, and it will never be destroyed. No matter what happens in the world or local politics, despite natural or personal disasters, the Lord's church—His kingdom—will stay. And *we* get to be a part of it!

—Michelle

> "The Lord's Church [will] rise in the last days as a small stone 'cut out of the mountain without hands.' 'Without hands,' meaning by divine intervention, the Lord's Church would increase in magnitude until it fills the whole earth, 'never [to] be destroyed . . . [but to] stand for ever.'"
>
> Ronald A. Rasband
>
> "Fulfillment of Prophecy," Apr. 2020

Daniel 3:17

Our God whom we serve is able to deliver us from the burning fiery furnace.

But If Not

For the first time in my life, I was afraid to talk to God. I knew He would answer—but did I have the courage to do what He asked? The doctors had told us there was nothing more they could do for our daughter. The decision whether to continue Elora's life support had been cruelly placed in our hands. How was I supposed to decide how and when my daughter's life would end? I couldn't. Standing at that crossroads without a clear path was torture. I wouldn't find peace without His help.

I gathered my courage and offered the hardest prayer of my life, begging Him one last time for a miracle. And then, I loosened my white-knuckle grip on what *I* wanted, laid every ounce of my will on the altar of trust, and offered my "but if not."

Heavenly Father asked us to do the hardest thing—to remove Elora's life support. I walked into the furnace of my daughter's death with trembling steps, unsure how or if I would survive, but clinging to my faith. And when the flames surrounded me and my family, God sent angels to stand with us in the fire. He has rescued me. And because of Him, I will one day be reunited with my daughter in a place where fire will have no more power to burn.

—Krista

> "They trusted in Jehovah for deliverance, 'but if not,' that is, even if God in His wisdom did not prevent their death, yet they would remain true to Him."
>
> D. Todd Christofferson
>
> "Worship," Apr. 2025

Daniel 4:3–4

Then they brought the golden vessels that were taken out of the temple . . . and the king, and his princes, his wives, and his concubines, drank in them.

Cover Your Eyebrows

In our family we say, "Cover your eyebrows!" before saying something that might be disrespectful. That way if you are struck by lightning, you won't look as weird afterward. In Daniel, there was a king who really got zapped for doing worse.

When Nebuchadnezzar's son took over as king, he had a feast. Perhaps out of disrespect to Daniel or his God, he used the sacred temple vessels for his party. A finger shot out and wrote on the wall MENE, MENE, TEKEL, UPHARSIN. The king asked all the wise men of the land to interpret it, but only Daniel could. It meant that the king would lose his station. Although the king dressed Daniel in a fine robe and a gold chain, that very night the Persians and the Medes took over the empire. Darius, who came to love Daniel but was tricked into throwing him in the lion's den, would become the next king, while Nebuchadnezzar's son and all his family were killed.

So the next time someone in my family begins with saying "cover your eyebrows," maybe they shouldn't continue. The Lord will hold people accountable for not keeping sacred things sacred.

—Christine

"Reverence for the sacred fosters genuine gratitude, expands true happiness, leads our minds to revelation, and brings greater joy into our lives."

Ulisses S. Soares

"Reverence for Sacred Things," Apr. 2025

Daniel 6:10

Now when Daniel knew that the writing was signed, he went into his house; and . . . he kneeled upon his knees three times a day, and prayed, and gave thanks before his God, as he did aforetime.

Integrity

To pay for college, I worked as a legal secretary during the summer. My boss yelled at me a lot. One morning, he asked me to send an important letter to a client before noon, but I forgot. Rather than tell him the truth, I quickly sent the letter off the next day. I felt sick when I returned home. After a fitful night's sleep, I decided to tell my boss the truth, even though I knew he would tear me apart for lying to him. He did yell at me, but keeping my integrity was worth the sacrifice.

Daniel was a man of integrity. His business life and spiritual life were one and the same. As a man of the world and as a man of God, no one could find fault in his actions. Presidents and princes were jealous of his success and wanted to destroy him. The only possible flaw they could find in him was his consistent following of the law of his God, for Daniel did not hide his prayers and talks with God.

Playing to the vanity of the king, the government advisors asked the king to establish a statute: for thirty days, no one in the kingdom was to petition any god or man save the king, or the man would be cast into the den of lions (Daniel 6:7–8). Daniel knew of the decree, but that did not change his devotions to God. He continued to pray three times a day with his windows wide open so that anyone could see him praying. Daniel was willing to face the lions rather than forsake being a man of integrity.

—Marianna

"As an Apostle of the Lord Jesus Christ, I bless you with the *confidence* to be a living testimonial of gospel values."

Dieter F. Uchtdorf

"Missionary Work: Sharing What is in Your Heart," Apr. 2019

Daniel 9:3

And I set my face unto the Lord God, to seek by prayer and supplications, with fasting, and sackcloth, and ashes.

Are You Prepared?

I've had different versions of the same bad dream since I was a teenager: I am starring in a live television skit show (or concert performance), and right before it's my time to go on, I suddenly realize that I never prepared. The panic over failing, fear about looking stupid, and frustration with myself because it all could have been prevented if I'd just prepared beforehand almost always woke me up. (If you're a therapist, please tell me what this means.)

On the other, and more important, hand, someone asked me once if I was prepared to meet Jesus today (not a threat, just a theoretical question). I confidently felt then and still do that I am. Not because I am perfect—I am not. But because I am prepared. I have and am trying to pray and fast and worship and repent. I serve and love and repent more. Because of this, I am not only ready to meet Jesus whenever it's time, but I am prepared to receive revelation from God today.

Heavenly Father and Jesus Christ don't require a perfect performance to connect with us today. We prepare by humbly seeking and we'll be ready when the time for revelation—and whatever else They lovingly have to give—comes.

—Michelle

> "Personal revelation is available to all those who humbly seek guidance from the Lord."
>
> Quentin L. Cook
>
> "The Blessing of Continuing Revelation to Prophets and Personal Revelation to Guide Our Lives," Apr. 2020

Hosea 3:1

Then said the Lord unto me, Go yet, love a woman beloved of her friend, yet an adulteress, according to the love of the Lord toward the children of Israel, who look to other gods, and love flagons of wine.

Being a Bride

Steve walked me over to the trail on BYU temple hill on the south side of campus overlooking the botany duck pond. When he knelt down and asked me to be his queen for all eternity, I immediately threw my arms around his neck and said, "YES!" It was the happiest day of my life. Being Steve's bride did not end with the wedding. I made a commitment that I would be true to our relationship throughout eternity.

Israel had made a covenant with God to be His chosen people, similar to the faithful promise of a bride to her bridegroom. But Israel had been adulterous with other gods, rather than being true to the God of Israel. They played the harlot and had relationships with other gods.

The major theme of Hosea is how much God loves Israel. God constantly shows how much He loves His people, but His people do not always show God the same love in return. Hosea symbolized the love of the Lord by a marriage with Israel. He is the bridegroom and Israel is the Lord's bride. During Hosea's time as a prophet, Israel had been unfaithful to her loving husband, always playing the harlot with other gods.

Are we faithful in our relationship with God?

—Marianna

"One who places loyalty to a party or cause ahead of divine direction worships a false god."

D. Todd Christofferson

"Worship," Apr. 2025

Hosea 6:6

For I desired mercy, and not sacrifice; and the knowledge of God more than burnt offerings.

Three Things

I recently visited the cherry blossoms in Washington, DC, with my sisters. It was the first time I'd been back to the city since I was about eight years old. All those years ago, we visited the Smithsonian. My parents encouraged each of us to learn three things from the experience and share them afterward.

My feet hurt, and the last thing I wanted to do was go to a boring museum. After my mother was out of sight, I went to the bathroom which had a couch and took a nice long nap. When it was time to leave, I found my family, and soon we went around the room each saying our three things. My older sisters had seen the First Lady's dresses, the Star-Spangled Banner flag, and gorgeous works of art. When it was my turn, I said my three things: the bathrooms are clean, the couch is comfortable, and I never want to go to another museum in my life. It was not well received.

I imagine the Lord felt something similar when the children of Israel did not understand the meaning behind the law of sacrifice. It was supposed to turn them to Christ and help them understand the plan of salvation. As we take the sacrament each week or renew our temple covenants, are we seeing the truths taught or simply napping?

—Christine

> "And to each of you who has made temple covenants, I plead with you to seek—prayerfully and consistently—to understand temple covenants and ordinances."
>
> Russell M. Nelson
>
> "The Temple and Your Spiritual Foundation," Oct. 2021

Hosea 13:6

According to their pasture, so were they filled.

Planting Your Pasture

One of my sons has the gift of asking great questions. At a recent family dinner, he asked, "If you could eat only one food for the rest of your life, what would it be?" We blurted out quick answers. "French fries!" or "Chocolate milk!" But the longer we discussed the possibilities, we realized there was more to consider than just naming a favorite food. Eating one food for the rest of your life could get very boring, or even unhealthy. So, what would be best? Choosing pizza would be fun because you'd have lots of variety. But salads might be a healthier long-term option.

This verse in Hosea is an analogy that offers similar "food for thought." Whatever you plant in your pasture is what you'll have to fill yourself with. So, what would you plant? Wheat? Rice? Ice cream sandwiches?

Now, because the scriptures are filled with symbolism, we know this verse doesn't only apply to produce. It's also about the pastures we plant in our hearts. So what are you putting in your pastures? Are you filling yourself with the best things? Are there attributes of Christ you'd like to grow and nurture in your life? We reap what we sow. Let's plant pastures of the best crops, things that fill us with the light and love of Christ.

—Krista

> "God enriches 'every thing to all bountifulness.' They 'which soweth bountifully shall reap also bountifully.'"
>
> Gerritt W. Gong
>
> "Ministering," Apr. 2023

Joel 2:23

Be glad then, ye children of Zion, and rejoice in the Lord your God.

Let's Be Joyous Today!

Recently I gave someone I love a gift. Her response surprised me. "I feel bad," she said with a frown. "That's too much. You didn't have to do that." She wasn't just being polite. She truly felt undeserving and, rather than feeling love, gratitude, and joy, she felt undeserving and even apologetic. It made me sad.

I wonder if we ever look at the gifts of forgiveness and grace the Savior offers and respond with, "Oh, I feel bad. That's too much. I don't deserve it." I wonder if it makes Him sad.

Jesus Christ *loves* us. He has so much He is trying to give us! How we receive it matters to us and to Him. He doesn't want us to feel guilt or shame or reject His gifts. He wants us to feel joy and gratitude and love. *He has freed us!* With our imperfect, outstretched arms, we can receive all He has to give with joy. We are loved. We are wanted. *He* decided before the world even was that we were deserving of His sacrifice. He *wants* us to have joy! So, let's be joyous!

—Michelle

"At the start of my journey of faith, joy in Jesus Christ was my first great discovery, and it changed my world. If you have yet to discover this joy, embark on its quest. This is an invitation to receive the Saviour's gift of peace, light, and joy—to revel in it, to wonder at it, and to rejoice in it every Sabbath."

Patrick Kearon

"Welcome to the Church of Joy," Oct. 2024

Joel 3:14

Multitudes, multitudes in the valley of decision: for the day of the Lord is near in the valley of decision.

Our Advocate With the Father

The Valley of Decision isn't a real geographic place. It's a symbolic name for the time when God will judge His children. Have you ever wondered what that day will be like? I have. And I have a lot of questions, especially about how it will feel to stand before God. But there's one thing I know for sure: Jesus Christ will stand beside me.

We often picture the final judgment as a day of strict justice, with God pronouncing sentences from His heavenly courtroom. But our Father is also a God of mercy. His plan has always included a Savior so that if we "sin and repent, we have an advocate with the Father" (JST, 1 John 2:1). As our Advocate, He will plead our cause, not by trying to prove we're innocent, but by pointing to how His perfect sacrifice has already paid the price for our sins (see D&C 45:3–5). With Christ at our side, justice is fulfilled and mercy is given freely.

I still have a lot of questions about Judgment Day, but knowing that my Savior—my Brother and Advocate—will stand with me in the Valley of Decision means I can face my Heavenly Father with confidence. And so, I will give Him my heart, my will, and my faith, looking toward that day with hope and peace.

—Krista

"As we know from modern revelation, all 'shall be judged . . . and every man shall receive according to his own works, his own dominion, in the mansions which are prepared.'"

Dallin H. Oaks

"Divine Love in the Father's Plan," Apr. 2022

Amos 3:7

Surely the Lord God will do nothing, but he revealeth his secret to his servants the prophet.

Our Secret Recipe

When we lived in Hershey, Pennsylvania, we heard stories of the extent early chocolate makers went to hide their secret recipes. For example, Forrest Mars stole the idea from Mounds and took it to Britain, calling his version Bounty, which is still a bestseller. Most people in the UK today have never heard of Mounds.

Fortunately, our prophets today share the Lord's secret recipe of how to prepare for His coming with all those who listen. In a recent address, President Nelson encouraged us to "grow in [our] confidence before the Lord." The three ingredients we need to add to our lives to do this are having more charity, letting virtue fill our thoughts and spending more time in the temple. As we do, "we will be filled with more joy, and [our] faith in Jesus Christ will increase." The way he said to accomplish this is to work on having more charity, letting virtue fill our thoughts, and spending more time in the temple.

In a culture of increasing political tension and open access to negative content, surely this is the *secret* we need for today. Luckily, we don't need to hide it like chocolate recipes. We can share it openly with anyone willing to give it a try so that we will be ready for that great day when Christ will come again.

—Christine

> "We do not know the day or the hour of His coming. But I do know that the Lord is prompting me to urge us to get ready for that 'great and dreadful day.'"
>
> Russell M. Nelson
>
> "Confidence in the Presence of God," Apr. 2025

Amos 6:1

Woe to them that are at ease in Zion, and trust in the mountain of Samaria, which are named chief of the nations, to whom the house of Israel came!

Taking It Too Easy

The prophet Amos warned the children of Israel that they were not living the Lord's standard. They were not worried enough about the future consequences of their behavior. He described the Israelites as those who "lie upon beds of ivory, and stretch themselves upon their couches, and eat the lambs out of the flock, and the calves out of the midst of the stall" (Amos 6:4-6).

When I went through a complicated surgery, I was stuck lying on my back for months and I hated it! As soon as I could, I got up and started moving. But after being stuck in bed for so long, my muscles were weak, and I was not able to work as long or as hard as I had before. That was the frustrating result of taking it too easy (out of necessity in this case). When I have a choice, I want to be hard at work, especially doing the work of the Lord.

Those who are at ease in Zion are taking it too easy rather than being anxiously engaged in His work: "They seek not the Lord to establish his righteousness, but every man walketh in his own way, and after the image of his own god, whose image is in the likeness of the world" (D&C 1:16). We can change our spiritual weaknesses into spiritual strengths by becoming more like the Savior. Developing Christlike attributes is the key to living a life that will help establish Zion. It cannot be done lying on a couch!

—Marianna

"We can live as a Zion people, if we wish to. Will it be hard? Of course it will."

David R. Stone

"Zion in the Midst of Babylon," Apr. 2006

Amos 8:11

I will send a famine in the land, not a famine of bread, nor a thirst for water, but of hearing the words of the Lord.

Feeding Souls

Last year, I suffered from an abdominal infection. As part of the healing process, I was on a very restrictive liquid diet for a few weeks. It was a challenging time. The lack of nutrition took its toll. I was physically depleted. The truly crazy thing was that I didn't realize how bad I felt until I could eat and began to feel better again—more like *me.*

There are people around us, right now, who are spiritually depleted. They feel lost, afraid, without purpose. Some don't realize how lost they feel. Others do and are longing for something to bring relief.

Thankfully, we don't have to endure a restrictive spiritual diet. We have the nourishment of the Atonement of Jesus Christ, with healing, guidance, strength, revelation, priesthood power, and so much more.

If you feel weak, feast on the gospel. If others around you are weak, offer them a taste. Let's find joy in feeding souls. No one has to go spiritually hungry anymore.

—Michelle

"Afflicted with anguish, some wander to and fro upon the earth in search of truth without knowing where to find it."

Neal A. Maxwell

"Shine as Lights in the World," Apr. 1983

Obadiah 1:21

And saviours shall come up on mount Zion.

Sven and Mrs. Sven

We once lived in a stake with a beloved tradition of spending an entire day together in the temple, as circumstances allowed. The year all our kids were finally in school, my husband, Travis, and I accepted the invitation. He took the day off work, and I arranged afterschool childcare. Together, we searched our family lines until we found a married couple who needed all their temple ordinances completed. Their names were incomplete—listed only as Sven and Mrs. Sven—but as we performed each ordinance on their behalf, from baptism to sealing, we felt their radiant joy. By the end of that day spent together across the veil, we knew and loved them. I fully expect that when Travis and I reach heaven, a couple will come running to greet us: "We're Sven and Mrs. Sven!" We'll hug and get to know each other better. It will be amazing.

Being a savior on Mount Zion is about restoring broken links, treasuring eternal identities, and extending God's mercy backward through time. It's a deeply personal way to know who we are, where we come from, grow gratitude for the lives and sacrifices of loved ones who came before, and become part of Christ's work of redemption, not just as a recipient, but as a participant.

–Krista

> "One by one, name by name, we offer beloved family members—ancestors—sacred ordinances and covenant blessings in the Lord's pattern of saviors on Mount Zion."
>
> Gerrit W. Gong
>
> "All Things for Our Good," Apr. 2024

Jonah 1:3

But Jonah rose up to flee unto Tarshish from the presence of the Lord.

Just Say Yes!

One of the greatest myths of all time is that if you do everything right, then your life will be without trials. Look at the most righteous men in history. Moses miraculously freed God's people, only to wander in the wilderness for forty years. Isaiah wrote some of the most beautiful truths ever, then was tied to a tree and sawed in half. Joseph Smith restored the gospel and was martyred. Christ Himself suffered pains and afflictions of every kind. Although their ultimate rewards are fabulous, their lives were filled with challenges.

Jonah hid from the Lord because he thought what the Lord asked of him was too hard. I know so many *Jonahs* today. Those who turn down callings because they think it will take too much time or those who stop attending their ward because the other members aren't as nice as they wish. Sometimes the Lord does ask hard things of us to test our faith. Unfortunately, the Lord doesn't always send a storm and a fish to get them back on the right path.

In some cases, He simply calls another and gives you the freedom to stray. Though it breaks His heart, part of the plan of happiness was to give us our free will. So let's not test the Lord. When we are asked to do hard things, let's just say yes!

—Christine

"The gospel is not a way to avoid challenges and problems but a solution to increase our faith and learn how to deal with them."

Massimo De Feo

"Rise! He Calleth Thee," Apr. 2024

Jonah 4:11

And should not I spare Nineveh, that great city, wherein are more than six score thousand persons that cannot discern between their right hand and their left hand and also much cattle?

Rejoicing After Surviving the Whale

The Jonah story can be seen as an analogy of our own mortal journey on earth rather than a true story about being swallowed by a big fish. The Savior Himself taught that Jonah's story was a type or model of the doctrine of resurrection (Matthew 12:40). Jonah's experience was to remind us of man's hope and joy for a resurrection or rebirth after death when man has been swallowed up in the belly of the earth. Then, why wasn't Jonah happy at the end of his story?

After having the covenant experience of being born again, Jonah successfully fulfilled his missionary call to command Nineveh to repentance. And they did! Shouldn't he rejoice? Instead, Jonah was angry at the Lord that these repentant sinners were not destroyed. Ask yourself: Did Jonah really change after his spiritual rebirth? Or did he return to the person he was before? How do we retain our spiritual rebirth in this life?

The Lord has called me to accomplish specific assignments as a daughter of God and as a member of His Church. The Relief Society asked me to help a sister clean her house. I did not want to, but after cleaning her home, I saw her happiness. It caused me to rejoice, rather than continue to complain, like Jonah.

—Marianna

"Stay on the covenant path. Your life will be easier, happier, and filled with joy."

Yoon Hwan Choi

"Do You Want to be Happy?" Oct. 2023

Micah 4:1

But in the last days it shall come to pass, that the mountain of the house of the Lord shall be established in the top of the mountains, and it shall be exalted above the hills; and people shall flow unto it.

Thrilling Indeed

Years ago, my dad was a sealer in the Oakland temple. One evening, he had the task of checking all the sealing rooms and turning off the lights at the end of the day. As he approached one of the sealing rooms, he thought he heard voices. He stood in the doorway, looking at an empty room. But he could hear and *feel* joyous laughter. He smiled at the room that looked empty but was filled with celebrating spirits, and turned off the light. He walked down the hall, still hearing their joy.

I wonder if sometimes we are under-thrilled at what happens in the house of the Lord. Perhaps we are too distracted by stress, numbed by grief, or impatient to get back to our day that we miss the miracles happening inside the temple. I wonder how thrilling it would be if we could actually see those that flow into the temple from the other side of the veil to witness the eternal connections that are made there every day. I think it would be thrilling indeed.

—Michelle

"Observing the Christian world in that day . . . we would have thrilled to see the glory of holy temples established again, with the Spirit, the ordinances, the power, and the authority to teach eternal truths, heal personal wounds, and bind families together forever."

Jeffrey R. Holland

"A Perfect Brightness of Hope," Apr. 2020

Micah 5:2

But thou, Beth-lehem . . . though thou be little among the thousands of Judah, yet out of thee shall he come forth unto me that is to be ruler in Israel; whose goings forth have been from of old, from everlasting.

Ordinary Folk

The Hobbit by J.R.R. Tolkien has resonated with readers for generations, and one reason is that the hero isn't who you'd expect. Bilbo—a small, humble halfling—is chosen by the wizard Gandalf to join a company of dwarves on a quest to retake their mountain home from a dragon. In the movie adaptation, the Elven queen Galadriel, puzzled by Bilbo's role, asks Gandalf, "Why the halfling?" He replies, "[The wizard] Saruman believes that it is only great power that can hold evil in check. But that is not what I've found. I've found it is the small things, everyday deeds of ordinary folk that keeps the darkness at bay."

Many ancient Jews expected the promised Messiah to arrive as a mighty military leader—riding on horseback, leading armies to deliver them from their enemies. But the prophet Micah foretold a different coming: the Messiah born as a baby in tiny, humble Bethlehem. A reminder that true power often arrives quietly, and greatness can come from the most unlikely places. Like Bilbo—and like Bethlehem—you and I are ordinary. But in following Christ, our small everyday deeds can make an extraordinary difference.

—Krista

"He is always calling upon us, and He uses us, His ordinary servants, to help bring His children to Him."

Gregorio E. Casillas

"God Loves All His Children," Oct. 2024

Nahum 1:15

Oh Judah, keep thy solemn feasts, perform thy vows; for the wicked shall no more pass through thee.

An Old Story

I remember when the musical *Hamilton* came out. The tickets were astronomically expensive, and everyone wanted to see it. They raved about the production, which was a modern retelling of the first treasurer of the United States. It seemed odd that an old story would find such relevance today, until I watched the show myself. The themes of diversity and ambition were exactly what modern audiences were grappling with. It resonated with their concerns.

The prophet Nahum used a similar tactic. Although he taught of the death of the Assyrians, he lived a hundred and fifty years after that. In his day, the Babylonians were trying to take over. Nahum warned the ancient Israelites to "keep [their] solemn feasts" and "perform [their] vows," which they did not do. As a result, those people became the lost ten tribes. Nahum's warning to his people of his day fell on deaf ears. The Babylonians took the remaining Jews captive for their same lack of temple service.

Today, we are facing a confusing era with prophesied destruction in our future. The covenants we make in the temple are key to keeping ourselves and our families safe no matter what comes our way. Nahum's old story still resonates with our modern concerns. Will we listen?

—Christine

"Everything we believe and every promise God has made to His covenant people come together in the temple."

Russell M. Nelson

"The Temple and Your Spiritual Foundation," Oct. 2021

Habakkuk 3:19

The Lord God is my strength, and he will make my feet like hinds' feet, and he will make me to walk upon mine high places.

Impossible Terrain

While driving through a canyon near my home in Utah, my family and I watched a mountain goat leap and climb its way up a sheer cliff. The ledges of rock were so thin they were nearly invisible, yet the goat scaled to a dizzying height like its feet were made of velcro.

In the verse above, hinds' feet are goats' feet, made for clinging to impossible places. Have you ever been there? In a place so uncertain that it turned your wide, shady path into a high mountain cliff? Maybe you've had days, or even years, of clinging to the thinnest of ledges, barely hanging on, terrified of falling.

This is the prayer and faith of the prophet Habakkuk: that the Lord can give us the feet of a mountain goat, steady on impossible terrain. He can help us scale cliffs, cross crags, and cling to the narrowest holds. He knows the best places to step and will guide us safely to the other side.

When life gets hard, I'll be praying for the Lord to bless both you and me with hinds' feet.

—Krista

> "Think of it! The Savior suffered 'pains and afflictions and temptations of every kind' so that He can comfort us, heal us, rescue us in times of need."
>
> Russell M. Nelson
>
> "Think Celestial!" Oct. 2023

Zephaniah 3:17

The Lord thy God in the midst of thee is mighty; he will save, he will rejoice over thee with joy; he will rest in his love, he will joy over thee with singing.

His Joy

Fun fact: If you read the Bible chronologically, Zephaniah would come *before Jeremiah*—during King Josiah's reforms, around 640–620 BC. Because he was a minor prophet, his book was tucked away toward the end. However, his message is equally important. His focus was warning the people of the impending judgment on Judah. But his message ends with hope and restoration for those who repent. While judgment is real, God's ultimate desire is to redeem and rejoice over His people. So much so that He sings over those who return to Him.

Repentance can be hard. But even when we feel unworthy, God hears us. He doesn't want to condemn, but to redeem and rejoice. He sings over us—not because we are perfect, but because we are *His*. Jesus Christ didn't die *because* of us. He died *for* us. And when we choose Him, He feels joy. He feels joy when we repent. It brings Him so much joy when we turn to Him. So, maybe don't try to do or be enough. Give Jesus joy simply by choosing to be close to Him and accepting His love and grace.

—Michelle

> "We speak often of the pain and suffering of Gethsemane and Calvary, but seldom do we speak of the great joy the Savior must have anticipated as He offered His life for us."
>
> Craig C. Christensen
>
> "There Can Be Nothing So Exquisite and Sweet as Was My Joy," Apr. 2023

Haggai 1:7

Thus saith the Lord of hosts: Consider your ways.

Course Correction

While on a trip, my husband, Travis, and I rented bikes to explore the city. I hadn't ridden since I was a kid, and I loved it. When we got home, I bought my first grown-up wheels: a mountain bike I named Breezy. Travis took me on my first dirt trail, and it was harder than I expected. But I wanted to learn, so I kept trying. After months of riding, something wasn't clicking, so I asked Travis to ride ahead and watch my technique. He taught me to shift gears more quickly, stand when going downhill, and use my legs as built-in suspension. Considering my ways—examining and adjusting—made all the difference. Riding became way more fun.

When the Israelites returned to Jerusalem after their captivity in Babylon, they began rebuilding the temple. But it wasn't long before they abandoned the project and turned their focus to rebuilding their own homes and lives. The temple lay in ruins. Through the prophet Haggai, the Lord advised them, "Consider your ways." He was asking them to examine their priorities, notice what needed to change, and refocus their hearts on Him. "Consider your ways" is a wake-up call—to stop, reflect, and turn back to God.

—Krista

"There is no treasure, nor any hobby, nor any status, nor any social media, nor any video games, nor any sport, nor any association with a celebrity, nor anything on earth that is more precious than eternal life. So the Lord's counsel to every person is 'consider your ways.'"

Terence M. Vinson

"True Disciples of the Savior," Oct. 2019

Zechariah 2:11

And many nations shall be joined to the Lord in that day, and shall be my people; and I will dwell in the midst of thee.

Many Nations Shall be Joined to the Lord

Although I always knew that before Christ comes again the gospel would be preached to "every creature" (Mark 16:15), I assumed that the missionaries would go to them. That may yet happen, but as I arrived at the London England Mission as a senior missionary, I was amazed at the number of young missionaries from all over the world. They represent dozens of nations "joined to the Lord" in His great work. I have met a wonderful sister from Pakistan, and elders from the Congo, Cambodia and Mongolia—just to name a few.

These young missionaries are not only learning the gospel at a deeper level, but they are learning to be future leaders in their own countries, allowing the gospel of Christ to fill the earth. Even as we visited our new ward southeast of the city, we met new friends from India, Afghanistan, and China. They were faithfully attending institute classes, had become close friends with other members, and were joining with the Saints as one people.

This is a worldwide Church and will become more so. Still, as we focus on Christ, we can become one people no matter the cultural or language barriers. I've seen it, and it is thrilling.

—Christine

> "Truly the blessings of the gospel are for every race, language, and people. The Church of Jesus Christ is a global church. Jesus Christ is our leader."
>
> Russell M. Nelson
>
> "Christ Is Risen; Faith in Him Will Move Mountains," Apr. 2021

Zechariah 4:13–14

And he answered me and said, Knowest thou not what these be? And I said, No, my lord. Then said he, These are the two anointed ones, that stand by the Lord of the whole earth.

Speculation

As a young adult, before I was married, I imagined what my future would be like. I pictured what my husband would look like, what my children would look like, how many children I would have, where our family would live, and even what our home would look like. Now that I am living that life, many parts of it are different from what I imagined, but most of my life is better than my dreams.

Prophets do not speculate or imagine. They are seers and revelators who can discern, through the Spirit of the Lord, what symbols mean and what will really happen. We can trust their words, predictions, and explanations. Our faith should be renewed as we see how perfectly they described the exact events that have already occurred, such as the Israelites' return to Jerusalem and the birth of the Savior. We can look forward to their other revelations coming to pass as well.

As we read Zechariah's words about the latter days, we should not speculate about how the Lord will get all His work done. Instead, we should roll up our sleeves and get to work.

—Marianna

"I am not saying that the days ahead will be easy, but I promise you that the future will be glorious for those who are prepared and who continue to prepare to be instruments in the Lord's hands."

Russell M. Nelson

"Embrace the Future with Faith," Oct. 2020

Zechariah 6:1

And I turned, and lifted up mine eyes, and looked.

Jesus Everywhere

After the sealing of my daughter to her new husband in the Seattle temple, I was sitting at my kitchen table, going over everything I still had to do to prepare and throw the reception later that day when my daughter-in-law asked, "Why is Jesus everywhere?" I thought the question was strange, as she'd been in my home many times and was familiar with the artwork of the Savior on my walls. But then, my husband came down the stairs and asked, "What's with all the baby Jesuses?"

Then, I saw it—a miniature rubber Jesus figure on my kitchen table, and my sister-in-law and daughter grinning. I was mildly confused but completely suspicious. With further investigation, I noticed a mini Jesus on my bookshelf, on my TV, on the counter. He really was everywhere. Why? Because my sister-in-law and daughter had hid fifty of them around my house—some right in front of me in plain sight.

When my mind was focused on my worldly obligations, I hadn't even noticed what was right in front of me. But once I knew what to look for and I put in the effort, I literally found Jesus everywhere.

—Michelle

> "And as we allow Him to direct us in all things, we receive testimony that 'all things denote there is a God,' because where we look for Him we will find Him—each and every day."
>
> Tracy Y. Browning
>
> "Seeing More of Jesus Christ in Our Lives," Oct. 2022

Zechariah 8:9

Let your hands be strong.

Hands Like His

My dad is a general contractor and one of the hardest workers I know. I've always loved his hands. They're strong—capable of building incredible things from raw materials, skilled at using heavy tools and machinery with precision, and pushing through injury and exhaustion without complaint. His hands have worked tirelessly to provide for our family.

But their strength isn't just physical. My dad's hands are strong in quieter, sacred ways, too. They serve without being asked. They fold in prayer. They lift others when they're down. They express love in the gentlest, most powerful ways.

I think that's the kind of strength the Lord wants for our hands, too. Hands that are willing to work hard, carry heavy loads, provide, protect, and create. But also hands that serve, bless, and comfort. Hands that reach out to those in need and do the quiet work of ministering one by one. The Savior's hands bear the marks of sacrifice. He used His hands to work, heal, lift, and love—and He asks us to use our hands to do the same.

—Krista

> "He extended His merciful hand to those who needed relief from their burdens, both physically and spiritually."
>
> Ulisses S. Soares
>
> "The Savior's Abiding Compassion," Oct. 2021

Zechariah 9:16

For they shall be as the stones of a crown, lifted up as an ensign upon the land.

As the Stones of a Crown

Gemstones are rare for three reasons. First, they need the right combination of ingredients to form. Next, heat and pressure combine to purify and strengthen the stone. Finally, the gemstone must push to the surface and be found, cut, and polished by a master to be of the greatest worth. Zechariah said that those who follow the Savior in the last days "shall be as stones of a crown, lifted up as an ensign upon his land."

For us to become those jewels, we may have to pass through a similar process. Often, as we follow promptings, we are put in situations we wouldn't expect, adding elements to our personalities that help us become who we are meant to be. Then, even with prayer, we face trials and the accompanying pressure. Often that stress comes because of the decisions we make to follow the Savior. Finally, as we grow closer to the master, He asks hard things of us. Sometimes we have to let go of things we enjoy so that we can serve Him as He asks.

But as we stay true, the promise is clear. We will become more than we ever thought. We will become His jewels. And Christ will "seal [us] His" (Mosiah 5:15).

—Christine

"In reality, the greatest happiness and blessing of mortality will be found in who we have become through God's grace as we make and keep sacred covenants with Him."

Gary B. Sabin

"Hallmarks of Happiness," Oct. 2023

Zechariah 9:9

Rejoice greatly, O daughter of Zion; shout, O daughter of Jerusalem: behold, thy King cometh unto thee: he is just, and having salvation; lowly, and riding upon an ass, and upon a colt the foal of an ass.

Shouting My Hosannas!

If I could travel back in time, I'd choose to shout *Hosannas* with the believers as Jesus Christ rode triumphantly into Jerusalem. Imagine the energy and joy of that moment! With palm fronds in hand, the crowd shouted, "Hosanna! Save us, we pray!" (see Matthew 21:9; John 12:13) and spontaneously offered their cloaks to line the path before Him. They had waited so long, hoped so faithfully, and finally, He had come, just as Zechariah had prophesied over five hundred years before.

Most of the time, my worship looks like folded arms and whispered prayers, but sometimes the Spirit stirs my heart and I long to shout His name from the rooftop and tell the world about His love and grace. I want to rejoice that He lives! And dance with joy in His radiant light!

And so, I wonder what I will do when He comes again as prophesied. Will I fall to my knees in reverent prayer, or will I run to Him and shout Hosanna? Either way, I want to be ready. I want to know Him when He comes and be known to Him. Until then, I will be courageous in speaking His name and shouting my Hosannas by the way I live and follow Him.

—Krista

"Sing hallelujah—for He shall reign forever and ever! Shout hosanna, to God and the Lamb!"

Gerrit W. Gong

"Hosanna and Hallelujah–The Living Jesus Christ: The Heart of Restoration and Easter," Apr. 2020

Zechariah 10:2

For the idols have spoken vanity, and the diviners have seen a lie, and have told false dreams; they comfort in vain; therefore they went their way as a flock, they were troubled, because there was no shepherd.

Ye Olde Curiosity Shop

Seattle's wharf has an old store with many curiosities, like a three-headed calf, a mer-monkey, and mummies. My children especially love the fortune teller. Even though she is obviously an animated doll, the fortune teller gives you a card that tells you your future. My children like to compare the futures that she gives them. Each one is very different.

But my children also realize that these predictions are false dreams and vain divinations. Their hopes and dreams are not based on this fanciful piece of paper.

Zechariah warns us not to turn away from our Savior because of pride and vanity. Our idols and false dreams may be rooted in how much money we make, or how many followers we have on the internet. When our focus becomes the world rather than the Savior, we inevitably become troubled.

Our Savior is the antidote to those feelings. He pleads with us: "Come unto me, all *ye* that labour and are heavy laden, and I will give you rest" (Matthew 11:28).

—Marianna

> "Troubles are part of the plan and do not mean you've been abandoned; they are part of what it means to be His."
>
> Michelle D. Craig
>
> "Wholeheartedness," Oct. 2022

Zechariah 13:6

And one shall say unto him, What are these wounds in thine hands? Then he shall answer, Those with which I was wounded in the house of my friends.

I'm Sorry I Hurt You

While serving as Relief Society president, I began to see an issue with talking during our Sunday lessons. I loved the sisterhood we had, but I could see it was frustrating for the teacher and other sisters. Wanting to help the class be a better all-around experience, and not wanting to embarrass any sisters, I decided to reach out to a handful of sisters personally rather than addressing the issue at the beginning of class.

The first sister I talked to laughed and apologized, admitting she knew she was prone to chatter. However, a few days later, this sweet sister reached out to me to tell me she actually had been hurt by my call. She felt singled out and unwanted.

It broke my heart to know that I had been the cause of someone's pain, especially since my efforts had come from a place of good intent. I humbly apologized and expressed love. We had a good conversation where we both felt peace.

There will be times in our lives when we might hurt or be hurt by others. As we address these experiences with honesty and humility, we have the opportunity to build each other up, strengthen relationships, and be the peacemakers God needs us to be.

—Michelle

"My beloved friends, in our shared ministry of reconciliation, I ask us to be peacemakers—to love peace, to seek peace, to create peace, to cherish peace."

Jeffrey R. Holland

"The Ministry of Reconciliation," Oct. 2018

Malachi 1:2

I have loved you, saith the Lord. Yet ye say, Wherein hast thou loved us?

Where's the Proof?

Have you ever heard a child say they're bored . . . *on Christmas Day* . . . after opening a mountain of gifts? Or witnessed a child standing in the checkout line next to a grocery cart brimming with food, asking for a candy bar—and when their mom says no, they pout, "You never buy me anything!"?

It's easy to chuckle (or bring out the "mom-glare") at that kind of unawareness. But if we're honest, we all have our moments. The adult version sounds a little different, but it comes from the same place:

"God, why don't You ever bless me?"

"Why is everyone else's life better than mine?"

"You're not answering my prayers."

Through Malachi, God reminded Israel, "I have loved you." But their hearts had grown cold. "How?" they asked. "Where's the proof?" They had forgotten their history, the countless evidences of His love. And sometimes, so do we.

If our hearts ever wonder, "Wherein hast Thou loved me?", let's pause. Look around. Remember. Write the evidence down. Because He has always loved us. More than we know.

—Krista

> "I love you, and I assure you that the Lord loves you and sees the great work you are performing."
>
> Russell M. Nelson
>
> "Embrace the Future with Faith," Oct. 2020

Malachi 2:17

Wherein have we wearied him? When ye say, Every one that doeth evil is good in the sight of the Lord.

Calling Evil Good

I hate the smell of tuna. It makes me want to wretch. Meanwhile, my husband thinks that tuna is ambrosia, the food of the gods. When I watch him enjoying his stinky tuna sandwich, I can't understand what is going through his mind. To me there is nothing more disgusting.

Unlike our personal preferences, good and evil are not based on internal feelings, tastes, or appetites, but on the wisdom of God. He warns us against those things which will drive away the Spirit. That's what is evil. Then He invites us to do the things which will bring us the most joy. That's what is good.

So, when the lines between black and white are blurred, remember good and evil are God's choice not ours. If not, eating tuna would be a sin.

—Christine

> "Most important for spiritual growth is the requirement to choose between good and evil. Those who choose good would progress toward their eternal destiny."
>
> Dallin H. Oaks
>
> "Divine Helps for Mortality," Apr. 2025

Malachi 3:7

Return unto me, and I will return unto you, saith the Lord of hosts. But ye said, Wherein shall we return?

The Law of Undulation

Life has its peaks and valleys. We experience times when all is going well and other times when life is not. C. S. Lewis described this as the Law of Undulation, or the peaks and valleys of mortality. In the *Screwtape Letters,* the senior devil, Wormwood, taught his apprentice about this fact: "Humans are amphibians—half spirit and half animal. . . . As spirits they belong to the eternal world, but as animals they inhabit time. . . . Their nearest approach to constancy, therefore, is undulation—the repeated return to a level from which they repeatedly fall back, a series of troughs and peaks" (C. S. Lewis, *Screwtape Letters,* Letter VIII, 1942).

Malachi is a special book of scripture expressing powerful messages from the Lord for us today. Malachi is a transliteration of a Hebrew word meaning "my messenger."

Malachi's message details the troughs and peaks that we will experience before the Savior's Second Coming. The undulations of life must not distract us from our preparations for the day when we return to His presence.

—Marianna

"Our Savior and Redeemer, Jesus Christ, will perform some of His mightiest works between now and when He comes again."

Russell M. Nelson

"Revelation for the Church, Revelation for Our Lives," Apr. 2018

Malachi 3:10

Bring ye all the tithes into the storehouse, that there may be meat in mine house, and prove me now herewith, saith the Lord of hosts, if I will not open you the windows of heaven, and pour you out a blessing, that there shall not be room enough to receive it.

Mr. Miyagi Teaches Tithing

I am an OG '80s teen. *Karate Kid* came out when I was thirteen. I saw it in the theaters and fell in love with Daniel. Now, as a grandma, I have a platonic love for Mr. Miyagi. I love his patience, his strength, and his humble teaching style. He didn't lecture. He gave Daniel opportunities to develop muscle style, strength, and memory by doing physical chores that seemed to have nothing to do with karate. And yet, when Daniel was conditioned, Miyagi challenged him, allowing Daniel to respond intuitively to his movements. It was here that Daniel realized that, in the middle of obediently doing his chores, he had become a karate student to a true karate master.

Sometimes we wonder if paying tithing makes a difference. Since God is not a vending-machine God, we can't always see our blessings. Paying tithing allows us to become people of faith in God, not results. It brings us closer to the Master so He can help us become who He knows we can be. Yes, we will be blessed in many ways, but the true blessing is who we are becoming, not what we are receiving.

—Michelle

"The windows of heaven open in many ways. Some are temporal, but many are spiritual. Some are subtle and easy to overlook. Trust in the Lord's timing; the blessings always come."

Neil L. Andersen

"Opening the Windows of Heaven," Oct. 2023

Malachi 3:11

I will rebuke the devourer for your sakes, and he shall not destroy the fruits of your ground.

Crickets and Seagulls

In Utah, we celebrate two fireworks-worthy holidays in July—Independence Day and Pioneer Day. On July 24, parades and picnics commemorate the brave Saints who crossed the plains and tamed the desert. One of my favorite Pioneer Day stories is *The Miracle of the Crickets and the Seagulls.*

In 1848, the first year after the pioneers settled in the Salt Lake Valley, their crops were threatened by a massive infestation of Mormon crickets—those really huge, creepy ones. The pioneers prayed for help, and soon after, flocks of seagulls arrived. To the Saints' amazement, the birds began eating the crickets. Many of the accounts say that the seagulls would gorge themselves, vomit, and return to eat more, saving much of the harvest.

The *devourer* of ancient times is still hard at work. Today, he comes in subtle forms: discouragement, financial strain, distractions, fear, wasted time, or unexpected setbacks that eat away at our hopes. But God's promise also endures: He will rebuke the devourer for our sakes. Just as He sent seagulls to preserve the pioneers' harvest, God can send help to preserve what matters most to us. And your harvest—your efforts, your dreams, your faith—will not be wasted.

–Krista

> "He has promised us that He will protect us from evil. These promises are so certain, the Lord declares, 'Prove me now herewith.'"
>
> Neil L. Andersen
>
> "Tithing: Opening the Windows of Heaven," Oct. 2023

Malachi 3:16–17

And a book of remembrance was written before him for them that feared the Lord, and that thought on his name. And they shall be mine, saith the Lord of Hosts, in that day when I make up my jewels.

Thinking on His Name

At Christmastime, many sing Handel's *Messiah* and repeat the words "And His name shall be called Wonderful, Counselor, Almighty God, the Everlasting Father, the Prince of Peace." Do we recall Christ's names? I actually think we should.

When I was grieving my stillborn child, He comforted me and was *Wonderful*!

When I didn't know whether to get my master's degree after I thought my family was complete, He opened my mind to a more beautiful way as a patient and wise *Counselor*!

When I see broken hearts touched, healed and changed, I know he is truly powerful, even an *Almighty God.*

And just yesterday when I wanted to strangle my husband because I felt he wasn't listening to me and prayed for patience, I was filled with peace, for He is the *Prince of Peace.*

Let's be more mindful of the Lord by recognizing and calling Him by the names that reflect how He manifests Himself in our lives each day—and let's share these names with others.

—Christine

"Our faith in Jesus Christ needs to be nourished daily. It is nourished as we pray daily, study the scriptures daily, reflect on the goodness of God daily, repent daily, and follow the promptings of the Holy Ghost daily."

Dale G. Renlund

"The Powerful, Virtuous Cycle of the Doctrine of Christ," Apr. 2024

Malachi 4:1

For, behold, the day cometh, that shall burn as an oven; and all the proud, yea, and all that do wickedly, shall be stubble: and the day that cometh shall burn them up, saith the Lord of hosts, that it shall leave them neither root nor branch.

Burning

I was making instant rice for dinner. I started by boiling water and poured in the rice. Then, children needed me. I began helping them—without turning off the stove. Not long after, smoke and a terrible smell came from the kitchen. The fire alarm went off. I ran into the kitchen and grabbed the pan, not realizing how hot it was. I burned my hand and tried to cool both the pan and my hand with cold water. This only caused the smoke to increase. The firefighters arrived, using their industrial-strength fans to get rid of the smell and the smoke.

The sensation of burning can last long after the heat source is removed from your skin because burns damage nerve endings, causing intense pain. The pain of sin can also linger long after the sin has been removed from your behavior. Your mind and spirit remember—until you have been washed clean through the Atonement of Jesus Christ. The Second Coming of the Lord will be a day of burning for those who have done wickedly. I don't know how literal or how figurative this burning will be, but I do know that they will feel it. People can heal from painful burns, if they are not too extensive. The Savior will rise with healing in His wings for all those who look to Him for relief from their pain.

—Marianna

"How could people so quickly forget the God who had blessed them so abundantly?"

David A. Bednar

"In the Space of Not Many Years," Oct. 2024

Malachi 4:5

Behold, I will send you Elijah the prophet before the coming of the great and dreadful day of the Lord.

She's Holding My Hand

A couple of years ago, I had the idea to do something I hadn't done before—all the ordinance work for a single person in a single day. Her name was Emma. I started in the baptistry. As I came out of the water, I smiled, hoping she was happy. I felt the Spirit during her confirmation that she was. The initiatory experience built upon that feeling. By the time I sat in the endowment room, I sensed her more. I wondered if she was there. After spending some time in the celestial room, I headed up to the sealing room, where I knelt as proxy as she was sealed to her parents.

After spending four hours with Emma, she was no longer a name but a woman I loved. I didn't just feel her; I felt her *there*, near me, in that moment. So much so that, as I walked down the hallway, I reached out my hand, expecting her to take it, as we walked in the temple together.

—Michelle

"Vital to the preparation for the Second Coming is the great redemptive effort on behalf of our ancestors. The Lord promised to send Elijah the prophet before the Second Coming. . . . Elijah did come as promised . . . [and] did indeed confer the promised priesthood, the keys for the redemption of the dead and the union of husbands, wives, and families across all generations of time and throughout all eternity."

D. Todd Christofferson

"Preparing for the Lord's Return," Apr. 2019

Malachi 4:6

And he shall turn the heart of the fathers to the children.

Good Grandpa

Granny and Gramps lived overseas when I was born, and though we didn't get to meet right away, they wrote me letters about how excited they were to be grandparents. My mom gave me the letters when I was in high school. I tucked them into a scrapbook and forgot about them until decades later when Gramps passed away.

The COVID-19 pandemic prevented us from being with him during his final days. I was heartbroken and angry that I wasn't allowed to kiss his cheek before he died. In my grief, I began searching through old scrapbooks, hungry for memories—and that's when I found the letters. Gramps had written: "Dear Krista Marie, I am so very proud to be called 'Grandpa Hansen,' although this new role does frighten me a bit. I do hope I can be a good grandpa."

Memories of my "good grandpa" filled my heart. For forty-five years, he had done exactly what he had hoped. His grandfather-heart had been turned to me from the moment of my birth. He was a pillar of my life, always involved, steady, constant in his love, and faithful in his example of how to follow Jesus Christ. I refolded the letter, looked toward heaven, and said aloud, "Gramps, you did it! You were so good."

–Krista

> "Perhaps the most essential of a father's work is to turn the hearts of his children to their Heavenly Father."
>
> D. Todd Christofferson
>
> "Fathers," Apr. 2016

Malachi 4:6

And he shall turn . . . the heart of the children to their fathers.

A Thinned Veil

Before the early nineteenth century, the only people interested in family history were those trying to claim the inheritance of a distant relative or those hoping to find a connection to royalty in their family tree. Oddly, that changed about the same year the Saints moved to Utah. All over the world, historical societies began to emerge, with people of all faiths gathering and preserving records of those who had gone before.

I believe this is a miracle in fulfillment of Malachi's prophecy, but only half of it. Simply having the records available doesn't turn my heart; it only opens the door for the possibility of it. As we do the temple work for our ancestors, our hearts become involved. When the sealing promises take effect, we feel a spiritual connection that wasn't there before. Their spirits can and do touch our hearts.

In the temple, the veil is thin. Multiple times, I have felt the joy of those crossing the veil as I've performed their temple work. I've felt the connection of family members who have passed on, and I've been inspired to learn more about them. I've felt encircled in the love of righteous generations, all through temple covenants.

—Christine

"It is through the sealing covenants in the temple that we can receive the assurance of loving family connections that will continue after death and last for eternity."

Henry B. Eyring

"All Will Be Well Because of Temple Covenants," Apr. 2024

Jeremiah 2:13

For my people have committed two evils; they have forsaken me the fountain of living waters, and hewed them out cisterns, broken cisterns,that can hold no water.

Fountain of Living Waters

During our reading of the Old Testament, we have looked at the teachings of prophets as they taught their people about the future coming of the Messiah—both His First and Second Coming. They often did this through symbols that were a part of their everyday life. One powerful symbol used throughout scripture is that of the Savior as Living Water, because He is the source of our spiritual survival.

Water is essential to all life on this earth, including plants, animals, and humans. A person's body weight is composed of 60–75 percent water. A loss of just 4 percent of total body water leads to dehydration, and a loss of 15 percent can be fatal. A person could survive a month without food but would not survive three days without water. Israelites experienced both the lack of water resources and the societal pressures of a spiritual drought. When they faced certain death from their lack of water, they humbled themselves and sought the Lord to send rain. When the Israelites faced spiritual death, the Lord's prophets taught them to seek the fountain of Living Water and drink freely from this source.

The words of Jehovah quench our thirst and fill us up with His love. The Old Testament prepares us for His Coming today.

—Marianna

> "He is the living water, fulfilling the deepest needs of our souls with His constant love and kindness."
>
> Jose L. Alonso
>
> "Jesus Christ at the Center of Our Lives," Apr. 2024

About the Authors

Marianna Richardson is not an accomplished gardener, but she knows the importance of planting seeds in fertile ground that will give young plants the nourishment they need to grow. She is so thankful that her twelve children, once young plants at home, have now been transplanted all over the country and have yielded thirty-three thriving grandchildren. She loves being their mom and grandma.

Marianna continues to encourage young things to grow as she teaches at Brigham Young University. Her husband of forty-eight years teaches computer science at BYU, too. They both love to teach the gospel to others together, which they did in Sao Paulo, Brazil, where they served as mission leaders, and in Orem, Utah, where they taught at the UVU Institute.

About the Authors

Christine Thackeray adores studying the scriptures, playing word games, and playing with her grandchildren while a few dogs and cats run around at their feet. She has taught all seven of her children in early-morning seminary, but her favorite calling is Primary chorister. Christine has enjoyed participating in the previous *Women Read Scripture* publications. Each has been a treat, rediscovering corners of the scriptures and seeing how life connects to those great truths. Recently, Christine was called to serve in the England London Mission as an MLS missionary with the young adults there. She served in London as a much younger missionary some forty-three years ago.

You can follow her adventures at https://thackeraysinlondon.blogspot.com/

About the Authors

Michelle Wilson is an inspirational author, editor, speaker, and teacher who loves sharing gospel truths through stories, insights, and humor. She enjoys a good hike followed by a huge bowl of ice cream and playing games. She lives in the Pacific Northwest with her husband. Their three adult children have all left home to pursue their own lives. Michelle has forgiven them, however, because she is getting grandkids out of the deal.

You can find her at www.MichelleWilsonWrites.com.

About the Authors

Krista M. Isaaconson is a felicitously married mother of six children, who has discovered that grandma-hood is even better than expected. She loves pumpkin spice, vintage children's books, and her mountain bike named Breezy. And according to her husband, she has a lot of words. As an author, nonfiction content writer, presenter, and inspirational speaker, her passion is to write, speak, and testify of how Christ has carried her through the deep waters of losing her two-year-old daughter to cancer, and raising a son with autism. With God's love and Christ's grace, she's found that every unbearable burden can become bearable.

Connect with her at KristaMIsaacson.com or on socialmedia: @KristaMIsaacson.

Notes

Notes

Notes

Notes

Notes